GENERATING SOCIAL CAPITAL

Generating Social Capital

Civil Society and Institutions in Comparative Perspective

Edited by

Marc Hooghe and Dietlind Stolle

GENERATING SOCIAL CAPITAL

First published 2003 by
PALGRAVE MACMILLAN™
175 Fifth Avenue, New York, N.Y. 10010 and
Houndmills, Basingstoke, Hampshire, England RG21 6XS
Companies and representatives throughout the world

PALGRAVE MACMILLAN is the global academic imprint of the Palgrave Macmillan division of St. Martin's Press, LLC and of Palgrave Macmillan Ltd. Macmillan® is a registered trademark in the United States, United Kingdom and other countries. Palgrave is a registered trademark in the European Union and other countries.

ISBN 1–4039–6219–7 hardback
ISBN 1–4039–6220–0 paperback

Library of Congress Cataloging-in-Publication Data Available from the Library of Congress

A catalogue record for this book is available from the British Library.

Design by Newgen Imaging Systems (P) Ltd., Chennai, India.

First edition: May 2003
10 9 8 7 6 5 4 3 2

Printed in the United States of America.

Contents

ACKNOWLEDGMENTS

This book addresses how civic attitudes that are recognized as important ingredients of the social capital concept are generated. Researchers from several countries, such as Belgium, Canada, France, the Netherlands, Norway, Sweden and the United States, provide answers and tests to this overall question. The answers are the result of various elaborate research projects, academic exchanges and meetings over the last three years that involved the contributors and other researchers. The editors would like to thank the University of Pittsburgh, McGill University, the Fund for Scientific Research—Flanders, the Free University of Brussels, the European Consortium for Political Research and the European Science Foundation (ESF) for providing the resources or opportunities for this international collaborative project. Two academic events stand out as essential for the completion of this volume. The editors organized a workshop for the Joint Sessions of the European Consortium for Political Research in Copenhagen in April 2000, where several contributors to this volume presented and discussed their work. The ESF workshop on social capital, organized by Dario Castiglione and Jan van Deth in September 2001, was another milestone in the shaping and testing of some of the arguments presented here. We thank all contributors to this volume and all participants in these conferences for stimulating discussions and insights. The editors also thank Jen Simington and Lisa Nevens for their tremendous work on editing and design. Finally, the editors thank each other for the steady exchange of ideas and mutual support, and since we contributed equally to this project, the order of our names is purely alphabetical.

MARC HOOGHE AND DIETLIND STOLLE

CHAPTER 1

INTRODUCTION: GENERATING SOCIAL CAPITAL

Marc Hooghe and Dietlind Stolle

Less than five years ago, a book like this would have started with an elaborate definition of the concept of social capital. Today, this no longer seems necessary. Not only in political science, but also in other academic disciplines it is now widely acknowledged that the presence of dense networks within a society, and the accompanying norms of generalized trust and reciprocity, allow citizens to overcome collective action problems more effectively. Social capital is seen as an important resource available to societies and communities. Even policy makers have overwhelmingly adopted the notion of social capital. In Britain, the Blair government has re-invigorated civic education in schools in order to promote social capital and to strengthen a civic culture that is believed to be endangered by the rising distrust in government institutions. The Public Broadcasting System in the United States proudly proclaims that its community-based television programs actively promote the creation of social capital. President Yoweri Museveni from Uganda talks about access to social capital as one of his goals in the fight for the eradication of poverty. And when the government of the Flemish autonomous region in Belgium unfolded its ambitious "21 Goals for the 21st Century," the creation of social capital figured prominently among them.

Policy initiatives of this kind—as catchy and modern as they sound—leave us to wonder a bit: We do not have access to reliable research results about how social capital is actually generated. Certainly there is no shortage of social capital studies—in fact they have evolved into a prospering subdiscipline, and, to a large extent, this is due to the success of Robert Putnam's volumes on social capital in Italy and the United States. Especially in his powerful study of civic traditions in Italy, Putnam demonstrated that groups of citizens that have accumulated social capital in terms of social interaction, shared norms and networks can use these resources to resolve their conflicts more easily. Social capital is important for various collective societal issues, such as neighborhood projects and volunteering, as well as interactions with persons outside of one's own intimate circle. At the same time, the logic of Putnam's argument entails that in regions or cities where people are distrustful in dealing with strangers, citizens will experience more difficulties when they try to work cooperatively toward social solutions. In turn, this would adversely affect matters such as regional economic development, crime prevention and the performance of regional institutions. In such regions or nations, generalized trust is not institutionalized; to the contrary, institutional norms might be explicitly directed against trust or reciprocity. Such systems instill the belief that distrust, caution and defection pay off most (Banfield 1958).

Given this logic, social capital has been defined and measured as generalized trust, norms of reciprocity and networks (Putnam 1993). We make here a distinction between structural (networks) and attitudinal (trust and reciprocity) components of social capital (see more in Stolle this volume). In this volume we mainly focus on the attitudinal aspects of social capital, particularly generalized trust, norms of reciprocity and other forms of civic attitudes. The reason is that not all types of networks are the solution to larger collective action problems and to the strength of democracy, and networks can therefore not be examined as goals in themselves. Networks might have the opposite effect, for example, by strengthening or empowering nondemocratic groups and organizations. Generalized trust and generalized reciprocity, on the other hand, can be considered as integral and probably irreplaceable parts of any democratic political culture, as they clearly indicate an inclusive and tolerant approach to the population at large. We consider these attitudes as important prerequisites for cooperative behavior and the successful solution of collective action problems.

Many of the previous writings on social capital have focused on definitions, measurement issues or the consequences of social capital; in this volume we look at a largely unexplored field: The various mechanisms and sources that are responsible for the generation of social capital. More specifically, we will focus on the attitudinal components of social capital and examine how and why such civic attitudes develop. Interestingly, there are already a number of studies on the origins of what we call the structural components of social capital: We know what kinds of factors determine participation and the formation of networks between citizens. Classic studies have found that individual-level resources such as education, status, gender, knowledge, civic skills as well as political institutions make a difference for various participation patterns (e.g., Dalton 1996; Verba, Nie and Kim 1978; Verba, Schlozman and Brady 1995). The development of the attitudinal components of social capital, however, thus far has been studied less systematically.

This book is intended to uncover carefully those aspects of social and political institutions that influence the development of social capital, with a clear focus on the attitudinal components of the social capital complex. We can distinguish at least two main approaches in the search for answers to this puzzle. On the one hand, the development of civic attitudes is mostly seen as being located in various forms of social interactions, such as membership in voluntary associations. We call such approaches society-centered, as social capital is seen as clearly linked to and influenced by social interactions. Institution-centered approaches, on the other hand, see social capital embedded in and shaped by governments, public policies and political institutions. If we want to fully understand the concept of social capital and if we want to be able to help develop and maintain it, then it is necessary and in fact essential to invest more research efforts into a careful examination of these two approaches.

If society-centered accounts are correct, and social capital is mainly produced by the day-to-day interactions between citizens, our main attention should be directed at fostering formal as well as informal types of social contact. Yet, we do not have sufficient knowledge about whether and how social interactions are most beneficial for the development of civic attitudes. If institution-centered accounts are correct, we should be looking at promising public policies and institutional structures that facilitate social capital. Yet, little research has been done to explore aspects of public institutions that might be supportive of the development of reciprocity and generalized trust. It is obvious that these puzzles require answers that are relevant for both public policies and progress in social science: We cannot arrive at a more complete understanding of the phenomenon of social capital if we do not fully explore its origins.

DEFINITIONS AFTER ALL—WHAT WE KNOW ABOUT SOCIAL CAPITAL

Why are we interested in social capital? The research that documents the consequences of social capital has given some convincing answers. If societies are to prosper, citizens not only need physical and human capital, but also social capital (Ostrom 2001). While physical capital refers to tangible resources, and human capital can be understood as skills and education, social capital "refers to connections among individuals—social networks and the norms of reciprocity and trustworthiness that arise from them" (Putnam 2000, 19). While the first two kinds of capital in general are individually owned, social capital resides in relationships and therefore is almost by definition a collective property. This implies that, like all common goods, it is more vulnerable to neglect and free-riding than other kinds of capital.

The benefits of social capital are by now well established, both at the micro and at the macrolevel. In the political sphere, generalized trust and other civic attitudes allow citizens to join their forces in social and political groups and enable them to come together in citizens' initiatives more easily. In the social sphere, generalized trust facilitates life in diverse societies and fosters acts of tolerance and acceptance of otherness. Life in diverse societies is easier, happier and more confident in the presence of generalized trust (Uslaner 2002). Children embedded in supporting social networks score higher on school attainment (Coleman and Hoffer 1988; De Graaf, De Graaf and Kraaykamp 2000), while some studies have also found a strong relation between mental and even physical health and network position (Putnam 2000, 226–235; Rose 2000). While these consequences for individuals certainly entail societal benefits, research has also shown a more direct link between certain aspects of social capital and large-scale outcomes, such as economic growth (Fukuyama 1995; Knack and Keefer 1997; Dasgupta and Sergaldin 2000), lower crime rates (Jacobs 1961; Wilson 1987) and more responsive government (Putnam 1993).

These various examples of the consequences of social capital are indicative of a seeming division within the pursuit of social capital research. It appears that the sociological tradition of social capital research is interested in a large variety of benefits that social capital provides for the individual or for selected groups of individuals. This view is far reaching and includes such diverse examples as a network of diamond traders, a network of concerned school parents and strong family relations as forms of social capital. These networks can benefit the individual member of the network and others who are not members (e.g., other parents at school), or alternatively sometimes these networks can be so exclusive that the benefits become some sort of club good only, excluding outsiders. The political science research on social capital seems to apply a relatively normative view as social capital is often linked to largely societal benefits, mostly defined in terms of democratic goals. But even in the latter approach, the concept is not inherently positive: Even societies might have very harmful collective goals, and the presence of social capital might allow them to reach those goals more easily. For example, in predominantly white neighborhoods, community organizations can be used to exclude racial and ethnic minorities. For both traditions, though it is true that social capital enables and facilitates collective action, the difference is that in the sociological tradition social capital and its benefits have been examined in a variety of contexts, whereas in political science social capital is often (though not exclusively) linked to democracy and wider societal payoffs. In other words, the radius of the benefits sometimes differs across these accounts.

Not all types of social capital are seen as beneficial, and only specific aspects of social capital might have positive effects for the wider society. For example, Granovetter introduced the useful distinction between strong and weak ties, arguing that the latter kind provides various benefits to its members, particularly in terms of job searches (Granovetter 1973). Weak ties allow for more effective information flows and are therefore particularly beneficial for facilitating collective action. Another distinction is based on the difference between bonding social capital, which results from interactions with people like oneself, and bridging interactions which are with people from a broad sampling of the population (Putnam 2000). Bridging is believed to instill tolerance and acceptance of otherness, one of the foundations of civic virtues. Also trust has various forms: Particularized trust, for example, is directed at members of one's actual or imagined group and it provides the necessary fabric for achieving group goals more efficiently. Generalized trust, on the other hand, is a rather encompassing value that reaches to include most people and is most beneficial in contact with strangers (Brewer 1981; Yamagishi and Yamagishi 1994; Uslaner 2002). There is an implicit assumption that weak ties, bridging interactions and generalized trust might be forms of social capital that benefit both the individual and the wider society.

One of the most interesting questions from the political science perspective then concerns the conditions and influences that facilitate, maintain or even destroy those aspects of social capital that benefit society at large. It is rather puzzling that this question is seldom explicitly addressed. Following Putnam's lead in his study on Italy (1993), some authors seem to rely on a path dependency model. Some countries or societies are simply seen as high on beneficial aspects of social capital, as a result of a civic tradition that is historically grown. Other societies, on the other hand, are inhabited by particularized trusters and are characterized by a lack of weak and bridging social interactions.

Empirical research indeed shows that patterns of trust and distrust, or generalized and particularized trust, tend to be persistent. As far as survey research goes back, the Swedes and the Dutch have always been generalized trusters, for example.

However, going beyond the assumption that only strong civic traditions can be behind the strong civic presence of today, it is very plausible that contemporary institutional arrangements as well might facilitate or disturb the development and maintenance of social capital. The study of institutional aspects and public policies that contribute to the maintenance of stocks of social capital, therefore, merits our further attention.

Moreover, social capital patterns are not exclusively stable and given once and for all. Not only do we observe important changes over time, but we also see marked differences within societies. These patterns already suggest that it is fundamental to study the factors that are behind these temporal and inter- as well as intraregional variations. If social interaction patterns and the accompanying norms were simply reproduced from one generation to the next, trust levels would remain stable over time throughout a variety of societies. Children would be just as trusting (or distrusting) as their parents. Research indeed shows that family background and education patterns strongly influence attitudes of young people at the individual level (Stolle 2002). This does not imply, however that these practices fully determine one's attitudes and values: At the aggregate level, time series show marked fluctuations in trust levels from one point in time to another. And in the United States at least, the fluctuations have been mainly downward for the past four decades. While in the early 1960s some 55 percent of all Americans agreed with the statement that "most people can be trusted," by the year 2000, this was down to 35 percent (Putnam 2000, 140). Somewhere during the past four decades, societal and cultural changes have led to a more distrusting outlook in the United States. As Putnam has shown, this is mostly a generational effect: Younger cohorts systematically report lower trust levels than their parents. In Europe, on the other hand, we do not have solid indications that generalized trust is declining just as rapidly. On the contrary, trust has been maintained at relatively high levels in Scandinavian countries, whereas it gradually increased in Germany, for example. Trust, therefore, is not simply some stable element of our national heritages, but some factors can be identified that generate, maintain or obstruct the development of generalized trust and other social capital-related attitudes.

Finally, in all societies that have been studied, trust levels vary enormously according to social class. Newton (1999, 185) summarizes the research quite neatly when he states that "Social trust is most strongly expressed...by the winners in society, in so far as it correlates most strongly with education, satisfaction with life, income, class, and race. For that matter social trust is the prerogative of the winners in the world." Trust levels are typically lowest among the segments of the population with low living standards, with little educational attainment, and among minorities (Verba, Schlozman and Brady 1995; Onyx and Bullen 2001). If trust was simply some constant background presence, there would not be any reason for these systematic differences.

In addition, if generalized trust was a mere reflection of the perceived trustworthiness of other citizens within the same society, in principle all the inhabitants of a country or region would have more or less the same perception of the trustworthiness of their fellow citizens, because they experience similar atmospheres of trustworthiness. Yet this is clearly not the case; even within a defined region or country, citizens differ in terms of the trust they develop for their fellow citizens. The variance within populations of the same region or nation calls for further explanation.

Identifying the causes of these variations, too, should give us more insight into the factors responsible for the creation of social capital. Therefore, the findings on the social stratification of generalized trust and other civic attitudes, the temporal changes as well as the individual, regional and national differences, suggest that there must be some clearly identifiable factors influencing the attitudinal component of social capital, both among individuals and among societies. In most chapters in this volume, we try to identify such factors.

ISSUES RAISED BY SOCIAL CAPITAL THEORY AND TACKLED IN THIS BOOK

The main goal of this volume is to reach a better understanding of the factors that might be important for the generation, or for that matter, the destruction of social capital. There are three main reasons why we want to focus on this topic. First, it allows us to address one of the main shortcomings of current social capital research. Attention has been focused almost exclusively on trying to measure social capital, or trying to ascertain its consequences. We do not deny that these are important issues, but we see no compelling reason why the question of how social capital might be generated, which is arguably the most important one from a policy point of view, has all but been neglected in most of the research. Governments and development corporations no longer need to be persuaded to consider social capital as part and parcel of any democratic development process. These policy makers, however, have access to few clues on how they might succeed in effectively generating social capital.

Second, developing a sound causal mechanism for the generation of social capital would allow us to answer one of the main points of critique against current concepts of social capital. The problem with social capital research to date is that the demonstration of strong relationships between social capital and positive outcomes did not deliver evidence about the causal direction of the relation. While Putnam assumes that face-to-face interaction with others, whether within voluntary associations or simply with neighbors or friends, will lead to the creation and generalization of trust, the other causal argument might be just as plausible: Those high on trust will find it easier or more appealing to interact with others. The argument about the effects of social capital on institutional performance might just as well be turned around: In areas where institutions work well, it is easier to develop trust and interactions. Even the path dependency approach might be accused of potential circularity: The main explanation for current high levels then simply becomes that a region has always been high on social trust, which is a weak argument (Foley and Edwards 1998). Identifying clear causal mechanisms for the generation of social capital would allow us to escape from this kind of circular reasoning.

Third, it is clear that we cannot draw any conclusions about the rise and decline of social capital without fully examining the origins and nature of the concept. In *Bowling Alone*, Putnam (1995, 2000) argued that participation levels and all other components of social capital are declining in the United States, and this clearly struck a sensitive nerve, not only in American society but also in the scientific community at large. Since this discussion started, a lot of articles, books and conferences have been produced arguing for or against the decline thesis (Norris 2002; Stolle and Hooghe 2003). These kinds of arguments cannot be conclusive. What we need, instead, is a more precise understanding of when certain aspects of social capital matter, and where social capital comes from in order to draw any final conclusions about its rise and decline. It does not make sense to make inferences from trends in associational memberships and other types of social interaction regarding the state of social capital if we do not even know which types of social interactions or which types of institutions really contribute to its creation. We must therefore untangle these relationships before we engage in arguments for or against social capital's decline (however, see the commentaries in Hall 1999; Kohut 1996; Ladd 1999; Putnam 1995, 2000 and 2002).

THEMES OF THE BOOK

Although the debate about the precise nature of social capital has been going on for the last ten years, it is mostly based on normative and ideological assumptions, and several questions remain unresolved due to a lack of thorough empirical research. If we are interested in forms of social capital that benefit the broader society rather than just a small segment of the population, several important questions arise. Following the society centered approach, the issue is *whether* and *how* various types of social interactions develop civic attitudes and skills that help to overcome collective action problems. In other words, we need to know which types of social interactions cause the development of social capital and how. Are all associations alike in their democratizing effects? What aspects of group life are particularly beneficial for generating norms of reciprocity and trust? What is the causal mechanism involved, and why would associations have a much stronger influence than other socialization contexts? These questions must be answered before we use various indicators of social capital interchangeably. The chapters in the first part of this book try to answer these questions.

However, following the institution-centered approach, we do not really know much about the facilitation of social capital outside of associational life. Which type of neighborhood composition, character of local political life, and governmental experiences are related to patterns and levels of social capital? Which degree of government involvement would be optimal for the maintenance and support of social capital? Which aspects of government and which characteristics of political institutions might be particularly beneficial in fostering trust and related cooperative values? The chapters in the second part of the book take a close look at these issues.

The aim of this volume is to explore how various societal interaction settings on the one hand, and institutions and government policy on the other hand, may contribute to the generation of social capital. The editors, and most of the authors involved, do not depart from a fixed preference for society-centered or institution-centered approaches. The underlying assumption of this volume is rather that both society and institutions play a role in the creation of social capital. The most promising research goal, therefore, is to know under what circumstances these two sources matter for social capital. The research reported in this volume suggests that even though certain types of memberships are related to civic attitudes, we should be cautious in viewing voluntary associations as the main *producers* of these attitudes. Aspects of governmental policy and political institutions as well as societal divisions have important effects on the level and patterns of social capital. The results warn us that the causal relations assumed in the theoretical literature are not always as clear and straightforward as is often suggested.

In the first five chapters, we investigate *whether* and *how* voluntary associations foster generalized trust and other attitudinal aspects of social capital such as norms of reciprocity. Contrary to previous research, all of these chapters search for the relationships between specific aspects of participation and civic attitudes, with a special focus on the effect of group types, as well as the characteristics and mechanisms behind the group socialization experience. The authors examine socialization characteristics such as the number of memberships (Mayer; Wollebæk and Selle; van der Meer); intensity of participation (Wollebæk and Selle); length of membership (Stolle); aggregate member characteristics (Hooghe) and informal interactions (Molenaers). In addition, an analysis at the level of countries and regions (van der Meer) allows us to disentangle micro and macro effects of membership and other aspects of social capital. These chapters examine the circumstances under which citizens effectively generate social capital in the realm of civil society.

This first part leads to the conclusion that there is indeed a relation between voluntary associations and attitudinal aspects of social capital. In particular, most authors conclude that multiple or overlapping personal memberships are an important aspect of group life that is obviously related to the development of civic attitudes. This finding is important from a theoretical point of view: Social capital studies tend to assume that bridging relations (uniting actors across social cleavages) are more important than bonding relations (creating bonds within homogeneous subcultures). The studies on the effect of multiple memberships suggest that the bridging character of relations is not necessarily produced in the association itself but could also be the result of overlapping memberships at the individual level. As can be gathered from the data in the chapters by Mayer and Wollebæk and Selle, a lot of people belong to more than one association, thereby effectively establishing their own form of bridging social capital. An individual belonging to, for example, a women's organization, a religious group and a trade union will be exposed to various cross-pressures, even if all of these organizations, considered independently, are homogeneous.

These chapters on the role of associations, however, also raise two important caveats. First, not all types of associations are equally related to attitudinal aspects of social capital. And second, not all types of interactions matter equally. For example, membership in social and hobby groups and memberships that entail face-to-face interactions are less distinctive in their effects on civic attitudes than is predicted by social capital theory.

The next five chapters investigate institutional determinants of social capital outside the realm of civil society: neighborhood characteristics, government policy, the character of bureaucracies and the role of the political and economic elite. These chapters document how government policy and institutions have an effect on trust and other indicators of social capital. The authors focus particularly on the effects of local socioeconomic conditions, local composition and local environment (De Hart and Dekker), income policies and income equality (Uslaner), fairness and impartiality of institutions (Rothstein and Stolle) and structures of political institutions versus historical factors (Huysseune). These chapters explore the ways in which government policy and institutional characteristics and cleavages produce or erode social capital. Patterns of income equality, regional segregation as well as fair and impartial institutions play a particularly important role. The research reported in these chapters, however, also cautions against unwarranted optimism: Institutional effects do not work overnight; rather, long-established institutional patterns and policies are behind successful cases of social capital.

The overall conclusion of these chapters is that under certain conditions, both society and institutions play a role in the development of social capital. This would leave at least some policy options available for strategic interventions in order to boost the amount of social capital in a given society (e.g., fighting income inequality, constructing fair institutions and procedures, influencing local infrastructure, etc.). At the same time, the research reported in this volume leads to the insight that there is no single "magic bullet" solution. The generation of social capital is dependent upon a sustained and synergistic interaction between civil society and government institutions. Although it might be useful to try to entice citizens to become more engaged in civil society (Putnam 2000), or to try to create more open and egalitarian institutions (Skocpol 1999), the presence and the amount of social capital is ultimately dependent upon the interplay between these two factors. While most of the theoretical debate so far suggests that predominantly either society or state institutions are responsible for generating social capital, the empirical research reported in this volume highlights that both society and state can and do play a role, depending upon historical and other circumstances.

The chapters assembled in this volume are all strongly empirically oriented and constitute a valuable complement to some of the recent, theoretically oriented literature on social capital. Not only do the authors use a range of methodological approaches and data sets to test major assumptions of social capital theory and to examine the sources of social capital systematically, there is also wide geographical variation. The research settings range from Sweden to Norway, the United States, Belgium, France, the Netherlands, Italy and Nicaragua.

BRIEF INTRODUCTION OF INDIVIDUAL CHAPTERS

The following chapter, by Dietlind Stolle, offers an overview of the current state of social capital research. Stolle examines the current debate about the potential sources of social capital in more detail. Two under-researched areas in the search for sources of social capital are identified: the lack of empirical research on associational structures and their varying effect on civic attitudes and the lack of research on the role of governments and political institutions to foster attitudinal aspects of social capital. This introductory chapter links the discussion about the social capital research agenda to the remainder of the book.

In the third chapter, Nonna Mayer examines the effects of memberships in voluntary associations in France on civic attitudes. As far as classical voluntary associations are concerned, in France at least, their members are neither more trusting nor more civic. Mayer's findings suggest that "civil" society is not necessarily "civic" society, especially not if one defines civicness narrowly, as an attachment to representative democracy, its institutions and its authorities. However, "joiners" are, indeed, more aware of politics; they pay more attention to and know more about political issues. Tocqueville's intuition about the role of voluntary associations as intermediaries, connecting the private and the public sphere, still holds true.

Dag Wollebæk and Per Selle expand the examination of voluntary associational membership to include the case of Norway, where many citizens hold passive memberships in associations. Based on a 1998 Norwegian survey, the authors investigate the different effects of passive and active membership, while also taking the intensity of the involvement into account. Contrary to some assumptions in social capital theory, the authors conclude that passive membership is just as effective as active membership in promoting civic attitudes. Therefore there seems to be no real need for face-to-face interaction among members of associations for trust and civic attitudes to thrive. The analysis also shows that the time intensity of participation is less important than, for example, the multiplicity of memberships an individual holds. This corresponds to the classic notion that embeddedness in multiple networks is conducive to successful integration in society. The analysis, however, offers little support for the claim that citizens should be actively involved in associations in order for associations to have a powerful effect on the formation of a democratic civic culture.

Even if we assume that associations really are important for fostering democratic attitudes, the existing literature still does not specify a causal mechanism that could explain the occurrence of this effect. Based on a 1998 Belgian face-to-face survey, Marc Hooghe suggests that some of the effects of associational membership can be explained using a socialization logic. Based on a review of the social psychology literature on group interaction, the author argues that these socialization effects are dependent upon member and group characteristics. Members learn civic (or uncivic) attitudes in associations as a result of the concentration of selected attitudes within a group. This would imply that not all kinds of associations can be considered as sources of social capital, but only those associations in which democratic value patterns predominate. At the same time, this causal mechanism suggests that membership in voluntary associations cannot fundamentally change people's beliefs and values.

In most of the literature on social capital, attention is focused on the role of formal voluntary associations. In third-world development projects, too, international organizations like the World Bank or various development corporations tend to seek partnerships with local nongovernmental organizations. Nadia Molenaers relies on innovative fieldwork in two remote Nicaraguan villages to demonstrate that voluntary associations do not always function as democratic sources of social capital. Network analysis shows that these nongovernmental organizations tend to distribute the material benefits they receive from outside donors mainly among their members and supporters, while neglecting other members of the community. The organizations also tend to manifest ideological, political and ethnic cleavages among the population. The analysis shows, furthermore, that informal exchange mechanisms, like those traditionally found among neighboring farmers, are much more effective in ensuring equal access to scarce capital goods. The theoretical relevance of this finding is that democratic participation should not be equated with membership in formal associations, as is often done: In some circumstances, informal networks have more powerful democratic effects. The study also questions the possibility of "artificially" creating an organized civil society through outside donor interventions.

Job van der Meer tackles a related assertion about the importance of voluntary associations. The "rain maker" argument states that the benefits provided by associations do not remain limited to the members themselves, but that these can be seen as a collective good, to the benefit of all individuals within a region or nation, whether members or not. Van der Meer puts this argument to the test by ascertaining whether nonmembers too, benefit from the presence of strong associational networks within their society. For some attitudes at least, this indeed proves to be the case. This conclusion would imply that there might be a collective benefit resulting from associational membership. It is therefore possible that most research on the importance of voluntary associations is misdirected: If associations really function as a pure collective good, we do not expect to find differences between members and nonmembers per se, but we rather expect to find societal differences, depending on the density of the associational networks within that society.

In the second part of this volume, attention is shifted from the role of voluntary associations to the effects of institutional and contextual variables on the formation of social capital. Joep de Hart and Paul Dekker examine the differences in social capital between a rural village and an impoverished city neighborhood in the Netherlands based on survey and focus group materials. The authors show that population characteristics as well as local factors pertaining to safety, diversity and public space largely explain differences in social capital in both regions. Yet different factors play a role for different aspects of social capital. They find that the city neighborhood, with a concentration of unemployed, poor groups and ethnic minorities, has few chances of developing a thriving civic community. Feelings of insecurity are very high in this place, and this seems to be one of the elements feeding this "vicious circle." It is argued that if we want to explain a lack of social capital in some neighborhoods, regions or countries, these economic backgrounds and cleavage structures should be taken into account.

Shifting from local patterns of social capital to national policies, Eric Uslaner explores the possibility that the nature of government policy could explain the observed relation between democratic governance and generalized trust levels. In an analysis of the World Values Survey, the author finds that trust is a deep-rooted attitude, formed early in life, which can be altered only slightly by later experiences. However, the author does observe a relationship between prolonged periods of democratic government (more than forty years of continuous democracy) and trust levels. Governments can foster these democratic attitudes, and even though it might not happen in the short run, they might "produce" more trusting citizens after several decades of democratic experience. Most importantly, Uslaner offers evidence that countries that implemented policies to reduce income inequality have higher levels of generalized trust. Creating social capital does not seem to be primarily a responsibility of the voluntary sector but rather the effect of sustained democracy and income equality.

This insight is taken up by Bo Rothstein and Dietlind Stolle, and they go further to ask about the causal mechanism between generalized trust and the institutions that implement public policy. Their main argument is that impartial and fair procedures practiced by government institutions have a positive effect on trust in a society. In particular, the authors explore the relationship between the character of the welfare state institutions and trust in society, as some welfare state institutions exhibit a more divisive and others a more encompassing and inclusive character. The authors support their argument with survey data from Sweden, demonstrating that confidence in welfare institutions and in law-enforcing institutions seems more relevant for explaining generalized trust levels than the confidence expressed in political institutions, such as the parliament, which are very distant from the day-to-day life of ordinary citizens. The authors conclude that if we want political institutions to have a positive effect on social capital levels, the character of bureaucracies and welfare state institutions would have to be our primary areas of interest.

Michel Huysseune, too, highlights the role of government policy by looking at the recent history of North and South Italy. According to this analysis, efforts to trace the differences in civic culture between northern and southern Italy to their different political histories during the Middle Ages fail to acknowledge the fact that at least for the nineteenth century, we observe no systematic differences between the economic and political development of the two parts of the country. Cultural path dependency therefore cannot be considered a satisfactory explanation for the observed contemporary differences. It is argued that the policy of the central government in Rome, and the power of the Christian Democratic party, helped to maintain a system of patronage in southern Italy. The influence of powerful political actors, like the Communist Party, also should be taken into consideration. Huysseune uses historical data and literature to support this thesis. At a theoretical level, a comparison is made between the situation in southern Italy and the challenge of contemporary developing countries to build social capital. The main argument here is that government policy and political parties play an essential role as sources of social capital and thriving civic communities.

In our conclusion, we integrate the various insights of the authors in these chapters and emphasize the fact that the limited potential of voluntary associations to generate civic values suggests two avenues for future research. On the one hand, along with the institution-centered approach that we present in this volume, we need more studies that disentangle the causal effects of institutions on civicness. The chapters in the second part of this volume clearly show that institutional characteristics cannot be left out of the social capital equation. On the other hand, in sync with the society-centered approach, the study of the effects of diverse networks, overlapping networks and more informal social interactions is also underexplored.

REFERENCES

Banfield, E. C. (1958). *The Moral Basis of a Backward Society*. New York: The Free Press.

Brewer, M. B. (1981). "Ethnocentrism and Its Role in Interpersonal Trust." pp. 345–360. In M. Brewer and B. Collins (eds.), *Scientific Inquiry and the Social Sciences*. San Francisco: Jossey-Bass Publishers.

Coleman, J. S. (1990). *Foundations of Social Theory*. Cambridge, MA: Harvard University Press.

Coleman, J. S. and T. Hoffer (1988). *Public and Private High Schools. The Impact of Communities*. New York: Basic Books.

Dalton, R. (1996). *Citizen Politics*. Chatham, NJ: Chatham House Publishers.

Dasgupta, P. and I. Sergaldin (eds., 2000). *Social Capital. A Multifaceted Perspective*. Washington, D.C.: World Bank.

De Graaf, N. D., P. De Graaf, and G. Kraaykamp (2000). "Parental Cultural Capital and Educational Attainment in the Netherlands: A Refinement of the Cultural Capital Perspective." *Sociology of Education* 73(2), 92–111.

Foley, M. and B. Edwards (1998). "Beyond Tocqueville: Civil Society and Social Capital in Comparative Perspective." *American Behavioral Scientist* 42(1), 5–20.

Fukuyama, F. (1995). *Trust: The Social Virtues and Creation of Prosperity*. London: Hamish Hamilton.

Granovetter, M. S. (1973). "The Strength of Weak Ties." *American Journal of Sociology* 78, 1360–1380.

Hall, P. (1999). "Social Capital in Britain." *British Journal of Political Science* 29, 417–461.

Jacobs, J. (1961). *Death and Life of Great American Cities*. New York: Random House.

Knack, S. and P. Keefer (1997). "Does Social Capital Have an Economic Payoff? A Cross-Country Investigation." *Quarterly Journal of Economics* 112, 1251–1288.

Kohut, A. (1996). *Trust and Civic Engagement in Metropolitan Philadelphia: A Case Study.* Washington: Pew Center for the People and the Press.

Ladd, E. (1999). *The Ladd Report.* New York: Free Press.

Newton, K. (1999). "Social and Political Trust in Established Democracies." pp. 169–187. In P. Norris (ed.), *Critical Citizens.* New York: Oxford University Press.

Norris, P. (2002). *Democratic Phoenix.* Cambridge: Cambridge University Press.

Onyx, J. and P. Bullen (2001). "The Different Faces of Social Capital in NSW Australia." pp. 45–58. In P. Dekker and E. Uslaner (eds.), *Social Capital and Participation in Everyday Life.* London: Routledge.

Ostrom, E. (2001). "Social Capital and Collective Action." Paper presented at the conference "Social Capital: Interdisciplinary Perspectives," Exeter University, September 15–20, 2001.

Putnam, R. (1993). *Making Democracy Work.* Princeton: Princeton University Press.

Putnam, R. (1995). "Bowling Alone: America's Declining Social Capital." *Journal of Democracy* 6(1), 65–78.

Putnam, R. (2000). *Bowling Alone.* New York: Simon and Schuster.

Putnam, R. (ed., 2002). *Democracies in Flux: The Evolution of Social Capital in Contemporary Society.* Oxford: Oxford University Press.

Rose, R. (2000). "How Much Does Social Capital Add to Individual Health? A Survey Study of Russians." *Social Science and Medicine* 51(9), 1421–1435.

Skocpol, Th. (1999). "How Americans Became Civic." pp. 27–80. In Th. Skocpol and M. Fiorina (eds.), *Civic Engagement in American Democracy.* Washington, D.C.: Brookings Institution.

Stolle, D. (2002). "The Social and Political Role of Schools and Families in the Creation of Generalized Trust." Current Rusell Sage Foundation Project.

Stolle, D. and M. Hooghe (2003). "Consumers as Political Participants? Shifts in Political Action Repertoires in Western Societies." In M. Micheletti, A. Føllesdal and D. Stolle (eds., 2003), *The Politics Behind Products: Using the Market as a Site for Ethics and Action.* New Jersey: Transaction Press.

Tarrow, S. (1996). "Making Social Science Work Across Space and Time: A Critical Reflection on Robert Putnam's Making Democracy Work." *American Political Science Review* 90, 389–397.

Uslaner, E. (2002), *The Moral Foundations of Trust.* New York: Cambridge University Press.

Verba, S. and N. Nie (1972). *Participation in America: Political Democracy and Social Equality.* New York: Harper and Row.

Verba, S., N. Nie and J.-O. Kim (1978). *Participation and Political Equality*. New York: Cambridge University Press.
Verba, S., K. Schlozman and H. Brady (1995). *Voice and Equality: Civic Volunteerism in American Politics*. Cambridge: Harvard University Press.
Wilson, W. J. (1987). *The Truly Disadvantaged*. Chicago: University of Chicago Press.
Yamagishi, T. and M. Yamagishi (1994). "Trust and Commitment in the United States and Japan." *Motivation and Emotion* 18, 129–166.

CHAPTER 2

THE SOURCES OF SOCIAL CAPITAL

Dietlind Stolle

INTRODUCTION

Have the citizens of Western democracies lost their trust in each other? If so, what are the sources of this unfortunate development and what are the consequences? Why can citizens in some regions or villages join together and solve their collective action problems while others cannot? These questions have been prompted in large part by the growing conviction that the answers are crucial both to political stability and to economic development.

In the 1990s, scholarly studies and polemical essays attempted to answer these difficult questions, drawing attention to resources that derive from the society itself, namely social capital. While many dimensions of the concept of social capital are far from new, major sociological and political science contributions in the late 1980s and early 1990s (Coleman 1988, 1990; Putnam 1993, 2000) have provoked new research and much debate over the last decade. Scholars have been increasingly concerned with this key social resource that seems to oil the wheels of the market economy and democratic politics. The existence and maintenance of social trust and networks in communities seems to lower the amount of drug use, criminal activity, teenage pregnancies and delinquency; to increase the success of schools and their pupils; to enhance economic development; and to make government more effective (Fukuyama 1995; Granovetter 1985; Hagan, Merkens and Boehnke 1995; Jencks and Peterson 1991; Kawachi et al. 1997; Knack and Keefer 1997; La Porta et al. 2000; Putnam 1993, 2000). In short, social capital is conceptualized as a societal resource that links citizens to each other and enables them to pursue their common objectives more effectively. It taps the potential willingness of citizens to cooperate with each other and to engage in civic endeavors collectively. As such, it has proved influential as a means of countering the strong emphasis on the atomized individual that was so characteristic of politics (and economics) during the 1980s in the United States and the United Kingdom.

Robert D. Putnam struck a sensitive nerve when he applied his argument to the United States and argued in *Bowling Alone* (1995a, 2000) that social capital has been in steady decline over the last four decades. His description of falling membership in voluntary associations, declining volunteerism, political apathy and rising political and social distrust seemed to confirm the civic disarray that people had experienced in recent decades in the West. Scholars have debated, contested and re-examined Putnam's alarming interpretations and warnings.[1] While the idea of social capital seems to capture what large numbers of people, politicians included, are feeling about the problems of early-twenty-first-century Western societies, there is considerable disagreement about the conceptualization and measurement of social capital and its sources and about exactly how and why it is important (Stolle and Hooghe 2002). Most of the key contributions to the debate have focused on the significance of associations and other social interactions that comprise "civil society" and their importance for the building of the attitudinal aspects of social capital, such as trust and cooperation. These formal and informal social interactions contribute to the emergence of societal norms and generalized values, even though not all types of interactions are equally productive of these traits. The role of political institutions has only recently been introduced into the discussion about the sources of generalized values such as trust and reciprocity. The remainder of this chapter assesses the current state of research on the sources of attitudinal aspects of social capital, more than half a decade after the revival of the social capital debate.[2]

THE SOURCES OF SOCIAL CAPITAL: AN OVERVIEW

How are the norms of reciprocity and values of trust generalized and institutionalized, and what is different among groups, regions and nations where this is not the case? This is the most under-researched area in social capital studies, supporting only a few hypotheses, all of which need more development and empirical testing. There has been debate about the extent to which local, regional or national patterns of social capital have been fixed and shaped by historical factors on the one hand, and about the feasibility of contemporary forces to change levels and forms of social capital on the other. The question is, of course, which contemporary factors influence social capital formation. There is some disagreement between those who view the source of social capital as residing mainly in the realm of civil society, centered chiefly on groups of voluntary associations and largely disconnected from the state and political institutions, and those who argue that for social capital to flourish it needs to be embedded in and linked to formal political institutions (Berman 1997; Foley and Edwards 1998; Levi 1998; Skocpol 1996; Tarrow 1996). According to the latter group of scholars, social capital does not exist independently in the realm of civil society: Governments, public policies, societal cleavages, economic conditions and political institutions channel and influence social capital such that it becomes either a beneficial or detrimental resource for democracy. In this account, the capacity of citizens to develop cooperative ties is also determined by the effects of state policy. This point of view would imply that institutional engineering might indeed be used to foster social capital.

In an attempt to bridge these camps, Putnam has recently argued that in the U.S. context, the combined effort of employers, the mass media, voluntary associations, individual citizens and government is needed to restore levels of social capital in the United States (2000, 402ff.; see also Putnam 2002). The debate about whether and how social capital can be intentionally developed is crucial for low social capital areas attempting to restore or facilitate this resource (Petro 2001). Special attention has been devoted to the potential of the state to erode and destroy social capital.

Although this debate has been going for some years, it is mostly based on normative and ideological assumptions, and several questions remain unresolved due to a lack of thorough empirical research. For example, following the argument of society-centered accounts, we do not really know whether or how voluntary associations influence their members' civic attitudes. Are all associations alike in their democratizing effects, and what aspects of group life are particularly beneficial for generating norms of reciprocity and trust? What is the causal mechanism involved, and why would associations have a much stronger influence than other socialization contexts? At the same time, following the institution-centered approach, we do not really know which aspects of government and which characteristics of political institutions might be particularly beneficial in fostering trust, related cooperative values and social participation. In the remainder of this chapter, we investigate these current debates in detail.

HISTORICAL FORCES VERSUS CONTEMPORARY FACTORS

Putnam (1993), Fukuyama (1995) and Banfield (1958) maintain that the capacity of a society to ensure cooperation among its citizens is determined by its historical experience. Putnam, for example, traces social capital to medieval Italy, explaining how, in the south, Norman mercenaries built a powerful feudal monarchy with hierarchical structures, whereas in the north communal republics based on horizontal relationships fostered mutual assistance and economic cooperation. Putnam seeks to demonstrate that the "civicness" of the north survived natural catastrophes and political changes. In addition, he points out that the civic regions were not wealthier in the first place. The implications of this view have left many social scientists and policy makers dissatisfied: If the amount of social capital in a society is so strongly path dependent, then there would seem to be few policy options available to stimulate the development of social capital. It is more likely that governments, and particularly oppressive regimes, can damage and destroy social capital, as the examples of the Norman kingdom in southern Italy and of several authoritarian and totalitarian regimes in southern and eastern Europe show. The most pessimistic view would be that societies that are low on social capital are simply stuck in a quagmire of distrust, and there seems to be little that can be done about it. However, in his later work Putnam makes clear that we need to make a distinction between short-term and long-term institutional influences on social capital. It might be true that generalized trust as well as forms and density of social interactions are shaped through historical forces, but present-day social and political institutions and local, regional and national governments are also able to make an impact. We will review two main debates and resulting research on societal factors, mostly voluntary associations, and on other institutional factors, mainly governmental, below.

THE ROLE OF VOLUNTARY ASSOCIATIONS

Most accounts of social capital rely predominantly on the importance of social interactions and voluntary associations in the manner originally suggested by Tocqueville. The most important mechanism for the generation of norms of reciprocity and trust is identified as regular social interaction (Putnam 1993, 1995a). Following the Tocquevillian tradition, associations are seen as creators of social capital because of their socialization effects on democratic and cooperative values and norms: Associations function as "learning schools for democracy."[3] For example, the settlement houses were often referred to as training grounds for the participants to shape and influence their social values and further political demands (Putnam 2000, 394ff.). Similarly horizontal voluntary associations are thought to have influenced the cooperative spirit of Northern Italians.

The claim is that in areas with stronger, dense, horizontal, and more cross-cutting networks, there is a spillover from membership in organizations to the cooperative values and norms that citizens develop. In areas where networks with such characteristics do not develop, there are fewer opportunities to learn civic virtues and democratic attitudes, resulting in a lack of trust. In this account, social capital is seen as important because it benefits the functioning of democratic institutions. At the microlevel, this entails the relationship between an individual's membership in associations and networks (structural aspects of social capital), and an individual's values and attitudes (cultural aspects of social capital). So far the social capital school has mainly used membership in voluntary associations or other types of networks as the indicator of social capital, *assuming* that such groups and associations function as a school of democracy, in which cooperative values and trust are easily socialized.[4] However, we do not have empirical proof of this function. In other words, we do not truly know whether voluntary associations act in this way, or, if so, how. In addition, we also do not know much about other aspects of social interactions that are sufficient and necessary for the institutionalization of cooperative values and generalized trust. The problem is that there is no microtheory of social capital that explicitly states which aspects of social interactions matter for the creation of generalized trust and norms of reciprocity. So, while the microrelationship between membership in voluntary associations, on the one hand, and trust and attitudes of cooperation, on the other, underlies contemporary theories of social capital, the efficacy of voluntary associations in creating trust and reciprocity has so far only been assumed in the literature and has not been empirically tested or explored.

The reason for this lacuna in social capital research so far has been that very few data sets actually combine these indicators of social capital, trust and cooperation with measures of the structure of individual associations or interactions, the content of their work and the degree of social contact that exists. National and cross-national surveys that include questions on generalized attitudes, like the National Election Studies in the United States, the General Social Surveys, or the World Values Surveys, do not give detailed information about the respondents' involvement in different types of associations. Some exceptions are the Belgian national survey (Hooghe 2003) and the time budget study in the Netherlands (Dekker and De Hart 1999). However, even the use of national-level survey data with more detailed associational indicators does not give much insight into the associational life of specific groups; hence, group-level characteristics as causes of social capital production cannot be directly identified. As a result, we do not know whether trust and cooperative attitudes increase linearly with the length of time spent in any type of association or other social interaction, or whether they are a function of a particular type of involvement or a special type of group.[5]

With these limitations, research on the consequences of social participation and associational membership has indicated a general relationship with the civic traits of the participants or members. Most empirical studies on the effect of voluntary associations showed that members of organizations and associations exhibit more democratic and civic attitudes as well as more active forms of political participation than nonmembers. Almond and Verba (1963) found that members of associations are more politically active, more informed about politics, more sanguine about their ability to affect political life and more supportive of democratic norms (Billiet and Cambré 1996; Hanks and Eckland 1978; Olsen 1972; Verba and Nie 1972). Others have noticed that the number and type of associations to which people belong, and the extent of their activity within the organization, are related to political activity and involvement (Rogers, Bultena and Barb 1975). In later research, Verba and his colleagues found that members of voluntary associations learn self-respect, group identity and public skills (Verba, Schlozman and Brady 1995; Dekker, Koopmans and van den Broek 1997; Moyser and Parry 1997). Similarly, Clemens shows how multiple memberships in women's organizations and additional training at the turn of the twentieth century fostered the transfer of civic and organizational skills and interpersonal ties. This web of formal and informal organizations provided the backdrop of the women's suffrage movement (Clemens 1999).

To these findings, the social capital school adds the insight that membership in associations should also facilitate the learning of cooperative attitudes and behavior, including reciprocity. In particular, membership in voluntary associations should increase face-to-face interactions between people and create a setting for the development of trust. This in-group trust can be utilized to achieve group purposes more efficiently and more easily. Furthermore, via mechanisms that are not yet clearly understood, the development of interpersonal trust and the cooperative experiences between members tend to be generalized to the society as a whole. In this way, the operation of voluntary groups and associations contributes to the building of a society in which cooperation between all people for all sorts of purposes—not just within the groups themselves—is facilitated (for empirical evidence regarding this relationship, see Almond and Verba 1963; Brehm and Rahn 1997; Hooghe and Derks 1997; Hooghe 2003; Seligson 1999; Stolle and Rochon 1998, 1999).[6]

The problem with the research to date is that even though individuals who join groups and who interact with others regularly show attitudinal and behavioral differences compared to nonjoiners, the possibility exists that people self-select into association groups, depending on their original levels of generalized trust and reciprocity. This is a classic problem of endogeneity. People who trust more might be more easily drawn to membership in associations, whereas people who trust less might not join in the first place.

Ideally one would track association members over time in order to filter out the separate influence of group membership on trust, controlling for self-selection effects. However, such longitudinal data are rarely available and are time-consuming and costly to collect. Another strategy is to compare those who are more active with those who are less engaged in associational life. In order to gain better insights into the relationship between self-selection and membership effects, Stolle collected a data set sampling nonmembers and members in various associations in three countries—Germany, Sweden and the United States—and carried out two comparisons, namely between nonmembers and members, and between those who had just joined and those who participated for longer periods. The finding is that membership does indeed influence trust toward the other group members and personal engagement within the group, but with regard to *generalized* trust, the self-selection effects were more pronounced than the membership effects (Stolle 2001a,b). This essentially means that people with higher levels of trust indeed self-select into associations. In other words, the strong emphasis placed by society-based accounts of social capital on traditional voluntary associations as the *producers* of generalized trust might not be warranted. In this volume we will find further qualifications of this statement (see chapters by de Hart and Dekker, Hooghe, Mayer, Wollebæk and Selle, Stolle and Hooghe, van der Meer this volume).

However, before we can draw any final conclusions about the efficacy of voluntary associations for trust and civic norms we need to consider the possibility that not all types of social interaction have similar effects on their participants. Some associations might have special characteristics that give rise to generalized trust. The reason this question arises is again that we do not have a microtheory that explains which aspects of associational life or other social interactions are important for learning generalized attitudes. We need to go one step further and look at the causal mechanisms behind this relationship and examine *how* the membership in associations or other types of social interaction might be able to influence generalized trust, if at all.

Several important hypotheses have been developed in social capital theory about specific group characteristics that might be responsible for the development of generalized values in voluntary associations. First and most important, face-to-face interactions should be more productive of civic attitudes than so-called "checkbook" organizations. Second, the group experiences might be even more pronounced in their impact when the members of the group are diverse and from different backgrounds. This type of group interaction, which is called "bridging" (Putnam 1993, 90), brings members into contact with people from a cross-section of society and, as a result, the formative experience is likely to be much more pronounced than if the association is itself a narrowly constituted segment of society (Putnam 1995b; Rogers, Bultena and Barb 1975).[7] Such bridging and overlapping ties characterized, for example, the development of women's organizations and the women's movement for suffrage in the early twentieth century in the United States (Clemens 1999). Third, memberships in hierarchical associations, such as the Catholic Church in southern Italy, which do not create mutuality and equality of participation, do not have the same effect as memberships in social capital–rich groups (Putnam 1995a). The reason is that relationships within vertical networks, because of their asymmetry, are not able to create experiences of mutuality and reciprocity to the same extent as relationships in horizontal networks.

So far, none of these hypotheses has been successfully confirmed by empirical research at the microlevel. However, some of the chapters that follow will specifically take these hypotheses up (e.g., Wollebæk and Selle this volume). The view that associations might be good schools of democracy because they bring together people from various social backgrounds has generally been contested. If diversity matters for the socialization of cooperative values, then voluntary associations might not be the place to look, as such groups have been found to be relatively homogeneous in character (Mutz and Mondak 1998; Popielarz 1999). Still, even if more-diverse associations are distinguished from less-diverse ones, the connection between group diversity and trust seems to depend much on the national context and is not a generalizable relationship throughout all Western societies (Stolle 2000). There is some evidence that suggests that bridging interactions in the neighborhood context might have beneficial effects on the formation of generalized trust. Political discussions with partners who hold opposing viewpoints also have been found to influence political tolerance (Mutz 2002).

Interestingly, at the collective or macrolevel, we find several theoretical models but only mixed empirical evidence supporting the idea of the importance of associations and social interactions for fostering civic values and attitudes and most importantly for overcoming collective action dilemmas. Here, the most developed literature examines social movements. In new social movement theory, for example, "submerged networks" of small groups from everyday life contexts help to create collective identities, which are essential for movement actions (Mueller 1994). Furthermore, van der Meer finds that in regions with higher associational density, citizens who are not even involved in associations have developed more trust in others and in political institutions (this volume). However, the relationship between regional membership density and generalized trust is not confirmed across settings (Stolle forthcoming). The additional fact that the evidence remains thin at the microlevel casts doubt on the causal relationship between associational membership and "civicness." The chapters in the first part of this volume will examine this claim.

Finally, the doubts regarding the obsessive focus on formal memberships and organizations have been echoed by scholars who work on gender relations, who argue that the research on formal and informal socializing is misguided because it looks in the wrong places. Women in particular tend to prefer more egalitarian networks, which is reflected in some examples of "feminist organizations" (Ferree and Martin 1995). The argument is made that true networks and forms of social engagement can be found in caring arrangements such as babysitting and other child-care circles (Lowndes 2000). Lowndes's point in particular urges us to consider how informal and small-scale care networks actually contribute to the maintenance of social cohesion within a society. A typical example would be that young mothers in the suburbs jointly bring their children to and pick them up from school. These kinds of arrangements are mostly informal and ad hoc, and therefore they usually are not registered in survey research on participation. Nevertheless, they are likely to contribute significantly to the maintenance of social cohesion and the advancement of quality of life within these suburbs. Lowndes therefore launches an appeal to include these kind of activities in the research on participation and social cohesion: "In order to investigate the links between social capital, political engagement and 'good government,' phenomena such as friendship, caring and neighborliness all have to be recast as legitimate objects of political enquiry" (Lowndes 2000, 537).

A number of these "female" participation patterns, which are often neglected in traditional participation research, have already been examined. Katzenstein (1998), for instance, develops the thesis that feminist activity does not necessarily translate into the formation of autonomous political organizations but can also express itself in feminist networks within larger institutions, like the military or the church. Political consumerism is another form of political engagement that can be cast in that light. Political consumers attach great importance to noneconomic, for example political, ethical and social, attitudes and values when they choose between products, producers and services (Micheletti, Føllesdal and Stolle, 2003). This means that they consider the market as an arena for politics and market actors as responsible for political and social development. Here it is particularly obvious that groups of the population that previously had not performed well on various scales of traditional participation, namely women and particularly housewives, are predominantly involved in this activity (Micheletti, 2003). However, no extensive data sources have so far captured these new phenomena of social/political engagement (however, see Andersen and Tobiasen, 2003).

In short, the actual potential of various social interactions for trust and cooperation development remain insufficiently tested by both the social capital school and its critics. The role of voluntary associations as creators of social capital, particularly of generalized trust, is not yet established by empirical evidence. The fundamental problem is that we do not have an established microtheory of social capital to support a causal link and to guide further analysis on this issue. Furthermore, there is considerable doubt that membership in voluntary associations captures the whole range of civic activities that constitute social capital.

THE ROLE OF THE FAMILY

The family is another potential source for generalized attitudes, such as trust and norms of reciprocity. It is important to note that thus far the family has been largely left out of the discussion about social capital. This relates to the historical separation of public and private in Western liberal democracies, which has meant that the family has posed difficulties for political and social theorists. John Rawls, for example, ruled it to be outside the "basic structure" of society (Moller Okin 1989). It is doubtful that the family can be considered part of civil society, yet the extent to which child-raising practices can be considered sources of civic engagement and society-regarding attitudes in the form of generalized trust and reciprocity is an important issue. The much-lamented decline in social capital has been discussed in direct relation to time budgets and the fact that women in particular have less time available for organizing and associating (whether this is a result of employment issues or unpaid work), yet there is also the possibility of the indirect effect that limited time budgets could have on child-raising practices. Bennich-Björkman (1998) provides a strong argument about the importance of child-rearing practices for the creation of generalized trust, and her argument can be extended to the building of civic engagement as well. In her account, child-care practices vary from generation to generation, with children being raised at present as a fun-loving generation that is very "I-oriented" (as opposed to "we-oriented"). The claim is that such orientations will have direct consequences for people's outlook in regard to others and their engagement with and for others. This of course fits well with, and adds precision to, Putnam's explanation regarding the loss of the "civic generation" (2000), another prominent hypothesis that he put forth, yet more systematic research is needed. For example, why do we see varying degrees of decline in social capital in countries that have similar shifts in child-raising "ideologies"?

Aspects of family life not only have potential explanatory power for the decline of social capital, but they are also useful in distinguishing differences among individuals in one country at one point in time and among individuals of various countries (Hooghe 2001). For example, in-depth interviews revealed that family background is the most influential determinant of the degree of trust developed by an individual (Stolle 2000; Wuthnow 1997). In addition, the extent to which parents told the respondents in their childhood to be careful with strangers emerges as one of the strongest predictors for generalized trust (Stolle 2001b). Certainly the literature in social psychology suggests that family experiences would have a considerable bearing on individuals' trust levels (Erikson 1963, 249ff.; Newton 1997; Renshon 1975). According to older research and more recent studies, we may expect parents to influence the attitudes and norms of their children in three major ways. First, children who are provided with a trusting and open parental environment and who are socialized in a self-respecting and tolerant atmosphere are more likely to be trusting and to want to reciprocate (Erikson 1963; Uslaner 2002). Second, parents teach their children how to judge others, and with whom to cooperate. Third, families function as actual arenas of learning where children experience first-hand episodes of cooperation or defection (Katz and Rotter 1969). In addition, parents' attitudes regarding openness toward strangers are transmitted to the child. They will create, for example, more or less open and cross-cutting networks of friends and acquaintances that function as "learning schools" for children. In sum, these three influences have been shown to be important sources of a child's development of trust, which presumably helps to determine their adult outlook on the world. It is probable that some of the national differences in trust levels can be traced to these differences in child-raising practices.

The importance of the family life for social capital raises the issue of who within the family is most responsible for the creation of the valuable resource. Watching out for children in the neighborhood has traditionally been associated with women, just as have the vast majority of child-raising concerns and the nature of values associated with raising children. In most accounts of the part played by the family in the creation of social capital, Coleman's included (1988), the reference is usually to the traditional, two-parent, male-breadwinner family, in which women take most of the responsibility for this work. The fact that the accumulation of social capital in voluntary associations and in families has depended disproportionately on women has gone mostly unnoticed in the social capital literature.[8] Hence the implications of the tensions and stress that are likely to arise with the rapid changes in both family form and the gendered division of paid (but not unpaid) work have not been adequately examined. This last discussion leads to our next theme, namely the role of the state and institutions as sources of social capital.

THE ROLE OF THE STATE AND POLITICAL INSTITUTIONS

The discussion about the role of the state and political institutions revolves around two main issues. First, there is a debate about the extent to which the state and state institutions exercise an independent influence on social capital, as opposed to the claim that social capital is purely a product of civil society. The bottom-up model that Putnam presents in his earlier work (1993) has been thoroughly criticized by Sidney Tarrow, for example, who argues that the "state plays a fundamental role in shaping civic capacity" (Tarrow 1996, 395). Similarly,

Margaret Levi disapproves of Putnam's exclusive concentration on societal factors as explanatory variables for institutional performance and suggests that policy performance can be just as much a source as a result of trust (Levi 1996). Theda Skocpol, Ganz and Munson (2000) also argue that historically the development of voluntary associations as large umbrella organizations depended on state support. Second, there is disagreement about the extent to which governments' intervention is beneficial or even detrimental to social capital. We will explore these issues in turn and consider whether incorporating a gender perspective might recast them.

To what extent do states have an independent effect on social capital? One state-related variable has been clearly identified as being related to social capital, namely democracy (Almond and Verba 1963; Inglehart 1997). Even stronger is the relationship between social capital as measured by generalized trust and the extent of political rights and civil liberties in a given country (Sides 1999). Generally, authoritarianism, or what Booth and Bayer Richard label "repression level" in their analysis of selected Central American countries, is found to have a strong, negative influence on social capital (Booth and Bayer Richard 1998). Repressive governments disturb civic developments in two other major ways: First, they discourage *spontaneous* group activity, and second, they discourage trust (Booth and Bayer Richard 1998, 43). Even though totalitarian governments, such as communist regimes, mobilize civil society through party and other governmental organizations, association is always state-controlled and often not voluntary. Generally, authoritarian and totalitarian governments seem partially to build their strength on the foundation of distrust among their citizens. A good example of this can be found in the activities of the German Democratic Republic's state-secret police, which pitted citizens against each other and provoked tight social control among friends, neighbors and colleagues, and even within families. No wonder that Sztompka talks about a "culture of mistrust" that has persisted in the post-communist societies of Eastern Europe and that will slow down the reform process of democratic development in those regions (Sztompka 1995). Sztompka elaborates some important aspects of the political system in Eastern Europe that might contribute to the strong development and persistence of mistrust in those societies, some of which will also point us to those aspects of institutions that are important for trust creation in democracies. He highlights the incredible uncertainty that citizens face in the adoption phase of the new democratic system, the inefficiency of monitoring institutions to guarantee law and order, the image of the new political elite as self-interested and, finally, the high expectations that have been raised in the transition years.

The Central American and Eastern European experiences stand for examples of negative influences of governments, which can lead to the erosion of social capital. Some social capital theorists generalize this notion to encompass the strength of government in general and fear that any form of government intervention is anathema to the healthy development of voluntary association and trust. Fukuyama (1999), for example, eschews any notion that government might help to build social capital in favor of a process of "spontaneous renorming."[9] This smacks of older arguments to the effect that the capacity of voluntary organizations and of the family to attend to social needs has been undermined by the state. However, the examples of overpowering regimes, such as communist regimes or the Norman kingdom in southern Italy, that caused a depletion of social capital also provide insights into how governments might be able to enhance and facilitate the development of generalized trust and civic activities in the course of transition to democracy, namely by highlighting the quality of monitoring institutions, the role of the political elite and the nature of the expectations that might be raised. When singling out democracies, the fact is that even though they usually score higher on measures of generalized trust, there are still significant differences among them in their ability to generate civic capacity. This variance needs to be explained. In fact, in response to those who are doubtful about governmental capacities to influence social capital, we will see below (and in later chapters) that social capital is most developed in strong welfare states.

So, what are the aspects of democratic government that matter for social capital? One influence on generalized trust has to do with inequalities that prevail within the society (Boix and Posner 1998). Differences in income distribution have been linked to the variance in welfare regimes, namely the differences between universalism and the means-testing in welfare states (Korpi and Palme 1998; Rothstein 1998) and the tax and social security policies associated with them. For example, in Scandinavian countries, where we find rather low levels of income and gender inequality, trust levels are significantly higher than in France and the United States. Also, temporal variations in trust levels strongly correlate with temporal variations in income equality in the United States (Uslaner this volume). Citizens who see their fellow citizens as equals and as "one of their own" might more easily make a leap of faith and give a trust credit to people who are not necessarily known.

Furthermore, the Johns Hopkins cross-national project on the "nonprofit" sector[10] provides some interesting additional evidence about the importance of welfare state institutions (Anheier 2001). Voluntary organizations have grown in number in most countries during the 1990s, a period of welfare state restructuring. However, in many countries, especially the United Kingdom, but also in Germany, it is those organizations that provide a service, usually under contract to a government department, that have increased in number the most. On the other hand, it is in the most institutionalized welfare states of the Scandinavian countries that the voluntary sector has grown primarily in its "social" dimensions, with increased numbers of volunteers and membership affiliation rates. Rothstein (1998) has argued that "just institutions matter," referring to the propensity of the Scandinavian welfare state to take redistribution seriously and arguing that this leads to a wider commitment to equality and trust in government. Accordingly, it seems that state intervention enables those voluntary organizations to flourish that can be characterized more properly as part of civil society than as alternatives to government social welfare providers.

Contrary to the doubts about the role of governments in social capital facilitation, Scandinavian welfare states exhibit the highest levels of social capital in the Western world. As far as we know, generalized trust levels are the highest in Scandinavia and have been maintained there even up to the present day, as opposed to the United States, where they strongly declined over the last decade (Putnam 2000). This is also true for membership in voluntary associations of various kinds (Rothstein 2002). Income equality, gender equality and the guarantee of relatively high material and personal security as well as high levels of socioeconomic resources are specific aspects of institutionalized welfare states (as opposed to residual welfare states). Research has shown that at the individual level, the existence of these resources is positively related to social capital, particularly social participation and trust (Verba, Nie and Kim 1978). The idea that particular forms of government intervention can enable rather than erode voluntary associations is important also with regard to women's participation in civil society. Women's involvement in both formal voluntary associations and informal ones, including those concerned with family, child-rearing and neighborhood issues, depends increasingly on their being able to reconcile paid work and unpaid family obligations. Again, the Scandinavian countries have taken the lead in legislation that recognizes unpaid care work by making both cash (in the form of parental leaves) and child-care services available.

Finally, the argument is made that governments can realize their capacity to generate trust only if citizens consider the state itself to be trustworthy (Levi 1998, 86). States, for example, enable the establishment of contracts in that they provide information and monitor legislation, and enforce rights and rules that sanction lawbreakers, protect minorities and actively support the integration and participation of citizens (Levi 1998, 85ff.). From a gender perspective, the emphasis is placed on the extensiveness of public policies in Scandinavia that are explicitly directed at women and the resulting trust women develop for such state institutions and policies (Svallfors 1996). Thus political and institutional trust enables women also to trust other citizens more extensively. More generally, political and institutional trust develops because people believe "that the institutions that are responsible for handling 'treacherous' behavior act in a fair, just and effective manner, and if they also believe that other people think the same of these institutions, then they will also trust other people" (Rothstein 2002; Rothstein and Stolle this volume; Stolle, forthcoming).

These differences in government and state capacity to monitor free-riding, to punish defection and to direct a relatively impartial and fair bureaucracy have not been examined thoroughly in an empirical and comparative way; however, they provide a plausible explanation for national differences in social capital levels, and also for differences among various types of democracies. Again, those aspects of social provision that determine the quality and inclusiveness of service delivery and the fairness of political institutions can cause differences in institutional trust and attitudes toward politicians, which in turn influence generalized trust. The reason for this, as Stolle argues in a study of three Swedish regions, is that citizens who are disappointed with their politicians and bureaucrats and who have experienced the effects of their dishonesty, institutional unfairness and unresponsiveness transfer these experiences and views to people in general (although not to people they know personally). Similarly, good experiences with government and fair political and social institutions can be generalized to other people who are not personally known (Stolle, forthcoming). However, the question remains as to precisely how these experiences are generalized to the public at large, and how institutional experiences are transmitted and socialized. Possibly parents play a role in transmitting their institutional experiences to their children. Parents report to their children their experiences of fairness with the police, the judicial system or the political system in general, which in turn influences how children think about political institutions and about other people.

CONCLUSION

Social capital is an important societal resource. In social science, the concept of social capital is currently receiving considerable academic attention, and rightly so, because it has been shown to play a considerable role in our political and social lives. Furthermore, the concept of social capital allows us to focus on specific aspects of political culture and to use political culture as an explanatory variable in cross-national settings.

We have shown here that the importance of voluntary associations as the center and main measure of social capital has been called into question. Second and moreover, we have also suggested that the assumption of most social capital theorists as to the efficacy of voluntary associations in producing generalized norms and values such as trust should be taken with caution at best. There is no strong empirical evidence to confirm the microrelationship between membership and trust. However, the chapters below will give us additional insights. It might be necessary to examine other types of social interactions in their potential to facilitate civic attitudes and behaviors. However, the broadening of the social capital concept to include various types of social interaction might constitute a conceptual problem as it becomes fuzzier and its relationship to democracy less obvious. The social and political consequences of various types of social interaction are not very well researched yet and remain on the agenda for future work.

Third, most accounts of social capital theory focus on stability and path dependency in the realm of civil society, though this essay showed that it is the institutional analysis of social capital that enables us to see the importance of contemporary factors. Indeed in building social capital theory, we also have to look outside organizations and social interactions *per se* for mechanisms that produce, foster and/or disturb developments of generalized trust and norms of reciprocity. In a cross-national perspective, the overpowering difference is not between joiners and nonjoiners or long-term joiners and short-term joiners, but among members of different nations and regions. There are features of political and social institutions in some countries and regions that make a more positive contribution to the development of civic values and attitudes. It is clear that the spread of generalized trust, and norms of reciprocity and social participation are complex phenomena and cannot be explained by one factor alone. Countries with highly developed institutionalized welfare states are also those with the highest levels of social capital in a cross-national comparison. Yet welfare states have typically been left out of analyses of social capital, or have even been characterized as threatening to social interactions within society. We suggest here that the link between welfare states and social capital should be specified more fully. The second part of this volume takes up these themes in fuller discussions.

Fourth, the role of the family in social capital creation has been mostly left untouched even though preliminary evidence suggests that the family plays an important role in influencing generalized and cooperative attitudes and possibly even societal engagement. Parents shape their children's trust and engagement as role models through their own institutional experiences and the way they teach their children to judge specific social situations. These differences in child-rearing practices possibly vary by country and region and certainly warrant further research.

Finally, whereas the concept of social capital has traditionally been located in the realm of civil society, our analysis here has shown that it is rather deeply embedded in the triangular relationship among the state, the family and civil society. The important aspects of civil society that have been highlighted by the rise of the social capital concept, such as generalized trust, social interactions, civic engagement, cooperation, tolerance, are all closely related and not separated from state institutions and family life. Only in connection with civil society, the nature of the state and the family is it possible to identify the various sources of social capital. The task is to examine more systematically which aspects of civic, familial, as well as social and political institutions create and possibly maintain low or high regional and national levels of social capital and to understand the gendered variations within this complex matrix.

NOTES

1. Generally, his work, even though highly praised, has been criticized for being too negative and too focused on society (as opposed to state and political institutions) and circular (see critiques in Berman 1997; Foley and Edwards 1998; Jackman and Miller 1998; Ladd 1996; Levi 1996; Portes 1998; Skocpol 1996; Tarrow 1996).
2. Earlier accounts are linked to the work of Tocqueville (1961), even though he does not use the term "social capital."
3. However, associations might also have external effects, as they link citizens to the political process (see Toqueville 1961 and Putnam 1993).
4. Another reason for this approach has been, of course, that indicators of memberships in associations as opposed to other types of social interactions or attitudinal data have been readily available.
5. However, see some group-level studies that investigate membership influences on political and social views and behavior (however, different from trust) by Eastis (1998) and Erickson and Nosanchuck (1990).

6. The theoretical relationship between membership in voluntary associations and democratic payoffs in the wider society has been discussed in Gundelach and Torpe (1997), Foley and Edwards (1996) and Boix and Posner (1998).

7. In the extreme case of homogeneity, the association may not only be narrowly constituted but may also have as its purpose the denial of equal rights or opportunities to others. In such cases, it is more than reasonable to doubt the effectiveness of associational membership in promoting generalized trust or reciprocity.

8. However, see Putnam's recent work, which has many more references to the role of women (2000).

9. Fukuyama does mention a few potential positive governmental influences on social capital, such as the provision of education and other public goods, property rights and public safety.

10. Definitions of the "nonprofit sector" and the "third sector" vary substantially and are not crucial to our argument here. However, it is important to note that the term "voluntary association" or "organization" is no longer an accurate description of the large and increasing number of organizations that rely as much on paid as voluntary labor, and on government funding more than voluntary giving.

REFERENCES

Almond, G. and Verba, S. (1963). *The Civic Culture*. Princeton: Princeton University Press.

Andersen, J. and Tobiasen, M. (2003). "Who Are These Political Consumers Anyway? Survey Evidence from Denmark." In M. Micheletti, A. Føllesdal and D. Stolle (eds.), *Politics, Products, and Markets. Exploring Political Consumerism Past and Present*. New Brunswick: Transaction Press.

Anheier, H. (2001). "Dimensions of the Third Sector: Comparative Perspectives on Structure and Change." Working Paper, Centre for Civil Society, London School of Economics, London.

Banfield, E. (1958). *The Moral Basis of a Backward Society*. New York: The Free Press.

Bennich-Björkman, L. (1998). "Strong Individuals, Weak Society? Child Rearing and the Decline of Social Capital after World War II." Paper presented at the ECPR Joint Sessions, Warwick, March 23–38.

Berman. S. (1997). "Civil Society and Political Institutionalization." *American Behavioral Scientist* 40, 562–574.

Billiet, J. and Cambré, B. (1996). "Social Capital, Active Membership in Voluntary Associations and Some Aspects of Political Participation." Paper presented at conference on social capital and democracy, Milan, October 3–6.

Boix, C. and Posner, D. (1998). "Social Capital: Explaining Its Origins and Effects on Government Performance." *British Journal of Political Science* 28(4), 686–695.

Booth, J. and Bayer Richard, P. (1998). "Civil Society and Political Context in Central America." *American Behavioral Scientist* 42(1), 33–46.

Brehm, J. and Rahn, W. (1997). "Individual Level Evidence for the Causes and Consequences of Social Capital." *American Journal of Political Science* 41, 999–1023.

Clemens, E. (1999). "Securing Political Returns to Social Capital: Women's Associations in the United States." *Journal of Interdisciplinary History* 30(4), 613–638.

Coleman, J. S. (1988). "Social Capital in the Creation of Human Capital." *American Journal of Sociology* 94, S95–S120.

Coleman, J. S. (1990). *Foundations of Social Theory.* Cambridge, MA: Belknap Press.

Dekker, P., Koopmans, R. and van den Broek, A. (1997). "Voluntary Associations, Social Movements and Individual Political Behavior in Western Europe." In van Deth, J. (ed.), *Private Groups and Public Life.* London: Routledge.

Dekker, P. and J. de Hart (1999). "Civic Engagement and Volunteering in the Netherlands." pp. 75–107. In J. van Deth et al. (eds.), *Social Capital and European Democracy.* London: Routledge.

Eastis, C. M. (1998). "Organizational Diversity and the Production of Social Capital." *American Behavioral Scientist* 42(1), 66–77.

Erickson, B. and Nosanchuck, T. A. (1990). "How an Apolitical Association Politicizes." *Canadian Review of Sociology and Anthropology* 27, 206–219.

Erikson, E. (1963). *Childhood and Society.* New York: Norton.

Esping-Andersen, G. (1999). *Social Foundations of Postindustrial Economies.* Oxford: Oxford University Press.

Ferree, M. M. and Martin, P. (eds., 1995). *Feminist Organizations.* Philadelphia: Temple University Press.

Foley, M. and Edwards, B. (1996). "The Paradox of Civil Society." *Journal of Democracy* 7, 38–53.

Foley, M. and Edwards, B. (1998). "Beyond Tocqueville: Civil Society and Social Capital in Comparative Perspective." *American Behavioral Scientist* 42(1), 5–20.

Fukuyama, F. (1995). *Trust: The Social Virtues and Creation of Prosperity.* London: Hamish Hamilton.

Fukuyama, F. (1999). *The Great Disruption. Human Nature and the Reconstitution of Social Order.* London: Profile Books.

Granovetter, M. S. (1973). "The Strength of Weak Ties." *American Journal of Sociology* 78, 1360–1380.

Granovetter, M. (1985). "Economic Action and Social Structure: The Problem of Embeddedness." *American Journal of Sociology* 91, 481–510.

Gundelach, P. and Torpe, L. (1997). "Social Capital and the Democratic Role of Voluntary Associations." Paper presented at the ECPR Joint Sessions, Bern, Switzerland, February 27–March 3.

Hagan, J., Merkens, H. and Boehnke, K. (1995). "Delinquency and Disdain: Social Capital and the Control of Right-wing Extremism among

East and West Berlin Youth." *The American Journal of Sociology* 100(4), 1028–1052.
Hall, P. (1999). "Social Capital in Britain." *British Journal of Political Science* 29(3), 417–461.
Hanks, M. and Eckland, B. (1978). "Adult Voluntary Associations and Adolescent Socialization." *Sociological Quarterly* 19, 481–480.
Hooghe, M. (2000). "Organizational Diversity and the Production of Social Capital. A Survey Analysis of Differential Socialization Effects in Voluntary Associations." Paper presented at the Annual Meeting of the American Political Science Association, Washington D.C., August 31–September 3.
Hooghe, M. (2001), "Not for my kind of people. Adaptive Preference Formation and Political Passivity." pp. 162–175. In P. Dekker and E. Uslaner (eds.), *Social Capital and Participation in Everyday Life*. London: Routledge.
Hooghe, M. (2003). "Participation in Voluntary Associations and Value Indicators." *Nonprofit and Voluntary Sector Quarterly* 32(1), in press.
Hooghe, M. and Derks, A. (1997). "Voluntary Associations and the Creation of Social Capital: The Involvement Effect of Participation." Paper presented at the ECPR Joint Sessions, Bern, Switzerland.
Inglehart, R. (1997). *Modernization and Postmodernization*. Princeton: Princeton University Press.
Jackman, R. and Miller, R. (1998). "Social Capital and Politics." *Annual Review of Political Science* 1, 47–73.
Jencks, C. and Peterson, P. (1991). *The Urban Underclass*. Washington: Brookings Institution.
Katz, H. and Rotter, J. (1969). "Interpersonal Trust Scores of College Students and Their Parents." *Child Development* 40, 657–661.
Katzenstein, M. (1998). *Faithful and Fearless. Moving Feminist Protest inside the Church and the Military*. Princeton: Princeton University Press.
Kawachi, I. et al. (1997). "Social Capital, Income Inequality, and Mortality." *American Journal of Public Health* 87, 1491–1498.
Knack, S. and Keefer, P. (1997). "Does Social Capital Have an Economic Payoff? A Cross-Country Investigation." *Quarterly Journal of Economics* 112, 1251–1288.
Korpi, W. and Palme, J. (1998). "The Paradox of Redistribution and Strategies of Equality." *American Sociological Review* 63, 661–687.
Ladd, E. C. (1996). "The Data Just Do Not Show the Erosion of America's Social Capital." *Public Perspective* 7(1), 5–6.
Laitin, D. D. (1995). "The Civic Culture at 30." *American Political Science Review* 89(1), 168–173.
La Porta, R. et al. (2000). "Trust in Large Organizations." pp. 310–324. In P. Dasgupta and I. Semageldin (eds.), *Social Capital*. Washington: World Bank.
Levi, M. (1996). "Social and Unsocial Capital: A Review Essay of Robert Putnam's Making Democracy Work." *Politics and Society* 24(1), 45–55.

Levi, M. (1998). "A State of Trust." In V. Braithwaite and M. Levi (eds.), *Trust and Governance*. New York: Russell Sage Foundation.

Loury, G. (1977). "A Dynamic Theory of Racial Income Differences." In P. Wallace (ed.), *Women, Minorities, and Employment Discrimination*. Lexington: Heath.

Lowndes, V. (2000). "Women and Social Capital." *British Journal of Political Science* 30, 533–540.

Micheletti, M. (2003). "Why More Women? Issues of Gender and Political Consumerism." In M. Micheletti, A. Føllesdal and D. Stolle (eds.), *Politics, Products, and Markets. Exploring Political Consumerism Past and Present*. New Brunswick: Transaction Press.

Micheletti, M., Føllesdal, A. and Stolle, D. (eds., 2003). *Politics, Products, and Markets. Exploring Political Consumerism Past and Present*. New Brunswick: Transaction Press.

Moller Okin, S. (1989). *Justice, Gender and the Family*. New York: Basic Books.

Moyser, G. and Parry, G. (1997). "Voluntary Associations and Democratic Participation in Britain." In J. van Deth (ed.), *Private Groups and Public Life*. London: Routledge.

Mueller, C. (1994). "Conflict Networks and the Origins of Women's Liberation." In E. Larana, H. Johnston and R. Gusfield (eds.), *New Social Movements: From Ideology to Identity*. Philadelphia: Temple University Press.

Mutz, D. (2002). "Cross-cutting Social Networks: Testing Democratic Theory in Practice." *American Political Science Review* 96(1), 111–126.

Mutz, D. and Mondak, J. (1998). "Democracy at Work: Contributions of the Workplace Toward a Public Sphere." Paper presented at the Annual Meeting of the Midwest Political Science Association Meeting, Chicago, April 23–25.

Newton, K. (1997). "Social Capital and Democracy." *American Behavioural Scientist* 40(6), 575–586.

Olsen, M. (1972). "Social Participation and Voting Turnout." *American Sociological Review* 37, 317–333.

Paxton, P. (1999). "Is Social Capital Declining in the United States?" *American Journal of Sociology* 105(1), 88–127.

Petro, N. (2001). "Creating Social Capital in Russia: The Novgorod Model." *World Development* 29(2), 229–244.

Popielarz, P. (1999). "(In)voluntary Association: A Multilevel Analysis of Gender Segregation in Voluntary Associations." *Gender and Society* 13(2), 234–250.

Portes, A. (1998). "Social Capital: Its Origins and Applications in Modern Sociology." *Annual Review of Sociology* 24, 1–24.

Putnam, R. (1993). *Making Democracy Work*. Princeton: Princeton University Press.

Putnam, R. (1995a). "Bowling Alone: Democracy in America at the End of the Twentieth Century." Nobel Symposium. Uppsala, Sweden.

Putnam, R. (1995b). "Tuning In, Tuning Out: The Strange Disappearance of Social Capital in America." *Political Science and Politics* 28, 664–683.

Putnam, R. (2000). *Bowling Alone: The Collapse and Revival of American Community.* New York: Simon and Schuster.

Putnam, R. (ed., 2002). *Democracies in Flux: The Evolution of Social Capital in Contemporary Society.* Oxford: Oxford University Press.

Renshon, S. (1975). "Personality and Family Dynamics in the Political Socialization Process." *American Journal of Political Science* 19(1), 63–80.

Rogers, D., Bultena, G. and Barb, K. (1975). "Voluntary Associations Membership and Political Participation." *Sociological Quarterly* 16, 305–318.

Rothstein, B. (1998). *Just Institutions Matter: The Moral and Political Logic of the Universal Welfare State.* Cambridge: Cambridge University Press.

Rothstein, B. (2002). "Social Capital and the Social Democratic State: The Swedish Model and Civil Society." In R. Putnam (ed.), *Democracies in Flux.* Oxford: Oxford University Press.

Schlozman, K. et al. (1995). "Gender and Citizen Participation: Is there a Different Voice?" *American Journal of Political Science* 39(2), 267–293.

Seligson, A. (1999). "Civic Association and Democratic Participation in Central America." *Comparative Political Studies* 32, 342–362.

Sides, J. (1999). "It Takes Two: The Reciprocal Relationship between Social Capital and Democracy." Paper presented at the Annual Meeting of the American Political Science Association, Atlanta, September 2–5.

Skocpol, T. (1992). *Protecting Soldiers and Mothers. The Political Origins of Social Policy in the United States.* Cambridge, MA: Harvard University Press.

Skocpol, T. et al. (1993). "Women's Associations and the Enactment of Mothers' Pensions in the United States." *American Political Science Review* 87(3), 686–701.

Skocpol, T. (1996). "Unravelling from Above." *American Prospect* 25, 20–25.

Skocpol, T., Ganz, M. and Munson, Z. (2000). "A Nation of Organizers: The Institutional Origins of Civic Voluntarism in the United States." *American Political Science Review* 94(3), 527–546.

Stolle, D. (2000). *Communities of Trust: Social Capital and Public Action in Comparative Perspective.* Ph.D. dissertation, Princeton University.

Stolle, D. (2001a). "Clubs and Congregations: The Benefits of Joining an Association." pp. 202–244. In Karen Cook (ed.), *Trust in Society.* New York: Russell Sage Foundation.

Stolle, D. (2001b). "Getting to Trust: An Analysis of the Importance of Institutions, Families, Personal Experiences and Group Membership." In P. Dekker and E. Uslaner (eds.), *Politics in Everyday Life.* London: Routledge.

Stolle, D. (forthcoming). "Communities, Social Capital and Local Government—Generalized Trust in Regional Settings." In P. Selle and A. Prakash (eds.), *Investigating Social Capital.* New Delhi: Sage India.

Stolle, D. and Hooghe, M. (2002). "Conflicting Approaches to the Study of Social Capital." *Ethical Perspectives* 9(2), in press.

Stolle, D. and Rochon, T. (1998). "Are All Associations Alike? Member Diversity, Associational Type and the Creation of Social Capital." *American Behavioral Scientist* 42(1), 47–65.

Stolle, D. and Rochon, T., (1999). "The Myth of American Exceptionalism: A Three Nation Comparison of Associational Membership and Social Capital." In J. van Deth et al. (eds.), *Social Capital and European Democracy*. London: Routledge.

Svallfors, S. (1996). *Välfärdsstatens moraliska ekonomi välfärdsopinionen i 90-talets Sverige*. Umeå: Boréa.

Sztompka, P. (1995). "Vertrauen: Die fehlende Ressource in der Postkommunistischen Gesellschaft." In B. Nedelmann (ed.), *Politische Institutionen im Wandel*. Opladen: Westdeutscher Verlag.

Tarrow, S. (1996). "Making Social Science Work Across Space and Time: A Critical Reflection on Robert Putnam's Making Democracy Work." *American Political Science Review* 90, 389–397.

Tocqueville, Alexis de (1961 [1835]). *Democracy in America*. New York: Schocken Books.

Uslaner, E. M. (2002). *The Moral Value of Trust*. Cambridge: Cambridge University Press.

Verba, S. and Nie, N. (1972). *Participation in America: Political Democracy and Social Equality*. New York: Harper and Row.

Verba, S., Nie, N. and Kim, J.-O. (1978). *Participation and Political Equality*. New York: Cambridge University Press.

Verba, S., Schlozman, K. and Brady, H. (1995). *Voice and Equality: Civic Volunteerism in American Politics*. Cambridge: Harvard University Press.

Wuthnow, R. (1997). "The Role of Trust in Civic Renewal." The National Commission on Civic Renewal, University of Maryland.

CHAPTER 3

DEMOCRACY IN FRANCE: DO ASSOCIATIONS MATTER?

Nonna Mayer

INTRODUCTION

In the recent debate about the concept of social capital, the civic and democratic role attributed to voluntary associations has received critical attention (Tarrow 1996; Portes 1998; Van Deth et al. 1999; Warren 1999). In line with Tocqueville's famous statement that "only by the reciprocal action of men upon another can feelings and ideas be renewed, the heart enlarged, and human mind developed... This, only associations can do" (Tocqueville 1986, 158), many authors perceive voluntary associations as an ideal school of democracy. Because of the horizontal and egalitarian type of face-to-face interpersonal relations they promote, they are supposed to bring together people from different backgrounds, generate communication and debate and foster self-confidence and confidence in others. Associations are also supposed to make their members aware of the power of collective action and therefore promote political involvement and mobilization. Yet this vision might be overoptimistic and simplified. The purpose of our chapter is to examine the role of voluntary organizations as important links between citizens and the political system. We conclude that their importance as creators of attitudinal aspects of social capital may have been exaggerated.

Our point of departure is the attitudinal effect that membership in voluntary associations is believed to have. It is assumed that membership in voluntary associations can create and shape various civic attitudes, such as generalized trust. The question is: Why should participation in associations also influence political trust? This idea has been clearly stated since the classical study of "civic culture" by

Almond and Verba (1963). For them, voluntary social interaction builds up feelings of confidence and safety in the social environment, which has political consequences. To them general social trust is translated into politically relevant trust (Almond and Verba 1963). And they report similar findings by Morris Rosenberg that trust is a general attitude toward others, "that those who score high in 'faith in people' are less likely than the low scorers to be cynical about politics and politicians" (ibid., 285). Yet horizontal trust between ordinary people is one thing: Vertical trust placed in politicians may be created differently, Ken Newton argues (Newton and Norris 2000; Newton 2001; Hardin 1999). And Putnam himself clearly keeps social trust distinct from trust in institutions and political authorities: "One can easily trust one's neighbor and distrust city hall, or vice versa" (Putnam 2000, 137).

Politics is a sphere of conflicting interests, and a certain dose of mistrust can even be civic. As stated by Citrin in his 1974 controversy with Miller about the declining trust of Americans in their government: "It is worth recalling John Stuart Mill's belief that a democratic political culture is characterized by a vigilant skepticism (or realistic cynicism) rather than an unquestioning faith in the motives and abilities of political authority" (Citrin 1974, 988). In addition, many associations are not politically neutral: Some are left wing, others right wing, and their relations to government can vary greatly according to which parties are in office. There is no apparent reason to assume, for example, that membership in associations that stand in opposition to or are critical of the government would lead to more trust in government. Possibly, association members of selected groups might be able to gain better insights into how the government works and become more knowledgeable and more interested in politics. Yet, the relationship between membership and political trust per se is more questionable (see van der Meer this volume).

Finally, in a recent book, Nina Eliasoph (1998) has questioned the very capacity of associations to breed interest in politics and create a public sphere of debate. Her careful observation of the interactions taking place in various types of American associations leads to exactly the opposite conclusion. Eliasoph describes an evaporation of politics: Political conversations are clearly avoided in these associations. Because of the urgency of solving daily problems, the focus on local action and the fear of disagreement on such matters, politics is kept backstage and local problems are not connected to the public sphere.

In this chapter then, we will present new French data on the relationship between participation in associations and various trust indicators. First we will examine this relationship at the aggregate level. While political and generalized trust are declining in France, active membership seems to be rising. Membership and trust levels evolve in opposite directions, and this already implies that they cannot be considered as simply different sides of the same coin. Furthermore, the analysis of our survey data shows that trust and membership are not significantly related at the individual level, but we do observe that membership is related to political interest. The pattern of these relations allows us to question the universality of the allegedly strong relation between participation and various trust indicators.

DISTRUST IN FRANCE

In France, the debate about social capital and its virtues is just starting. In the tradition of Simmel and Durkheim, French sociologists have given more importance to the wider concept of "sociability," defined as the general pattern of social interactions, including family, friendship, neighborhood, professional and religious relations, etc. (Degenne and Forsé 1998; Mendras 2001). Pierre Bourdieu uses the concept of social capital in a different sense, as part of a theory of class reproduction and political domination. Bourdieu defines social space by the volume, structure and evolution of three forms of capital: Economic, cultural and social, the latter mainly amplifying the effects of the two first forms of capital (Bourdieu 1979, 109–185; 1980).

Yet France is an interesting case for the test of the effects of associational life on civic attitudes. It has for a long time been considered as a "civic desert" compared to the vibrant community life of Anglo-Saxon and Scandinavian countries (Barthélémy 2000, 19). World Values Surveys (WVS) show that France has extremely low rates of generalized trust, as measured by the answers to the question "Generally speaking, would you say most people can be trusted or that you can't be too careful in dealing with people?" And while the level of generalized trust between the first WVS wave in 1981 and the second one in 1990 has risen in nearly all of the countries studied, France is (with Spain) the only country where it declined, and this decline still seems to continue. In France the proportion of the sample choosing the trusting answer fell from 25 percent in 1981 to 21 percent in 1999 (Galland 1999, 46–47; 2000, 28).

In the past ten years, there has also been a sharp decline in electoral participation and a drop in the level of political trust. Only one French adult out of four feels well represented by a political leader or a political party (compared with 39 and 35 percent in 1989), and the feeling that elected representatives and politicians are "somewhat corrupt"

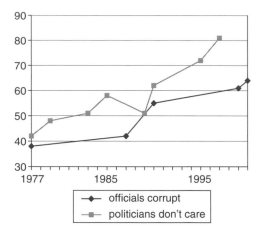

Figure 3.1   Political distrust in France (1977–2000)

Note: Percentage of respondents answering that "elected representatives and public officials" are mostly corrupt, and percentage stating that "on the whole, politicians" don't care "what people like you think." For each year: *n* = 1,000. SOFRES 1998, 246 and 2000, 278–279.

Source: SOFRES polls, 1977–2000.

and do not care what people think has risen in a spectacular way (see Figure 3.1).

Given the general decline in political and institutional trust, one might expect that participation in voluntary associations, too, is declining in France. After all, if voluntary associations are really that important for creating trust, as is often claimed, it would be a logical step to assume that the decline in trust is caused at least partially by the fact that these associations no longer function properly or that they do not succeed in attracting enough members. Furthermore, in most of the literature on the decline of social capital, little distinction is made between the structural and attitudinal components of the concept (see Stolle this volume). Authors seem to assume that the relation between these components is constant, which would imply that the two fluctuate together. In other words, if social capital were really a fixed and stable complex, with invariant relations between its components, trust and participation levels would have to move in sync over time.

In the remainder of this chapter, we first ascertain whether participation has indeed declined in France before we investigate the link among participation, trust and civicness. Drawing on official statistics and survey data, we shall show that social capital, defined by membership in voluntary associations, is not declining in France and that the members of voluntary associations are not more civic, although they are more politicized.

THE VITALITY OF VOLUNTARY ASSOCIATIONS

France's associational deficit has certainly been exaggerated. Historians like Maurice Agulhon have shown the vitality of networks and "circles" in the south of France (the so-called "southern sociability") and the political role they played between the Revolution and the Second Republic (Agulhon 1970, 1977; Huard 2000). However, the legal recognition of these networks and circles occurred later in France than in the United States or other European countries. The spirit of the French Revolution was to suppress all intermediary bodies between individuals and the state, out of fear that the reconstitution of the Ancien Régime's guilds and the development of factions might distort the general will. The 1789 Declaration of Rights did not proclaim the right to associate. The 1791 Le Chapelier law even forbade the formation of workers' or employers' associations. For more than a century, all governments perceived associations as a threat to the social and political order, and they repressed their development. The Right was afraid they would strengthen the rising power of the working classes, and the Republicans were anxious to counter the influence of the Catholic Church. Legal recognition came only in 1884 for professional unions and in 1901 for associations in general, after some forty unfruitful attempts of developing a legal framework (Merlet 2001).

The Waldeck-Rousseau republican law of 1901, still in force today, is very liberal. It defines associations broadly as a contract by which two or more people put together their knowledge or their activity, with "another purpose than profit" (Article 1). Associations can form freely, they do not need to ask for an authorization, and they do not even need to be declared (Article 2). But only the declared associations are considered legal entities, with the *personnalité civile* that entitles them to go to court, own property, etc. Only religious congregations, caught in the midst of a fierce battle between church and state, were kept under a more strict form of control. The 1901 law enabled the numerous associations that had appeared at the turn of the century to develop and prosper. The most spectacular associational boom started in the 1970s: In the wake of the new social movements, feminist, environmental, antinuclear and humanitarian networks were the first ones to grow. The rise of individualistic postmaterialist values also expanded the sports, culture and leisure sector. After the socialist victory in the elections of 1981, foreigners recovered the right to associate that they had been deprived of in 1939. This reform led to the emergence of a wave of associations defending the rights of immigrants and their children. With the 1982 decentralization act, associations gained more influence at the local level. Finally, the economic recession and the emergence of the "new poor" led to the development of new associations, which often replaced the state in the sector of welfare and health.

Nowadays, some 70,000 associations are declared every year, three times more than in the 1960s and ten times more than at the beginning of the twentieth century (Degenne and Forsé 1998, 106–107; CNVA 2000, 53–55).[1] Of course many of these associations will not last and their disappearance is not registered. In order to get a more precise picture of the density of associational life, Viviane Tchernogog launched a large postal survey in 1,400 municipalities, giving a detailed account of 13,000 associations. On this base, she estimates the actual number of active associations in France at 880,000, or one association for every sixty inhabitants (Tchernogog 2001).[2] The non-profit sector in France is well developed in comparison with its European counterparts, with a little over 20 million members, the equivalent of a million full-time salaried employees and almost as many volunteer workers, and its operating expenditures constitute 3.7 percent of the gross domestic product (GDP) (Archambault 1999, 82–83).

Survey data confirm the vitality of associational life in France. According to the periodic surveys of the Centre de Recherche pour l'étude et l'observation des conditions de vie (CREDOC), conducted since 1979 on national representative samples, 43 percent of the adult population living in France belonged to at least one association in 1997, compared with one third in 1967 (Hatchuel and Loisel 1999). The experimental survey on "Democracy, Toleration and the Strains of French Politics," conducted in the summer of 2000 by Gérard Grunberg, Paul Sniderman and myself, confirms the vitality of associational networks.[3] Only one-third of the respondents claimed no membership at all, and one-third belonged to one association and one-third to more than one. Even if one weighs the sample to correct for the educational bias that one finds in every survey, the figures hardly change.[4] Although questions were asked by reading a list of associations and determining for each one whether the respondent was a member, which may have facilitated positive answers, the figures remain impressive.[5]

Clearly there are no indications that the membership of voluntary associations has declined in France. The erosion of associations therefore cannot be held responsible for the decline of social and political trust that took place in the last ten years. Peter Hall, studying the British case, arrives at the same conclusion: Membership in voluntary associations is not declining, the new generations are not less inclined to participate, yet overall levels of social trust have declined from 56 percent in 1959 to 44 percent in 1990 (Hall 1999, 432). While political participation and interest in politics remain stable, feelings of political efficacy and trust also declined in Great Britain. Hall concludes that "the erosion of social capital that Putnam and others find in the American case is not a uniform phenomenon across the industrialized democracies ... the loose coupling found in Britain between levels of associational membership and political participation, on the one hand, and social trust and political trust, on the other raises some questions about precisely how associational involvement affects civic engagement" (Hall 1999, 457–458).

The figures presented in this section clearly indicate that participation and trust levels do not evolve jointly or in the same manner. This already allows us to be skeptical about the alleged close relationship between these two aspects of social capital. To substantiate this skepticism further, in the next section we will use our survey data to examine how exactly associational involvements affect civic and political attitudes.

TRUST, CIVICNESS AND POLITICIZATION

In a first step, we present the bivariate relations between membership and various indicators of trust and civicness. To measure the structural aspects of social capital, we will use a simple indicator, the number of associations to which one belongs: None, one, or more, which splits the sample in three groups of fairly equal size (35 percent, 33 percent and 32 percent). While many authors seem to assume that social and political trust go together, as part of an overall attitude of faith in people, in this analysis we have separate indicators for the various forms of trust. One is about generalized trust, with classical questions about how much faith one has in strangers. The two other indicators are about political trust, with questions about the perception of politicians, on the one hand—how honest, how caring and therefore how reliable they appear—and about confidence in public institutions, on the other, even more central for the functioning of democracy for they last, while politicians come and go (Newton and Norris 2000). Lastly we will study the relationship between membership in voluntary organizations and civicness. The latter is measured with questions about the perceived importance of basic institutions in a representative democracy, such as voting or the existence of political parties and of a parliament, about commitment to fundamental democratic values, such as tolerance or social justice, and about engagement in public affairs, a dimension that is part of Putnam's comprehensive social capital index (Putnam 2000, 291), and that we measure here by the interest paid to politics, the degree of political knowledge and the recognition of the left–right cleavage. The correlations between membership in voluntary organizations and these different indicators are summarized in Table 3.1.

Table 3.1 Trust, civicness and politicization by membership in associations: bivariate relations

Voluntary associations membership	None $n = 750$	1 $n = 701$	2+ $n = 697$	Correlation
	TRUST			
High generalized trust	18	21	24	.07*
High trust in politicians	38	40	47	.07**
High trust in institutions	53	57	57	.04
	CIVICNESS, DEMOCRATIC COMMITMENT			
Voted in all/almost all elections since age to vote	72	77	81	.10**
Extremely/very important for democracy that people vote regularly	75	81	80	.08**
Extremely/very important for democracy that there are political parties	43	49	48	.03
Extremely/very important for democracy that the state guarantees a minimum income	57	54	56	.01
Extremely/very important for democracy to demonstrate in order to defend one's claims	63	61	61	.00
A strong man who does not bother with Parliament or elections is what the country really needs for a leader (Agrees very much/somewhat)	43	42	40	−.09**
Low score on intolerance scale (= high tolerance)	26	31	34	.08**
	POLITICIZATION			
High score on political knowledge scale	18	24	29	.11**
Left–right identification (versus nonidentifiers)	55	65	70	.13**
Very/fairly interested in politics	34	41	52	.16**

Note: Entries in columns 2–4 are percentage of the respondents, $n = 2,148$. Entries in column 5 are Pearson bivariate correlations (* = $p<.01$; ** = $p<.001$).

Source: CEVIPOF survey, May–June 2000 ($n = 2,148$).

Our indicator for generalized trust combines the answers to two questions: "Generally speaking, would you say that most people try to take advantage of you when they can, or that they do their best to behave decently?" and "Would you say that most people are ready to help others or that they only care about themselves?" The coded answers varied between 0 (people who give the distrusting answer both times) and 2 (give the trusting answer both times). France, as we saw, is traditionally very low on generalized trust, like other Latin Catholic countries such as Italy or Portugal. Inglehart suggests that religion could be the explanation for this pattern, by contrasting the hierarchical and centrally controlled Roman Catholic organization as it exists in France with the horizontal locally controlled Protestant churches (Inglehart 1999, 92). Whatever the reason, in our survey, only one respondent out of five has the maximum score of 2 and can be described as high on generalized trust. Most importantly, joining one or more voluntary associations does not make a real difference.

To measure political trust, we constructed an indicator of perceived politicians' trustworthiness (to what extent are they seen as "honest" and "caring what people like us think"), varying between 0 and 2. Because of the many embezzlement scandals involving parties and political leaders of the Left and of the Right since the beginning of the 1990s, the French political elite has a very negative image. Only 12 percent of our sample has a score of 2 on the index, and whether they belong to one or more associations does not make them more confident. The scale on trust in public institutions (courts, police, the National Assembly, civil service) ranges between 0 and 4. As far as government is concerned, the evaluation is more positive, maybe because France traditionally is a highly centralized country where citizens expect a lot from the state. According to World Values Surveys, France displays a fairly high level of trust in public institutions, which has even increased between 1981 and 1999.[6] France, once more, can be considered as an exception to the general pattern found in most other countries. Usually high levels of institutional trust are associated with high levels of generalized trust, probably because institutions provide security and establish rules (Offe 1999, 65; see also Rothstein and Stolle in this volume). In France the opposite phenomenon occurs: A high level of trust in institutions contrasts with a very low level of generalized trust (Galland 2000, 45; 1999, 50) at the aggregate level, and in this regard, on the microlevel too, there is not much difference between members and nonmembers.

To measure civicness and democratic commitment we included questions about the importance of elections and representative democracy (whether individuals vote regularly, find voting important for a democracy to function well, are attached to the existence of the parliament and parties and are against authoritarian leadership) and about basic democratic values such as tolerance. Members of associations vote a little more often, and they are slightly more tolerant if one looks

Table 3.2 Distribution of the membership

Variables	% of those who are members
GENDER	
Male	70
Female	60
AGE	
18–24	63
25–34	57
35–49	67
50–64	67
65+	71
DEGREE	
None, primary school	57
Vocational degree	61
Baccalaureate	66
Bac + 2 years	68
University	77
INCOME	
7,500 Frs and below	57
7,501–10,000 Frs	61
10,001–15,000 Frs	67
15,001–20,000 Frs	69
20,001 Frs+	75
RELIGION	
Regular practicing Catholic	81
Irregular practicing Catholic	70
Nonpracticing Catholic	62
No religion	61
Other religion	67
POLITICAL ORIENTATION	
Left	71
Right	67
Neither left nor right	58
Total sample	65

Note: Entries are percentage of the respondents belonging to at least one association in indicated category.

Source: CEVIPOF survey, May–June 2000 ($n = 2{,}148$).

at their scores on a scale of intolerance combining questions about the death penalty, acceptance of foreigners and immigrants, and rights for Moslems to practice their religion (Table 3.1). Some authors have claimed that democratic commitment should go beyond the norms and procedures of representative democracy by encouraging self-expression and participation and by ensuring a fair and equal distribution of goods. However, members of associations attach no more importance than nonmembers to collective participation (demonstrate to defend one's claims), nor do they appear more attached to social equality (guaranteed minimum wage).

The figures in Table 3.1 show that bivariate relations exist but they are not really impressive. However, these relations should be controlled for background variables: The population involved in associational networks clearly differs from the general population. Our survey confirms what previous studies have shown: Membership is more frequent among men, older people, the more educated and those with a higher income, and also among religious people (Hatchuel and Loisel 1999). Political leaning makes little difference; left-wingers are but slightly more involved than right-wingers. The main cleavage opposes those with a clear political identification against those who have none (Table 3.2).

MULTIVARIATE ANALYSIS

These background variables clearly determine participation behavior, and therefore we have to include them as control variables if we want to arrive at a more solid assessment of the relation between participation and attitudes. If we run a logistic regression to check the influence of membership in voluntary associations and social cultural background on our indicators of social trust, political trust and commitment to democratic procedures and values, the result is clear cut. Controlling for gender, age, educational level, religion and income, being involved in associations has no impact whatsoever on these variables (Table 3.3). Generalized trust increases with social and cultural resources, among educated and well-off respondents, and also among the elderly. Trust in public institutions mainly reflects the level of education. And trust in politicians depends on age, level of education and gender, dropping to exceptionally low levels among younger people, women and respondents without the baccalaureate.

The only conclusion we can draw from the regression results presented in Table 3.3 is that membership of voluntary associations is not significantly related to social, political or institutional trust, once we control for relevant background variables. While associations do not

Table 3.3   Associational membership and trust indicators: a multivariate analysis

	Generalized trust	Political trust	Institutional trust
INCOME	**	n.s.	n.s.
Less than 7,501Frs	.66**	1.09	.78
7,501–10,000Frs	.71*	1.04	.88
10,001–15,000Frs	ref	ref	ref
15,001–20,000Frs	.91	1.38*	.84
+20,000Frs	1.14	1.35	.83
DEGREE	**	***	**
Primary school	.86	.91	.85
Vocational	.86	.86	1.04
Baccalaureate	ref	ref	ref
Bac +2	1.38	1.22	1.03
University	1.33	1.77***	1.66**
RELIGION	n.s.	*	n.s.
Regular churchgoer	1.36	1.32	1.15
Irregular churchgoer	1.07	1.04	.86
Nonpracticing Catholic	ref	ref	ref
No religion	1.17	1.30*	1.02
Other religion	1.11	1.67**	1.01
ASSOCIATIONS	n.s.	n.s.	n.s.
None	1.04	1.05	.92
1	ref	ref	ref
2+	1.12	1.17	1.01
AGE	***	***	n.s.
18–24	.75	.72*	1.02
25–34	.88	.68**	1.13
35–49	ref	ref	ref
50–64	1.14	2.11***	1.04
65+	1.65**	2.40***	1.22
GENDER	n.s.	***	n.s.
Male	.94	1.63***	1.06
Female	ref	ref	ref
Cte	1.50	.34	1.29

Note: Entries are logistic regression coefficients. The reference category is a woman, between thirty-four and fifty years old, belonging to one association, a nonpracticing Catholic, with the baccalaureate and a monthly income between 10,000 and 15,000 francs (indicated by italicized entries). Entries are exp.(B). $* = p < .05$; $** = p < .01$; $*** = p < .001$.

Source: CEVIPOF survey, May–June 2000 ($n = 2,148$).

seem to have any effect on trust, they do have an effect on politicization, as the analysis reported in Table 3.4 demonstrates. In this analysis, too, we used three indicators. One measures political knowledge, based on the answers to a short quiz at the end of the interview.[7]

Table 3.4   Associational membership and political indicators: a multivariate analysis

	Political knowledge	Political interest	Ideological sophistication
INCOME	***	*	*
Less than 7,501Frs	.55***	.99	.74*
7,501–10,000Frs	.83	1.15	.79
10,001–15,000Frs	ref	ref	ref
15,001–20,000Frs	1.31	1.38*	1.11
+20,000Frs	1.46*	1.49*	1.13
DEGREE	***	***	**
Primary school	.39***	.41***	.63**
Vocational	.52***	.61***	.69**
Baccaluareate	ref	ref	ref
Bac +2	1.02	1.10	1.00
University	1.97***	1.55**	.99
RELIGION	n.s.	*	n.s.
Regular churchgoer	1.26	1.37**	1.04
Irregular churchgoer	.90	1.63*	1.08
Nonpracticing Catholic	ref	ref	ref
No religion	1.10	1.23	.86
Other religion	.77	1.20	1.18
ASSOCIATIONS	n.s.	***	***
None	.82	.90	.73**
1	ref	ref	ref
2+	.89	1.40**	1.12
AGE	***	***	***
18–24	.47***	.63**	.76
25–34	.76*	.84	.70**
35–49	ref	ref	ref
50–64	2.28***	2.74***	1.51**
65+	3.40***	2.60***	1.15
GENDER	***	***	***
Male	3.17***	2.28***	1.42***
Female	ref	ref	ref
Cte	.84	.35	2.33

Note: Entries are logistic regression coefficients. The reference category is a woman, between thirty-four and fifty years old, belonging to one association, a nonpracticing Catholic, with the baccalaureate and a monthly income between 10,000 and 15,000 francs (indicated by italicized entries). Entries are exp.(B). * = $p < .05$; ** = $p < .01$; *** = $p < .001$.

Source: CEVIPOF survey, May–June 2000 ($n = 2,148$).

The second indicator is the classical question on how interested respondents are in politics. The third indicator measures the ideological sophistication of the respondent. It opposes those who are capable and willing to define themselves as "somewhat right wing" or "somewhat left wing" to those who refuse to answer or answer "neither left nor right." The left–right cleavage in France is the main political marker, equivalent to party identification in Britain or in the United States. Here we are interested not in the political orientation of the respondents but in their ability to acknowledge this divide and choose their side. The question is whether associational membership is related to the respondent's knowledge about politics, interest in politics, and their ability to define themselves politically. The results show that being involved in associations does not make participants better informed.[8] However, associational membership has a significant impact on the two other indicators, the level of political interest and the recognition of the left–right cleavage, even though age, gender and education have far more influence.[9] In other words, members give more attention to politics and are more likely to take sides for the Left or the Right than nonmembers (see Table 3.4).

One can make two objections to these results. First, there are many types of associations, and we do not expect that each and every one of them has the same effect. One would expect that militant movements, fighting for a cause such as human rights or workers' interests, have stronger politicizing effects than associations just providing services, for example, in the sports and leisure sector. This is indeed the case: Members of unions and human rights associations are more politicized. Respectively 62 and 68 percent declare themselves very or somewhat interested in politics, with the proportion falling to 50 percent among members of consumers and women's associations, 47 percent in environmental associations, 45 percent in Parent-Teacher Associations (PTAs) and sports and leisure associations. Members of human rights organizations and unions are also more capable of defining themselves politically as left wing or right wing. Yet, whatever the type of association they belong to, members are always more politicized than nonmembers.

The second objection is that a survey, conducted at one point of time, does not allow us to tell whether politicization is a cause or an effect of involvement in voluntary associations. Most probably it works both ways (see Hooghe this volume). Ongoing microsociological and longitudinal studies (Broqua et al. 2000; Fillieule and Broqua 2001; Hamidi 2002) show that the observed effects are dependent upon the type of association, its leadership and its degree of internal democracy. But even associations that have nothing to do with politics provide an opening on the political world, a familiarization with public talk, and an incitement to further commitments in other associations, unions or even parties. Therefore it is safe to conclude that all kinds of associations have some politicization effect, but with strong variations according to the type of organization.

THE TEST OF THE "COLEMAN" EXPERIMENT

The last step we take in this chapter is to probe deeper into the characteristics of political trust. Taking advantage of the computer-assisted telephone interviewing methodology (CATI), which allows more flexibility and interactivity than standard surveys, we included in our survey several experiments testing the consistency of public opinion by changing the framing and wording of the questions. One of them is the "Coleman" experiment, so called in reference to Coleman's seminal work on political influence as a resource deriving from trust, defined as "an investment in another which allows influence to take place, in which alter (the influenced) believes that ego (the influencer) will act in ways beneficial to alter, from alter's point of view" (Coleman 1963, 66). In Coleman's utilitarian perspective, trust is not so much a psychological feature of the truster but a rational decision, balancing expected losses and expected gains (Coleman 1990, 99). Along these lines, the point of our experiment was to go beyond stereotypes about politicians and general statements about democratic institutions and procedures and to test trust invested in governmental agencies as opposed to nongovernmental agencies, in concrete situations differently designed. The domain chosen is a sensitive one, involving nuclear risk and the health hazards of nuclear plants. This is a topical debate in France since the Chernobyl nuclear plant accident in April 1986. The government at that time was accused of having hidden the truth from the population, of having underrated the risk of radioactive clouds and of not having taken basic safety measures. Periodically an independent association, the Commission de Recherche et d'Information Indépendantes sur la Radioactivité (CRIIRAD), makes its own estimates of radioactivity in the vicinity of nuclear plants and contests the official measures. A suit has recently been filed against three former ministers, Charles Pasqua (interior), Michèle Barzach (public health) and Alain Carignon (industry), by a young man with a cancer of the thyroid, which he attributes to the passage of the Chernobyl radioactive cloud.[10] Clearly, nuclear risks are still a highly salient issue in French public opinion.

In our experiment, the interviewees were told that health problems
have been noticed in the vicinity of nuclear power plants and that an
investigation is being conducted to determine the extent of the risk.
What we wanted to test is their degree of confidence in the investigators. The experiment consists in varying randomly both the serious-
ness of the health problem and the authority in charge of the
investigation. The health problem is very minor (allergies) for half the
sample, while for the other half it is very serious (birth defects). And
the authority in charge of the investigation can be governmental (the
ministry of industry in one case, the *minister* of industry in the other
to see if personalization of responsibilities matters) or nongovernmental (the European Atomic Agency in one case, a panel of independent scientists on the other). This gives us a total of eight different
versions of the story that can be presented to the interviewees, randomly selected by the computer. The first aim of this experiment was
to understand the actual level of trust in French public officials, while
at the same time it allows us to examine whether members of voluntary networks are more trusting in general, whatever the authority
concerned.

The main result is that people appear less inclined to trust the
results of the investigation when it is undertaken by a governmental
body. In the two subgroups told that the Minister or the Ministry of
Industry are in charge, less than half of the interviewees feel confident
in the Ministry findings (Table 3.5). Conversely, in the two groups
told that a European agency is leading the investigation, a majority
trusts their conclusions, despite the fact that European institutions in
France are usually not very well known and are perceived as distant
and technocratic. But the most trusted agency is by far "an association
of independent scientists," with almost two-thirds of respondents
in that group giving a confident answer. The threat scenario was not
significantly influential for confidence responses.

If, on the whole, educated, wealthy and middle-class respondents
are slightly more confident, whatever the agency or the risk involved,
the differences are minor and not significant (results not shown). But
participation in voluntary associations makes no difference either:
Joiners do not find the investigators more reliable, whoever they are.
And just as nonjoiners, they tend to have less trust in public officials
than in nonpublic ones. The only significant differences come from
the level of social and political trust. High scorers on our indicators
of generalized trust, trust in political officials and trust in public institutions are systematically more confident in the results of the inquiry,
whatever the authority in charge. But the most interesting result is

Table 3.5 The Coleman experiment

	A slightly higher rate of allergies has been observed in the vicinity of nuclear power plants in France.				An increase in birth defects has been observed in the vicinity of nuclear power plants in France.			
%	The European Atomic Agency	An association of independent scientists	The Minister of Industry	The Ministry of Industry	The European Atomic Agency	An association of independent scientists	The Minister of Industry	The Ministry of Industry
...are conducting an investigation on the problem. How confident are you in the results of this investigation?								
Total confident	56	64	45	46	54	63	47	49
Total not confident	44	36	56	52	45	36	53	50
n	251	255	259	269	303	264	270	277

Note: Percentages do not always add to 100 percent because of the category "no answer."

that the structure of the answers remains the same: Even high "trusters" have more confidence in the inquiry conducted by an association of independent scientists or an European agency than in the inquiry of governmental agencies (for a detailed presentation of these results see Mayer 2002).

Some individuals appear more trusting than others, with a general attitude of confidence in other people, ordinary citizens, politicians, governmental and nongovernmental agencies. But this confidence does not stem from structural social capital measured by involvement in voluntary associations. Respondents seem to have a political and rational approach to the problem: Even the most trustful do not have as much confidence in the government as they do in nongovernmental agencies, presumably from remembering its past performance on the issue. As the memories of the Chernobyl cloud linger on, since at the time the government did not react properly, French government has over time eroded its capital of trust as far as nuclear matters are concerned.

CONCLUSION

Associations clearly are not the only providers of social capital; there are many other sources of social connectedness (see chapters in the second part of this volume). As far as classical voluntary associations are concerned, in France at least, members are neither more trusting nor more civic. Socioeconomic status and generation prove better predictors of generalized trust and norms of reciprocity (Table 3.1). Respondents with high levels of income and education have more faith in their fellow citizens. As Putnam reminds us, "survey reports about honesty and trust should be interpreted prima facie as accurate accounts of the respondent's social experiences. In virtually all societies 'have-nots' are less trusting than 'haves,' probably because haves are treated by others with more honesty and respect" (Putnam 2000, 138). And younger people, brought up in a context of economic recession, prove less trusting than the elderly, in the same way that they are more pessimistic about the future.

Civil society is not necessarily "civic" society, especially if one defines civicness narrowly as an attachment to representative democracy, its institutions and its authorities. In the 1990s, various militant radical associations developed in France, fighting for the right of the "without"—without papers *(les sans papiers)*, without a job, without a home—or in the growing sector of the antiglobalization movement, such as the Association for the Taxation of Financial Transactions (ATTAC). The supporters of these new associations might even be less "civic" in the sense that they contest the usual channels of participation and the legitimacy of elected representatives in the name of a stronger, more participative democracy (Barber 1984). Joiners therefore cannot be considered automatically as trusters, especially not with regard to the political system.

But joiners are indeed more aware of politics and they pay more attention to them. This is not the case just in France but also in other Western countries. Data from the World Value Surveys and the Eurobarometers show a positive relation between political interest and membership in social movement organizations (environment, human rights), social and welfare organizations as well as in interest groups, unions and political parties (Van Deth 2000a, 128).[11] Maybe voluntary associations are not really that successful as learning schools of democracy, but Tocqueville's intuition about the role of voluntary associations as intermediaries, connecting the private and the public sphere, still holds true.

NOTES

1. The trend is just starting to slow down: In France the peak was reached in 1996 with 67,778 creations, compared with 64,918 in 1995 and 62,897 in 1997 (CNVA 2000, 53).

2. She also studied their mortality rate. Her study shows that half the associations present in 1980 are still active ten years later, between 10 and 20 percent are there but asleep and the last third has disappeared (Tchernogog 1999).

3. Co-ordinated by Gérard Grunberg (Centre d'étude de la Vie Politique Française, CEVIPOF), Paul M. Sniderman (University of Stanford) and myself, a CATI-type survey was conducted on the phone between May 8 and June 27, 2000, on a national random sample of 2,148 respondents, representative for the population aged eighteen or older, living in metropolitan France. Phone numbers were selected from a France-Télécom file respecting stratification by district and urban/ rural areas. There were up to ten recalls, eight during week hours, two during the weekend. Respondents were selected within each household according to the "birthday method" (the person aged eighteen and above whose birthday was celebrated most recently). The survey benefited from grants by the National Science Foundation (SES-9818742 and SES-0111715) in the United States and by a consortium of institutions in France (Fondation Nationale des Sciences Politiques, FNSP; CEVIPOF; and Service d'Information du Gouvernement, SIG).

4. We systematically checked the results by giving the uneducated their proper weight. The level of membership in voluntary associations only slightly decreases (38 percent of the weighted sample belong to no association, 32 percent to one and 31 percent to more). We present here the unweighted data because weighting introduces another bias, as it assumes that the uneducated who refused to take part in the survey hold the same opinions and behaviours as the uneducated who accepted.

5. For instance in the survey conducted by CSA for the commemoration of the 1901 law on associations, people were first asked if they belonged to at least one association and subsequently only the respondents who had given a positive answer were read out a list of associations. The proportion of the sample declaring membership in at least one voluntary association in this survey dropped to 37 percent (telephone survey, November 8–9, 2000, national sample of 1,042 people representative of the population of fifteen years and above). The presence of the very young in this sample (fifteen to eighteen years), however, also brought down the level of membership (INJEP 2001, 18–25).

6. After the socialist victory in 1981, the proportion of left-wing voters trusting the army, the police and the civil service went up, catching up and sometimes exceeding the level of trust among right-wing voters (Bréchon 2000: 122).

7. Ten statements were proposed, five correct, five incorrect, mostly about French institutions (electoral rules, length of presidential mandate, powers of prime minister, party funding), European institutions and general political knowledge.

8. Knowledge seems to depend mostly on gender, followed by age and education. Women know less about politics, or choose not to answer, far more often than men, even controlling for their level of education, age and income. There is a clear gender gap here, not specific to France, that far from disappearing seems to be developing even further (see Van Deth 2000a).

9. The generational effect is decisive. Compared to the reference category (woman, middle aged, with the baccalaureate, middle-range income, nonpracticing Catholic and belonging to one association), the younger respondents (eighteen to twenty-four years old) are four times less likely to be interested in politics than the seniors (sixty-five years old and above), as shown in our logistic regression model (Table 3.4). They also are four times more likely to have low trust in politicians (Table 3.3). There is a clear-cut cleavage between the generations who discovered politics at the time of the May 1968 social movements, and remained interested and confident in politics, and those who came later, with each new cohort appearing less interested and more critical than the previous one. This is shown by the cohort analysis in the period 1978–2000 done by Etienne Schweisguth in a book I coedited (Schweisguth 2002, 70–79).

10. *Libération*, 16 and 17–18 June 2000. The Court of Justice of the Republic has decided that the suit could not be taken into consideration.

11. Van Deth makes the interesting observation that we should make a distinction between political interest and the saliency of politics. Unfortunately our data do not allow us to make this distinction in this chapter. Reconciling Eliasoph's and Tocqueville's theoretical insights, Van Deth (2000a) shows that while subjective political interest increases with social connectedness and associational membership, the saliency of politics decreases.

REFERENCES

Agulhon, M. (1970). *La République au Village*. Paris: Plon.
Agulhon, M. (1977). *Le Cercle dans la France Bourgeoise. Etude d'une Mutation de Sociabilité*. Paris: Armand Colin.
Agulhon, M. and M. Bodiguel (1981). *Les Associations au Village*. Arles: Actes Sud.
Almond, G. and S. Verba (1963). *The Civic Culture*. Princeton: Princeton University Press.
Andrieu, C., G. Le Béguec and D. Tartakowski (eds., 2001). *Associations et Champ Politique, La Loi de 1901 à l'Epreuve du Siècle*. Paris: Publications de la Sorbonne.
Archambault, E. (1999). "France. From Jacobin tradition to Decentralization." pp. 81–97. In L. Salamon et al. (eds.), *Global Civil Society. Dimensions of the Nonprofit Sector*. Baltimore: John Hopkins Center for Civil Society Studies.

Barber, B. (1984). *Strong Democracy.* Berkeley: University of California Press.

Barthélémy, M. (2000). *Associations: Un Nouvel Age de la Participation.* Paris: Presses de Sciences Po.

Bourdieu, P. (1979). *La Distinction. Critique Sociale du Jugement.* Paris: Editions de Minuit.

Bourdieu, P. (1980). "Le Capital Social. Notes provisoires." *Actes de la Recherche en Sciences Sociales* 31, 2–3.

Bréchon, P. (2000). "L'Univers des Valeurs Politiques: Permanences et Mutations." pp. 104–128. In P. Bréchon (ed.), *Les Valeurs des Français. Evolution de 1980 à 2000.* Paris: Armand Colin.

Broqua, C., S. Duchesne, C. Hamidi, O. Fillieule and N. Mayer (2000). *Dynamique de l'Engagement et Elargissement des Solidarités.* Paris: MIRE/ Fondation de France.

Citrin, J.(1974). "Comment: The Political Relevance of Trust in Government." *American Political Science Review* 58(3), 973–988.

CNVA (Conseil National de la Vie Associative) (2000). *Bilan de la Vie Associative en 1996–1999.* Paris: la Documentation française.

Coleman, J. S. (1963). "Comment on 'On the concept of influence.'" *Public Opinion Quarterly* 63–82.

Coleman, J. S. (1990). *Foundations of Social Theory.* Cambridge: Belknap Press of Harvard University Press.

Degenne, O. and M. Forsé (1998). "Vers une Sociabilité Négociée." pp. 90–116. In O. Galland and Y. Lemehl (eds.), *La Nouvelle Société Française. Trente Années de Mutations.* Paris: Armand Colin.

Eliasoph, N. (1998). *Avoiding Politics. How Americans Produce Apathy in Everyday Life.* Cambridge: Cambridge University Press.

Fillieule, O. and C. Broqua (2001). "Désengagement et Conséquences Biographiques de l'Engagement." pp. 157–162. In CRESAL, Actes du colloque *Actions Associatives, Solidarités et Territoires.* Saint Etienne: Publications de l'Université de Saint-Etienne.

Galland, O. (1999). "Les Relations de Confiance." *Revue Tocqueville* 20(1), 45–57.

Galland, O. (2000). "Les Français Entre Eux: Des Relations Electives et Sélectives." pp. 28–47. In P. Bréchon (ed.), *Les Valeurs des Français. Evolution de 1980 à 2000.* Paris: Armand Colin.

Grunberg, G., N. Mayer and P. Sniderman (eds., 2002). *La Démocratie à l'Epreuve, une Nouvelle Approche de l'Opinion des Français.* Paris: Presses de Sciences Po.

Hall, P. (1999). "Social Capital in Britain." *British Journal of Political Science* 29(3), 417–462.

Hamidi, C. (2002). *Les Effets Politiques de l'Engagement Associatif. Le Cas des Associations Issues d'Immigration.* Paris: Ph.D. Dissertation.

Hardin, R. (1999). "Do We Want Trust in Government?" pp. 22–41. In M. Warren (ed.), *Democracy and Trust.* Cambridge: Cambridge University Press.

Hatchuel, G. and J. P. Loisel (1999). "La vie associative: participer mais pas militer." *Données Sociales* 359–365.

Huard, R. (2000). "Political Association in Nineteenth Century France: Legislation and Practice." pp. 135–153. In N. Bermeo and Ph. Nord (eds.), *Civil Society before Democracy. Lessons from Nineteenth-Century Europe.* Lanham: Rowman and Littlefield.

Inglehart, R. (1999). "Trust, Well-being and Democracy." pp. 88–120. In M. Warren (ed.), *Democracy and Trust.* Cambridge: Cambridge University Press.

INJEP (Institut National de la Jeunesse et de l'Education Populaire) (2001). *L'Image de la Vie Associative en France.* Paris: Institut national de la jeunesse et de l'education populaire.

Mayer, N. (2002). "Les Dimensions de la Confiance." pp. 87–108. In G. Grunberg, N. Mayer and P. Sniderman (eds.), *La Démocratie à l'Epreuve, une Nouvelle Approche de l'Opinion des Français.* Paris: Presses de Sciences Po.

Mendras, H. (2001). "Le Lien Social en Amérique et en Europe." *Revue de l'OFCE* 76, January, 179–187.

Merlet, J. F. (2001). *Une Grande Loi de la IIIème République, la Loi du 1er Juillet 1901.* Paris: LGDJ.

Newton, K. (2001). "Trust, Social Capital, Civil Society and Democracy." *International Political Science Review* 22(2), 201–214.

Newton, K. and P. Norris (2000). "Confidence in Public Institutions: Faith, Culture or Performance?" pp. 52–73. In S. Pharr and R. Putnam (eds.), *Disaffected Democracies: What's Troubling the Trilateral Countries?* Princeton: Princeton University Press.

Offe, C. (1999). "How Can We Trust Our Fellow Citizens?" pp. 42–87. In M. Warren (ed.), *Democracy and Trust.* Cambridge: Cambridge University Press.

Pharr, S. and R. Putnam (eds., 2000). *Disaffected Democracies: What's Troubling the Trilateral Countries?* Princeton: Princeton University Press.

Portes, A. (1998). "Social Capital: Its Origin and Applications in Modern Sociology." *Annual Review of Sociology* 22, 1–24.

Putnam, R. (1993). *Making Democracy Work.* Princeton: Princeton University Press.

Putnam, R. (1995). "Tuning In, Tuning Out: The Strange Disappearance of Social Capital in America." *Political Science and Politics* 28(4), 664–683.

Putnam, R. (2000). *Bowling Alone. The Collapse and Revival of American Community.* New York: Simon and Schuster.

Salamon, L. et al. (1999). *Global Civil Society.* Baltimore: John Hopkins Center for Civil Society Studies.

Schweisguth, E. (2002). "La Dépolitisation en Questions." pp. 51–86. In G. Grunberg, N. Mayer and P. Sniderman (eds.), *La Démocratie à l'Epreuve, une Nouvelle Approche de l'Opinion des Français.* Paris: Presses de Sciences Po.

SOFRES (1998). *L'Etat de l'Opinion 1998.* Paris: Seuil.

SOFRES (2000). *L'Etat de l'Opinion 2000.* Paris: Seuil.

Stolle, D. (2001). "Clubs and Congregations: The Benefits of Joining an Association." pp. 202–244. In K. Cook (ed.), *Trust in Society*. New York: Russell Sage Foundation.

Tarrow, S. (1996). "Making Social Science Work Across Space and Time: A Critical Reflection on Robert Putnam's *Making Democracy Work*." *American Political Science Review* 90, 389–397.

Tchernogog, V. (1999). "Trajectoires Associatives. Premiers Eléments sur la Mortalité des Associaitions." *Revue des Etudes Coopératives, Mutualistes et Associatives* 272.

Tchernogog, V. (2001). "Quelles Ressources et Quels Emplois dans les Associations? Réflexions à Partir d'une Enquête de Cadrage." pp. 21–35. In CRESAL, Actes du colloque *Actions Associatives, Solidarités et Territoires*. Saint Etienne: Publications de l'Université de Saint Etienne.

Tocqueville, A. de (1986 [1840]). *De la Démocratie en Amérique*, Tome 2. Paris: Gallimard.

Uslaner, E. (1999). "Democracy and Social Capital." pp. 121–150. In M. Warren (ed.), *Democracy and Trust*. Cambridge: Cambridge University Press.

Van Deth, J., M. Maraffi and K. Newton (eds., 1999). *Social Capital and European Democracy*. London: Routledge.

Van Deth, J. (2000a). "Interesting but Irrelevant: Social Capital and the Saliency of Parties in Western Europe." *European Journal of Political Research* 37, 115–147.

Van Deth, J. (2000b). "Political Interest and Apathy: The Decline of a Gender Gap?" *Acta Politica* 35(3), 247–274.

Van Deth, J. (ed., 1997). *Private Groups and Public Life. Social Participation, Voluntary Associations and Political Involvement in Representative Democracy*. London: Routledge.

Warren, M. (ed., 1999). *Democracy and Trust*. Cambridge: Cambridge University Press.

CHAPTER 4

THE IMPORTANCE OF PASSIVE MEMBERSHIP FOR SOCIAL CAPITAL FORMATION

Dag Wollebæk and Per Selle

INTRODUCTION

Advocates of the virtues of participation assert that in a true democracy, citizens should be able to take an active part in civic matters, at least on the local level (Patcman 1970; Macpherson 1977). Regular elections and the existence of formal rights are by themselves not sufficient for democracy; they need to be supplemented by opportunities for direct democratic influence. On the other hand, pluralists emphasize how a diverse range of associations may act as representatives on the political scene, regardless of the activity level of the participants (Almond and Verba 1963). National political systems are too large to allow face-to-face discussion between all citizens. Therefore, the presence of associations is an institutional requirement if the combined values or interests of individuals are to be mediated.

There are evident influences from both strands of thought in Robert D. Putnam's (1993, 1995, 2000) important work on associations and social capital. His view of associations as intermediary institutions between citizens and the state and the weight he attaches to networks cutting across subcultural divides reveal a clear inspiration from writers in the pluralist vein. His emphasis on the necessity of active participation for the socialization of democratic virtues is, by contrast, related to participant-oriented approaches to democratic theory (Selle and Strømsnes 2001). The core contribution of associations is to provide social connections between their participants, which in turn produce trust and civic engagement. Thus, intensity has priority over scope. This leads him to dismiss politically oriented organizations with mainly or only passive members as relatively unimportant for the formation of social capital. In a pluralist perspective, by contrast, the passive supporter is important not only as a source of numerical strength and legitimacy for the associations but as part of the democratic process. Furthermore, weak and multiple affiliations ensure that most members belong to several overlapping networks. This implies that views will be moderated as a result of cross-pressures.

In this chapter, we analyze empirically whether only intensive participation can generate the resources so highly valued by Putnam, or if passive support may be more important than no support at all, as pluralists would argue. The data stem from a postal survey undertaken in Norway in 1998, a country where passive membership is particularly widespread among the population. Before moving on to the empirical analyses, however, we need to take a closer look at the hypothesized nature of the relationship between attitudinal aspects of social capital and participation in associations.

THE IMPORTANCE OF FACE-TO-FACE INTERACTION

One of the most important changes in the voluntary sector over the past decades has been the growth of what Putnam calls "tertiary associations" at the expense of "classic secondary associations" (Putnam 1995; Selle and Strømsnes 2001; Maloney 1999, 108). Tertiary associations are characterized by centralized, paid-staff leadership; they tend to be nondemocratically structured, and the support of the members tends to be channeled through money rather than time. This implies a trend in which the intensity of associational involvement is declining.

Putnam (2000) dismisses the growth of tertiary associations as a potential countertrend to the decline of social capital in the United States. The main reason given is that, although the members may feel a common attachment to symbols and values, they do not interact face to face. In his view, social capital can mostly be formed and transmitted through direct interaction. Furthermore, tertiary groups consist of vertical rather than horizontal networks. Their structure is better characterized as client–patron relationships than as interaction among equals (Maloney 1999, 109), and "two clients of the same patron, lacking direct contact, hold nothing hostage to each other" (Putnam 1993, 175). Putnam does admit that tertiary associations may have important external effects on the wider polity. Passive supporters play an important role in providing associations with economic support and numerical strength, which gives more weight to their arguments.

However, the internal effects on the participants are thought to be weak or absent. This leads Putnam to dismiss passive support as a source of social capital, which may be problematic on several accounts.

First, Putnam does not directly address secondary associations within which many or even most members are passive. In many countries, especially outside the United States, this is very common. The high amount of passive memberships is one of the main structural characteristics of the voluntary sector in Scandinavia and the Netherlands (Dekker and van den Broek 1998). Although "tertiary" organizations are gaining ground here too, most associations are still of the classic "secondary" form, which are democratically structured internally and which rely on the support of active (in addition to many passive) members.

Thus, passive members may belong to institutions within which large stocks of social capital are embedded. Although empirical evidence is scanty, some studies do suggest that passive members feel neither alienated nor disconnected from these social systems (Selle and Strømsnes 1998; Wollebæk 2000). If Putnam's emphasis on face-to-face contact for the socialization of civic values is correct, the level of social capital should nevertheless be observably higher among the core of activists than among the passive supporters, even within the same association.

Moreover, one of Putnam's sources of inspiration, Almond and Verba's *Civic Culture* (1963), attributes an importance to passive memberships that exceeds their focus on external effects. In their classic study, passive members displayed a significantly higher level of civic competence than nonmembers across five countries. Passive members were also more supportive of democratic norms than outsiders and shared a higher sense of political efficacy. This suggests that passive memberships may indeed have "internal" effects, a notion that is corroborated by other studies. Godwin (1992) emphasizes that even the most passive form of participation, financial support through check writing, "...reduces political alienation, as contributors believe their contributions make a difference. This, in turn, reduces the support for aggressive political participation" (cited in Maloney 1999, 113).

Furthermore, why should a sense of community or identification with a cause, which may be conducive to trust in compatriots, presuppose face-to-face contact? The theory of imagined communities provides a clue to how social capital of this kind can develop without personal interaction (Anderson 1991; Newton 1997; Whiteley 1999). The imagined community is a group to which one feels a psychological affinity, even though it is too large to allow face-to-face contact between all its members. Therefore, imagined communities are based on an abstract form of trust rather than on thin or thick trust (Newton 1999). In this vein, Whiteley (1999, 31) shows that those who most strongly identify with the imagined community (e.g., express patriotism) are more likely to express a generalized sense of trust in other people than individuals whose patriotism is weaker.

Although the nation is given as the typical example of the imagined community, the concept is transferable to other social systems with similar properties. The relations between a passive member and his/her association and the citizen and his/her nation clearly share important characteristics. Associations with passive members and nations are both social systems that are too large to allow face-to-face contact, but their members/citizens may still feel a common affinity to symbols or values, or share a commitment to a cause. To the degree that individuals hold overlapping memberships in associations, their sense of identification and abstract trust may be transferred to several contexts, and possibly to society as a whole.

THE IMPORTANCE OF MULTIPLE AFFILIATIONS

Another aspect in which individuals differ with regard to their participation in associations is the number of affiliations they hold. It is possible to identify two ways in which multiple affiliations may contribute more to attitudinal aspects of social capital than singular affiliations do. These can be labeled as moderating and cumulative effects.

First, at the societal level, the more overlapping and interlocking networks that exist, the higher the probability that people from different backgrounds will meet. To the degree that associations create horizontal networks that span underlying cleavages, they may have a moderating effect on the level of conflict in society. It is hypothesized that associations are particularly able to generate cross-cutting, multiple networks because the relationships between those involved are characterized by weak ties of relatively low intensity (Granovetter 1973).

This moderating effect occurs as a result of cross-pressures experienced through participation in multiple networks (Putnam 1993, 90). When interacting with individuals of diverse backgrounds, goals and preferences, each person is forced to moderate his or her own attitudes in order to create a lasting social contract in the different settings. Dense, overlapping and interlocking networks thus contribute to compromise and negotiation. Second, at the individual level, multiple affiliations mean more and broader interaction. Consequently, it should have a cumulative effect on an individual's trust and other attitudinal aspects of social capital. Almond and Verba (1963, 264–265) did find the number of memberships held by an individual to affect civic competence positively: "Membership in one organization increases an individual's sense of political competence, and membership in more than one organization leads to even greater competence." In fact, the number of multiple affiliations discriminated more clearly between the "civic" and less "civic" countries in their study than did the proportion of the population holding memberships or the level of membership activity.

Intensity and scope do not always move in accord, and although they are related, they should be treated as two separate aspects of participation. On the one hand, intense involvement in one association may foster an interest to take part in others. On the other hand, highly intense involvement may build barriers against outsiders and consequently narrow the scope of the networks created. Although Putnam emphasizes both scope and intensity of involvement, it follows from the weight attached to face-to-face interaction that intensity has first priority. Passive memberships in several associations are seen as less productive for social capital than active membership in one. In the analyses to come, this proposition will be put to the test.

DOES TYPE MATTER?

Until now, the discussion of the impact of participation in associations on attitudinal components of social capital has focused on form rather than content. However, given the immense variety of different purposes for which associations exist in Western countries, the question of the type of activity also needs to be taken into consideration.

At a glance, Putnam's contention seems to be that the type of association is virtually irrelevant for the extent to which social capital is developed (Putnam 1993, 90). On the surface, this is identical to Almond and Verba's (1963, 265) assertion that memberships even in nonpolitical associations lead to a more competent citizenry. However, if type means little in Putnam's work, structure means everything. The demands of horizontality, face-to-face interaction and the ability to transcend subcultural barriers will be met more often by nonpolitical, leisure-oriented associations than by associations with a manifest political purpose. Politically oriented associations are often products of cleavages in society and centralized in structure and have a large minority or even a majority of passive members. Thus, in Putnam's understanding of how to make democracy work, a choral society or a bird-watching club play a vital role, while the contribution of social movements, labor unions and political parties is downplayed (Foley and Edwards 1996). This somewhat counterintuitive notion stems directly from Putnam's distinction between external and internal effects, of which the latter appears to be given priority (Putnam 1995, 71).

This view is, naturally, contested. With regard to the internal effects of participation, Quigley (1996, 3) claims that nonpolitical associations cannot foster the civic skills necessary to promote social capital and strengthen democracy as much as organizations that contest state authority. Foley and Edwards (1996) and Rueschemeyer (1998) emphasize that externally, nonpolitical associations cannot play the role of a counterweight to the state like political associations or social movements do. Finally, Selle and Strømsnes (2001) question the degree to which associations can act as intermediary institutions between the individual and the state, if they are nonpolitical in purpose and often local in structure. Nevertheless, if Putnam's contention is correct, we might expect that members of political associations display a lower level of generalized trust than members of associations without an expressed political purpose. Given these disagreements it seems vital to examine the impact of the type of associations on attitudinal aspects of social capital, as we will in the remainder of the chapter.

MEASUREMENTS

The independent variables are measurements of the scope, intensity and type of association involvement. Scope is operationalized as the number of associations with which each individual is affiliated. Although most volunteers hold memberships, some do not. These affiliations also need to be accounted for, and the scope of the involvement includes both memberships and volunteering.[1] The intensity of the involvement is operationalized as the combined amount of time spent participating and volunteering in associations over the past year. This provides a reasonably accurate measure of the extent of face-to-face contact to which the member/volunteer has been exposed. As one additional hour of participation does not necessarily mean the same for highly active participants as for the more passively affiliated, an ordinal variable dividing the sample into four approximately equal groups is used rather than a linear measure of the number of hours spent participating.

Type is operationalized as the main purpose of the association(s) with which a person is affiliated. On the one hand, we have the pure nonpolitical associations, primarily involved in sports, culture or leisure (e.g., football clubs, music or arts groups, hobby associations, fraternity groups). Religious associations are rarely involved in politics in the Norwegian society. However, they are sufficiently different from leisure-oriented associations, both in purpose and structure, to deserve a separate subcategory of the nonpolitical type. At the other end of the scale, we find the organizations whose main purposes are political, namely political parties and unions. In between, there are a number of associations with a more or less manifest political purpose: For example, local community associations, humanitarian associations, environmental associations or advocacy groups for disabled persons. These are given the somewhat unsatisfactory "semipolitical" label. Many are affiliated with more than one type of association, and the categories must allow for this variation. Therefore, two additional categories are in order: Those who are affiliated with both a nonpolitical and a semipolitical association are classified in the first combinatory type, while those affiliated with non or semipolitical associations and a political association are grouped in the second type.

In this chapter, we decompose Putnam's formulation of the attitudinal aspects of social capital into two core elements: Trust and civic engagement. Trust is further divided into generalized trust and vertical trust (or trust in institutions).[2] Trust in institutions is not conventionally considered to be an attitudinal aspect of social capital. However, political trust constitutes an important link between citizens' participation in associations and their influence on the performance of political institutions as examined in Putnam's book on Italy (see also Paxton 1999 and Stolle and Rochon 1999). Generalized trust is measured by a single question: "In general, would you say that most people can be trusted, or that you can't be careful enough in dealing with other people." A variable indicating the level of vertical trust, that is, trust in institutions, is also included. This is measured by an additive index with four components: Trust in politicians, state authorities, municipal authorities and for-profit companies (Chronbach's alpha = .66).[3] Finally, civic engagement is operationalized as the level of expressed civic and political interest. In order to measure this, three items are used in a composite index: Voting behavior, readership of news material in daily newspapers and political interest.

In summary, with the exception of vertical trust, the indicators chosen to measure the subdimensions of social capital are mostly identical to the ones that Putnam uses (generalized trust, voting behavior and newspaper readership). Furthermore, they comply with the logic of the social capital concept in measuring potentials or resources, not end products. It therefore seems sound to conclude that the definitory validity of the indicators used is high. In addition, a set of common background variables (gender, education, age, employment, marital status, residential stability and population density) was included in order to control for the impact of other potential sources of social capital.

THE DATA

The analyses are based on the Survey on Giving and Volunteering, a nation-wide survey carried out by the Norwegian Centre of Research in Organization and Management (LOS Centre) in the spring of 1998, as part of the Johns Hopkins Comparative Nonprofit Sector Project (Wollebæk, Selle and Lorentzen 2000). This survey is the most comprehensive data gathered on the involvement of individuals in voluntary associations in Norway. The survey was administered by means of mailed questionnaires to 4,000 randomly selected Norwegians aged between sixteen and eighty-five. The respondents were contacted four times—a postcard one week before mailing the questionnaire, the mailing of the questionnaire itself and two follow-ups. The last follow-up was carried out by telephone. In all, we received 1,695 valid responses, which equals a response rate of 45 percent (adjusted gross sample). This response rate is somewhat lower than is the case for most mailed surveys in Norway. However, there is no systematic over-representation of active participants, and the bias toward middle-aged and higher-educated respondents is compensated by weighing the results.

RESULTS: INTENSITY, SCOPE AND TYPE OF PARTICIPATION AND SOCIAL CAPITAL

Our main research question is whether participation in associations contributes to attitudinal components of social capital. Our inclusion of voting adds a behavioral dimension. Furthermore, we are interested in finding out whether active participation contributes to the formation of social capital more than passive membership does. How necessary is active participation for the formation of social capital? How does the importance of activity compare to the effects of multiple affiliations and type of associations?

Table 4.1 presents regression analyses of three different indicators of social capital, wherein the impact of different dimensions of participation—high vs. low intensity and nonpolitical vs. other purpose—is controlled for standard background variables.

Table 4.1 Regression analysis of measures of social capital

Variables with coding	Generalized trust		Vertical trust		Civic engagement	
	Entire sample	Only members and volunteers	Entire sample	Only members and volunteers	Entire sample	Only members and volunteers
Women (=1)	.02	.04	.06*	.05	-.06*	-.08**
Age (years)	.06	.03	.07*	.08*	.37**	.31**
Education (1-3)	.13**	.15**	.13**	.12**	.13**	.12**
Population density (1-3)	.03	.04	.04	.04	.11**	.11**
Residential stability (1-5)	.004	.04	.04	.07*	-.04	-.02
Working full-time (=1)	.03	-.002	.01	.02	.001	-.03
Married/co-habitant (=1)	.07**	.07*	.04	.03	.09**	.09**
Active participant (>1 hr./week) (=1)	.22**		.12**		.13**	
Passive supporter (<1 hr./week) (=1)	.15**		.02		.10**	
Level of activity (1-4)		.05		.07*		-.01
Number of affiliations (1-4)				.08*		.09**
Nonpolitical/political association (0-1)		-.02		-.03		-.002
r^2	.070	.047	.042	.048	.185	.146

Note: $n = 1456/1114$ (generalized trust), $1415/1088$ (vertical trust), $1470/1124$ (civic engagement index), listwise deletion of cases. Significance: $* = p < 0.05$; $** = p < 0.01$.

Source: Norwegian Survey on Giving and Volunteering. LOS Centre Bergen, 1998.

With regard to the overall question of whether participation in associations contributes to social capital, confirmatory answers are given for all indicators. Joiners are consistently more trusting and more civically engaged than nonjoiners. Furthermore, even though other factors, notably age and education, prove to be at least as important predictors of social capital as participation, the relationship is still present when adjusted for the potential effects of sociodemographic and contextual variables. Thus, the weight attached to the role of voluntary associations in the formation of social capital in Putnam's theory is corroborated by empirical results at the individual level.

Our expectations are also confirmed with regard to the question of whether multiple affiliations have a cumulative effect on social capital. In fact, the scope of the involvement is a more powerful predictor of trust and civic engagement than the intensity. When controlling intensity and scope against each other in the analyses, including only members and volunteers, multiple affiliations contribute more to social capital than singular affiliations, while activity level fails to distinguish between members with the same number of affiliations. Only the results concerning levels of vertical trust give reason to conclude that both scope and intensity have an impact, even when controlled against each other.

The assumption that participation in nonpolitical associations is more conducive to social capital than participation in associations with more expressed political purposes is not strengthened by the results. The regression analyses including only members and volunteers showed no positive, significant effects of participation in associations with a nonpolitical purpose.

On the contrary, participation in leisure or cultural associations needs to be accompanied by an affiliation in semipolitical or political organizations in order to have an impact. The members of only leisure-oriented associations fail to distinguish themselves from the population at large in terms of trust and civic engagement (Table 4.2). This serves as a specification of the argument above: The most productive form of participation with regard to the formation of social capital seems to be not only participation in several associations but multiple affiliations in associations with different purposes.

Finally, and most importantly, the question of whether time-intensive, active participation is more conducive to social capital than passive support is, contrary to expectations, given a negative answer. The only exception is institutional (vertical) trust, where the highly active put more faith in institutions than the less active (see another

Table 4.2   Type of affiliation and levels of social capital

	Percent who say most people can be trusted	Vertical trust index (mean 0–100)	Civic engagement index (mean 0–100)	N (lowest)
Not affiliated	54	49.4	58.3	359
Member/volunteer	74	53.2	66.1	1235
Total entire sample	69	52.4	64.3	1594
Member or volunteer in...				
Nonpolitical, culture and recreation	67	49.5	62.1	340
Nonpolitical, religious	73	51.6	59.6	52
Semipolitical organizations	65	49.2	68.1	122
Political organizations (parties and unions)	75	55.2	67.9	128
Both nonpolitical and semipolitical	80	53.9	65.2	195
Both non/semipolitical and political	81	57.3	70.2	389

Note: All differences between types of affiliations are significant at the 99 percent level.

Source: Norwegian Survey on Giving and Volunteering. LOS Centre Bergen, 1998.

take on this relationship in Mayer this volume). With regard to generalized trust, activity level had an impact among younger volunteers and members, but there was no such relationship among those aged twenty-five or older. The weak relationship between trust and activity level among members and volunteers disappears when controlling for background variables and scope of participation. Concerning civic engagement, there was no relationship whatsoever between activity level in associations and civicness, while members consistently ranked above nonmembers on all indicators.

Thus, there is not much in the data to suggest that active participation, compared to passive, strengthens civic engagement, and the relationship between trust and intensity of involvement is tenuous at best. Even passive memberships had a positive influence on all of the indicators presented above, though the effects are slightly smaller compared to active memberships. Thus, at least based on the present data, a preliminary negative answer must be given to the question of whether active participation, that is, face-to-face interaction, is necessary for the formation of social capital. This is a highly surprising and to some extent counterintuitive finding that needs to be investigated in more detail.

UNDERSTANDING PASSIVE SUPPORT

In order to reach a clearer understanding of why individuals choose to be passive members of associations instead of not being members at all, we need to devote particular attention to two questions. First of all, what is the rationality behind passive support? Which reasons do passive members give for joining, and to what extent do their motives differ from those of active members? Second, once inside, how do they relate to their associations? Are they as alienated, indifferent and marginalized as Putnam would suggest?

The analyses are based on a series of questions concerning why members choose to join, how they view the internal life of the association and their role in it, and in which arenas they think the association should primarily exercise its potential external democratic function. The responses are cross-tabulated with level of activity and the type of association with which the member is affiliated. We now exclude those who are not affiliated with any associations and concentrate on the relationship between members and their organizations. The answers pertain only to the affiliation the members considered to be the most important. The indicator used to distinguish between active and passive supporters is, in contrast to the analyses above, their self-reported level of activity. Thus, neither the passive nor the active members are entirely representative of the group of members as a whole, and their subjective evaluations of activity level may not always correspond with the indicators used above (number of hours they have spent volunteering or participating). When contrasting the passive members with the active participants, we are therefore more in search for an answer to what passivity might entail than for generalizable answers to what passivity is.

What are the most common reasons for becoming a member, and how do passive members differ from active ones? Wollebæk (2000) shows that the two highest-ranking reasons for active members to join an association are personal fulfillment (e.g., to keep in shape or learn new things) and social contacts. Among passive members, on the other hand, economic or work-related advantages are the most important reasons given for joining. However, this applies almost exclusively to union memberships. The second and third most important motives are to influence decisions and to gain membership benefits (including access to information).

Thus, personal and "egoistic" motives generally rank above "altruistic" causes for joining associations (such as "helping others") among active and passive members alike. The motives among the passive members are more explicitly instrumental than among the activists, for whom opportunities for socializing predictably play a more important role. The most surprising finding, however, is that passive members are slightly more likely to join associations in order to influence decisions than active members. This is not due to the fact that political associations rely more on passive support than nonpolitical associations do. It is especially within nonpolitical and semipolitical associations that political influence emerges as more important for passive members than for the more active ones, while the relationship is the other way around among members of political organizations.

In addition to the slight difference in the weight attached to political influence as a motive, there is also a difference in scale between passive and active participants (for details, see Wollebæk 2000). When asked at which political level their association should primarily try to exert influence, active members tend to emphasize institutions in their immediate environment. Passive members, on the other hand, express a stronger interest in decisions at the national or international level. While twice as many of the active members emphasize living conditions in the local community compared to national or international agencies, the passive members consider the two arenas to be equally important. These results underline that, perhaps even more for passive members than for activists, associations may serve as institutional links between citizens and the larger political system. Whereas activists are strongly oriented toward the local community, passive members place more weight on issues of a larger scale. When regarding associations as networks providing links from the individual to decisions at the political scene, as the neo-Tocquevillian approach does, passive support may be at least as important as active.

With regard to the marginal role attributed to the passive supporter in Putnam's work, we might expect that passive members were fairly indifferent to the operations of the associations, and that activists would regard passive contributions as relatively unimportant. The results in Table 4.3, which summarize the members' attitudes toward the internal life of their respective associations, show that this is clearly not the case.

Statements A through C aim at capturing the importance members attribute to the internal democratic structure of the association. The responses reflect that internal democracy is still, despite recent developments in the voluntary sector in Norway, a core value among the members (Selle 1998). More interestingly in this context, however, passive members place no less weight on internal democratic structure than active members, except for a slight difference between the two

Table 4.3 Attitudes toward most important association (percent of respondents)

		Nonpolitical, leisure		Nonpolitical, religious		Semipolitical		Political (parties/unions)		All members	
		Passive	Active	Passive	Active	Passive	Active	Passive	Active	Passive	Active
A. Democratic structure important	Agree	86	86	83	84	84	87	89	96	87	87
	Disagree	3	4	8	8	2	1	0	2	3	4
Difference significant?*			.83		.98		.96		.01		.09
B. Leaders often act on their own	Agree	23	20	42	23	8	17	26	31	22	22
	Disagree	51	66	59	68	39	68	43	59	44	54
Difference significant?*			.01		.03		.00		.01		.00
C. Too little debate and discussion in organization	Agree	20	21	29	30	13	26	25	34	21	25
	Disagree	33	56	42	47	34	50	39	57	34	54
Difference significant?*			.00		.85		.03		.00		.00

D. Passive membership also important contribution	Agree	83	56	79	48	91	67	81	66	85	59
	Disagree	8	28	7	33	1	21	7	26	5	37
Difference significant?*		.00		.05		.00		.00		.00	
E. Would take part in specific activities, but not regular meetings	Agree	55	27	50	11	53	15	44	27	50	24
	Disagree	26	60	19	78	15	73	26	59	22	63
Difference significant?*		.00		.00		.00		.00		.00	
N (lowest)		117	300	12	52	87	77	136	129	348	588

Note: "Strongly/mildly agree" and "strongly/mildly disagree" are collapsed into "agree" and "disagree" respectively. "Neither/nor" and "don't know" not shown.
*Significance tests based on chi-squares.

Source: Norwegian Survey on Giving and Volunteering. LOS Centre Bergen, 1998.

groups among members of political associations. As reflected in the responses to statements B and C, active supporters express slightly more satisfaction with the way democracy works in their associations (disagree more with the statements) than passive members do.

With regard to the responses given to statement D, predictably, passive members consider their support to be more valuable than active members do. However, there is also a majority among the active members who think that passive memberships represent important contributions to the organizations. Statement E is the only question about which the opinions of active and passive members differ substantially. A majority of the passive members who have an opinion agree that they would gladly take part in specific activities but do not have the energy to attend ordinary meetings, while a majority of the active supporters with an opinion disagree. The propensity to participate actively when needed, but reluctance to enter a binding obligation with the organization, reveals two important features of passive membership. First, passive members display what is probably the most modern attitude. While being able to exert some influence on the organization and step in when needed, the member also preserves her individual autonomy. Second, from the association's point of view, it indicates that the passive members represent a reserve of activists from which the association can draw when carrying out specific, short-term activities. The latter underlines the importance of viewing passive memberships dynamically (Selle and Strømsnes 2001). The passive member of this year might be the active member of yesteryear, or next year. Individuals drift in and out of different roles and functions in the associations, depending on their life situation, their motivation and current resources.

In sum, the reasons for joining given by passive members were less oriented towards social rewards than among the active members, while opportunities for political influence played a comparatively more important role among inactive supporters. Passive support is also related to a more politicized view of the association's role in democracy, while active members tend to emphasize conditions in their immediate surroundings. Passive members care about how the associations operate, they do not see themselves as marginalized in relation to internal processes, and they say they are prepared to take an active part in specific activities if asked. Active members, on the other hand, value the contributions of passive support only slightly less than the passive members do themselves. Thus, the results suggest that passive members are neither alienated from, nor uninterested in, nor unimportant for the affairs of their associations.

The results presented in this chapter demonstrate that passive support cannot be left out in any comprehensive analysis of participation in associations. Regardless of whether passive support is seen as an independent, intermediary or dependent variable, it needs to be taken more seriously in social science than has been the case until now.

DISCUSSION

In summary, Putnam's basic contention, that participation breeds social capital, is generally supported by the findings from the empirical analyses. Equally, his claim that multiple involvements generate more social capital than singular involvements is strengthened. Although the direction of causality is naturally open to question, an issue we cannot address in this chapter (however, see Stolle this volume and see Stolle 2001), the above assertions find support in our results. The empirical backing, however, stops there.

First, contrary to expectations, participation in nonpolitical associations contributed to attitudinal aspects of social capital such as trust and civic engagement only when accompanied by involvement in associations with more manifest political purposes. Second, with the exception of vertical trust, which is located at the fringe of most definitions of social capital, active participation did not contribute significantly more to social capital than did passive support. Thus, the central tenet of Putnam's thesis, that it is through face-to-face contact in networks of secondary associations that social capital is created, finds little or no support in the empirical results. In addition, the comparison of the motives and attitudes of active and passive supporters revealed a picture quite contrary to the impression given by Putnam. The passive members were not indifferent to the internal life of the associations, and they were prepared to take on temporary active roles if necessary. Their involvement was rooted in a commitment to a cause, an interest in exerting influence and—like active members—a possibility of personal rewards. The absent effect of face-to-face contact has particularly important implications in the Norwegian context. The "broad" voluntary sector, a concept that has been used to describe associational life in Scandinavia (Dekker and van den Broek 1998), is characterized first and foremost by extensive and multiple memberships but comparatively low activity rates. Moreover, passive support may become even more prevalent in the years to come, due to tendencies toward centralization and professionalization in Norwegian associations (Selle 1998).

An interpretation of the absent effect of face-to-face contact is that the role of voluntary associations in the formation of social capital is overstated in Putnam's work. If active participation does not have an

impact on trust and civic engagement over passive support, this sufficiently proves that Putnam is mistaken in placing voluntary associations at the center of his social capital thesis. In this interpretation, the
observed relationship between passive affiliations and social capital is
seen as spurious. The differences between joiners and nonjoiners stem
from members having resources of some kind that outsiders do not
possess. Although we do not believe the relation to be purely spurious, there is some empirical support for this claim. The explained
variance in the regression models fluctuated between 5 and 15 percent, leaving 85 to 95 percent of the variation unaccounted for.
Assuming that social capital is not randomly distributed in the population, other causes not included in the analyses, such as childhood
experiences or psychological factors, or even different experiences
with the state are most likely at work. Some of these alternative
sources of social capital will be explored in the second part of this volume. Furthermore, the indicators used to measure other sources of
social capital, such as education and integration in the work force,
may be too crude in order to claim that the impact of status or
employment has been controlled. A spurious relationship between
participation and social capital would not be completely contrary
to common sense. After all, associational involvement is, for most
people, compared to other activities in which we take part on a more
frequent basis, of a rather low intensity measured both in time and
emotional commitment. At the very least, the relationship needs to be
qualified. Specifically, Putnam's view of participation in bird watchers'
associations or bowling leagues as the hallmark of civic engagement
and a vibrant democracy is not given much support by the data we
have analyzed.

However, considering the numerous studies that, like this one,
have found participation in associations as a whole to be related to
trust and civic engagement—even when controlling for a wide range
of factors—it does not seem plausible to dismiss the entire relationship
as spurious.[4] In particular, the presumption that social capital comes
from face-to-face interaction should be subjected to critical examination. Our interpretation, therefore, is that the results show that voluntary associations contribute to social capital, but not necessarily by
means of direct interaction between members. This implies that even
passive affiliations may have internal effects on those participating.
How might this occur? It is possible to distinguish between four
understandings of the relationship between the passive supporter and
his/her association: The associations as social systems, imagined
communities, information systems and networks of political influence.

When regarding the passive member as part of a social system, it is implied that socialization may take place even if she/he does not interact with other members within the context of the association. Many passive members are likely to socialize with activists, but in social settings other than the organization. This way, they keep in touch with the association by way of their networks of contacts with activists. Although this will certainly not always be the case, and the socialization is of a less-intensive character than is the case for active participants, it is a possibility that should not be ruled out a priori. Second, the affiliation may develop a sense of identification with and commitment to a cause. As discussed above, associations relying on passive support resemble Anderson's (1991) idea of an imagined community, a concept referring to all social systems too large to allow face-to-face contact, wherein members nonetheless share emotional ties to a community. Passive affiliations may foster a sense of affinity to a cause, which the individual knows is not only important to him/herself, but also to others. If the association is successful, the membership, regardless of activity level, conveys a sense of the value of cooperation for common purposes, of political efficacy and of a shared belonging to something important. Clearly, these virtues are all conducive to social capital.

Third, associations may function as information systems. Norwegian nationwide voluntary associations publish more than 17 million journals and newsletters annually, or almost five per person in the adult population (Wollebæk, Selle and Lorentzen 2000). Furthermore, the information networks in the new tertiary associations founded in the past couple of decades, which rely almost entirely on passive support, are at least as comprehensive as in traditional voluntary associations (Selle and Strømsnes 2001). This implies that the passive member is not necessarily out of touch with the goings-on of the association, nor will he be in the future. The extensive networks of information disseminate knowledge about current issues and how the association relates to them. As such, they may serve as "schools in democracy" and promoters of civic engagement—even though the members do not interact personally.

Finally, associations might serve as networks of political influence, even for those not actively involved. As demonstrated previously, passive members are not entirely marginalized with regard to internal decisions in the associations. If they hold multiple affiliations, as many do, they have the opportunity to exert influence on many arenas at the same time. Furthermore, one should be aware of the high turnover in membership one finds in Norwegian voluntary organizations.

The normal turnover is between 10 and 20 percent a year, but in some types of organizations it is even higher (Selle 1998).

The "participation by proxy" exercised by many passive supporters may be of no less significance for democracy than active participation. Maloney (1999, 117) suggests that "... citizens are becoming *participatory dualists*, seeing local political matters as being best addressed by individual action, and national matters of concern such as human rights and the global environment as best addressed by 'group' action" (italics in original). The empirical findings support this notion of "contracting out" the democratic participation function. There is an observable difference in scale between active and passive supporters with regard to which issues they believe the association should address. While activists are strongly oriented toward living conditions in their immediate surroundings, passive members regard national and international issues as equally important. This indicates that the associations in many cases function as intermediary institutions between the citizen and the larger political system even more for passive members than for actives. The small scale of many of the associations in which active participation takes place may inhibit them from having much bearing on political issues of a larger scale: "Thus neighbourhood associations may thrive and be effective in advancing their interests locally, but such participation often has little or no political impact at the regional and national level" (Rueschemeyer, Rueschemeyer and Wittrock 1998, 13). The notion that the passive members' affiliations with extensive information networks, "imagined communities" and networks of political influence leave them unaffected in terms of trust and civic engagement is an assumption, which so far has not been supported by empirical results. Pending evidence to the contrary, the postulation that only face-to-face contact within the realms of voluntary associations has internal effects on those affiliated, should not be too readily accepted.

NOTES

1. If a person has reported membership as well as volunteering for the same association, this is only counted once.
2. For a more thorough discussion of the selection of these indicators, see Wollebæk (2000).
3. Trust in politicians ranges from "few politicians are trustworthy" (1) to "most politicians are trustworthy" (4). Trust in the state, municipal authorities and companies are measured by five-point scales, ranging from "no trust" (1) to "very high trust" (5). The response "don't know" is given the middle value (3). In order to ease interpretation, the index was recoded to run from 0 to 100.

4. See Dekker and van den Broek (1998); Whiteley (1999); Torcal and Montero (1999) and Stolle and Rochon (1999) for studies corroborating the positive relationship between association membership and social capital. Van Deth (1997) provides an overview of studies of the relationship between participation in associations and political involvement, among which the majority report positive correlations.

REFERENCES

Almond, G. and S.Verba (1963). *The Civic Culture: Political Attitudes and Democracy in Five Nations.* Princeton: Princeton University Press.

Anderson, B. (1991 rev. ed.). *Imagined Communities: Reflections on the Origins and Spread of Nationalism.* London: Verso.

Berman, S. (1997). "Civil Society and the Collapse of the Weimar Republic." *World Politics* 49(3), 401–429.

Dekker, P., R. Koopmans and A. van den Broek (1997). "Voluntary Associations, Social Movements and Individual Political Behavior in Western Europe." pp. 220–241. In J. van Deth (ed.), *Private Groups and Public Life.* London: Routledge.

Dekker, P. and A. van den Broek (1998). "Civil Society in Comparative Perspective: Involvement in Voluntary Associations in North America and Western Europe." *Voluntas* 9(1), 11–38.

Foley, M. and B. Edwards (1996). "The Paradox of Civil Society." *Journal of Democracy* 7(3), 38–52.

Godwin, R. K. (1992). "Money, Technology, and Political Interests: The Direct Marketing of Politics." In M. Petracca (ed.), *The Politics of Interests.* Colorado: Westview Press.

Granovetter, (1973). "The Strength of Weak Ties." *American Journal of Sociology* 78, 1360–1380.

Macpherson, C. B. (1977). *The Life and Times of Liberal Democracy.* Oxford: Oxford University Press.

Maloney, W. (1999). "Contracting Out the Participation Function. Social Capital and Cheque-Book Participation." In J. van Deth et al. (eds.), *Social Capital and European Democracy.* London: Routledge.

Mouzelis, N. (1995). *Sociological Theory: What Went Wrong. Diagnosis and Remedies.* London: Routledge.

Newton, K. (1997). "Social Capital and Democracy." *American Behavioral Scientist* 40(6), 575–586.

Newton, K. (1999). "Social Capital and Democracy in Modern Europe." pp. 3–24. In J. van Deth et al. (eds.), *Social Capital and European Democracy.* London: Routledge.

Pateman, C. (1970). *Participation and Democratic Theory.* Cambridge: Cambridge University Press.

Paxton, P. (1999). "Is Social Capital Declining in the United States?" *American Journal of Sociology* 105(1), 88–127.

Putnam, R (1993). *Making Democracy Work: Civic Traditions in Modern Italy.* Princeton: Princeton University Press.

Putnam, R. (1995). "Bowling Alone: America's Declining Social Capital." *Journal of Democracy* (6)1, 65–78.

Putnam, R. (2000). *Bowling Alone. The Collapse and Revival of American Community.* New York: Simon and Schuster.

Quigley, K. (1996). "Human Bonds and Social Capital." *Orbis* 40(2), 333–343.

Rothstein, B. (1998). "Varifrån kommer det sociala kapitalet?" *Socialvetenskaplig tidskrift* 3(2), 164–171.

Rueschemeyer, D. (1998). "The Self-Organization of Society and Democratic Rule: Specifying the Relationship." In D. Rueschemeyer, M. Rueschemeyer and B. Wittrock (eds.), *Participation and Democracy.* Armonk: M. E. Sharpe.

Rueschemeyer, D., M. Rueschemeyer and B. Wittrock (eds., 1998). *Participation and Democracy.* Armonk: M. E. Sharpe.

Selle, P. and K. Strømsnes (1998). "Organised Environmentalists: Democracy as a Key Value?" *Voluntas* 9(4), 319–343.

Selle, P. and K. Strømsnes (2001). "Membership and Democracy: Should We Take Passive Support Seriously." In P. Dekker and E. Uslaner (eds.), *Social Capital and Politics in Everyday Life.* London: Routledge.

Selle, P. (1998). "Organisasjonssamfunnet—ein statsreiskap?" In T. Grønlie and P. Selle (eds.), *Ein stat? Fristillingas Fire Ansikt.* Oslo: Samlaget.

Stolle, D. (2001). "Clubs and Congregations: The Benefits of Joining an Association." pp. 202–244. In K. Cook (ed.), *Trust in Society.* New York: Russell Sage Foundation.

Stolle, D. and T. Rochon (1999). "The Myth of American Exceptionalism. A Three-Nation Comparison of Associational Membership and Social Capital." pp. 192–209. In J. van Deth et al. (eds.), *Social Capital and European Democracy.* London: Routledge.

Tocqueville, A. de (1954 [1835/40]). *Democracy in America.* New York: Random House.

Torcal, M. and J. Montero (1999). "Facets of Social Capital in New Democracies: The Formation and Consequences of Social Capital in Spain." pp. 167–191. In J. van Deth et al. (eds.), *Social Capital and European Democracy.* London: Routledge.

Torpe, L. (1998). *Lokal organisasjonsdeltakelse og demokrati. Mellem individ og fællesskab samt borger og styre.* Bergen: LOS-senteret.

van Deth, J. (1997). "Introduction: Social Involvement and Democratic Politics." In J. van Deth (ed.), *Private Groups and Public Life.* London: Routledge.

Whiteley, P. (1999). "The Origins of Social Capital." In J. van Deth et al. (eds.), *Social Capital and European Democracy.* London: Routledge.

Wollebæk, D. (2000). *Participation in Voluntary Associations and the Formation of Social Capital.* University of Bergen: Ph. D. Dissertation.

Wollebæk, D., P. Selle and H. Lorentzen (2000). *Frivillig Innsats.* Oslo: Fagbokforlaget.

Chapter 5

Voluntary Associations and Democratic Attitudes: Value Congruence as a Causal Mechanism

Marc Hooghe

Introduction

In most of the recent research on social capital, a positive correlation is observed between membership of voluntary associations and the adherence to democratic value patterns. However, we have access to few research results, which could explain the causal mechanism that is responsible for this positive correlation. Two models seem to predominate the current literature on social capital (see Stolle this volume). Some authors clearly rely on a *socialization* logic: Because of the interaction with others, members of voluntary associations are socialized into more democratic and more social value patterns. Subsequently, these positive attitudes are transferred to society as a whole: Members do not only learn to trust their fellow members, but they also develop a generalized trust in other citizens. In this view, voluntary associations or other societal contexts function as learning schools for democracy, as de Tocqueville called it. Putnam (1995, 666) echoes this view when he states: "the causation flows mainly from joining to trusting."

This line of reasoning has been received with much skepticism. Some empirical research expresses doubts about the existence of a significant relation between membership and civic attitudes (Berman 1997; Mondak and Mutz 1997), calling our attention to other societal contexts in which civic attitudes are shaped, whereas other research demonstrates that the relationship is at best weak (Brehm and Rahn 1997; Claibourn and Martin 2000; Mayer this volume). Levi (1996) has drawn our attention to the fact that not all associations will have positive effects: Some might just as well have negative consequences, and the existence of this "dark side of social capital" has been acknowledged in some of the more recent studies on social capital (Putnam 2000, 350–363).

Other authors are critical about the claims of the socialization school, and they stress the importance of self-selection (Newton 1997, 1999; Stolle 1998, 2002; Whiteley 1999; Uslaner this volume). Persons with antisocial attitudes will refrain from joining voluntary associations, and these associations will recruit members who are already relatively high on civic attitudes. This pattern of self-selection is taken to explain the positive correlation between membership and democratic value patterns. Uslaner (1998) follows the same logic when he states that some people have a more optimistic and more trusting outlook toward life (due to youth experiences) and therefore will be more inclined to join all kinds of associations.

At the present state of research, the debate between socialization and self-selection approaches remains unsolved (Dekker 1999). The problem is that neither the authors of the socialization school nor most of their critics have explained the causal mechanism that is responsible for this admittedly weak correlation pattern (Hooghe 2000). Within the literature on civic participation, no one really denies that a process of self-selection takes place: It seems self-evident that not everyone will have the same inclination to join voluntary associations. The basic research question, however, is to know whether voluntary associations have an *additional* socialization effect (Stolle 2000): Even after discounting the recruitment effect, is there still some influence from participation left, and, if so, what causal mechanism is responsible for this effect? Only if such an additional effect can be documented can we safely conclude that voluntary associations indeed play a key role in generating social capital and should not just be considered as indicators for the presence of social capital. In this chapter we want to explore the relationship between participation and the attitudinal components of social capital by using data from a recent Belgian face-to-face survey with 1,341 respondents (representative of the Dutch-speaking population of the Flemish autonomous region in Belgium).

The central question in this chapter is whether membership in voluntary associations leads to a reduction of feelings of ethnocentrism, and, if so, what causal mechanism could be responsible for this effect. Another ambition of this chapter is to introduce some of the recent social psychological concepts and research results about group processes into the social capital debate. This line of research suggests that interaction within groups does lead to socialization effects, but it does not support the claim that this kind of interaction automatically leads to the development of more social norms. Any effect groups might have is dependent upon the characteristics of the group and its members. As the Belgian survey included a large number of questions about associational participation, we can ascertain whether all kinds of associations have similar socialization effects, or whether these effects are context specific.

THE EFFECTS OF GROUP INTERACTION

In the current research on the relation between voluntary associations and the formation of citizenship attitudes, one can witness an intriguing lack of communication. On the one hand, authors inspired by the work and the insights of de Tocqueville and Putnam claim that interaction within voluntary associations has distinct effects on the value patterns of the members, and thus should be seen as a source of social capital. But on the other hand, we have access to an extensive body of empirical research about what actually goes on in primary and other groups, and what are the effects of these kinds of interaction. This line of research, however, is all but neglected in the current social capital debate.

The claim that interaction within groups has positive socialization effects is based on the assumption that members develop trust in their fellow members as a result of the sustained interaction within the association, which in turn is generalized toward society as a whole (Stolle 2000). Both assumed mechanisms are highly problematic. To start with, there is no evidence whatsoever that prolonged interaction in groups would actually lead to higher trust levels within the group.[1] Furthermore, given the fundamental difference between knowledge-based trust and generalized trust (Yamagishi and Yamagishi 1994), is seems unlikely that particularized trust would be converted that easily into generalized trust. We do not develop trust in total strangers, about whom we have no information, because we trust people we actually know (Uslaner 2000). But even if this was the case, it only adds to the problem. If particularized trust could be converted into generalized trust, there is no reason to assume that interaction within voluntary associations would be a privileged source of generalized trust. In that case, interaction within families, schools, neighborhoods or work environments would function just as well as a source of generalized trust (Whiteley 1999). In sum, the causal mechanism assumed does not seem entirely plausible.

We can rely on an enormous body of literature and research about the effects of group interaction (Tajfel 1981; Forsyth 1983; Turner et al. 1987; Hendrick 1987; Paulus 1989; Robinson 1996). The social-psychological literature on group interaction, however, does not offer support for any of the basic tenets of social capital theory. There is no indication whatsoever that interaction with other group members would automatically lead to the development of a more socially oriented value pattern, to a rise in trust levels, or to the abandonment of prejudices (Goslin 1969; Mills and Rosenberg 1970; Duncan and Fiske 1977; Ajzen and Fishbein 1980; Turner 1984; Turner et al. 1987). There are even some laboratory experiments showing that membership of a group can lead to an enhancement of prejudices against members of outsider groups (Skinner and Stephenson 1981; Haslam et al. 1999). We do not have any indication that group interaction automatically leads to a more socially desired value pattern, and this lack of research data should question the important role social capital theory assigns to voluntary associations.

This does not imply that interaction with other group members could not produce socialization effects. It does imply that these effects will be dependent upon context characteristics: The process is endogenously induced—the value changes are not exogenous. Members of a group are subjected to socialization experiences because they are influenced by the values of other group members, resulting in a process of value congruence within the group (Tajfel 1981; Turner et al. 1987; Levine and Russo 1987; Abrams and Hogg 1991). This form of "personal influence" within groups is already described in the classical study by Katz and Lazarsfeld: "We are led to expect that an individual's opinions will be substantially affected by the opinions of others whose company he keeps, or whose company he aspires to keep" (Katz and Lazarsfeld 1955, 53). During the past decades, this argument has received support from numerous experiments, demonstrating the existence of processes of value congruence within groups (for a review, see Levine and Russo 1987). Youth research demonstrates time and time again the importance of the effect of peer group members on the attitudes of individual actors

(Adler and Adler 1998; Bankston and Caldas 1996), and although we can assume that the magnitude of these effects will be less pronounced among adults, we have no reason to expect that socialization will not occur at all (Williams 1975). Following this logic implies that the socialization effects of organizations or groups do not originate from outside the group: The interaction does not introduce qualitatively new values into the group but enforces already existing values, as Katz and Lazarsfeld (1955, 96) already stated. The presence of and the interaction with other group members will influence the values and judgments of individual actors: "The sight and sound of others doing the same thing as oneself functioned as conditioned social stimuli to release and augment learned reaction tendencies previously existing in individuals... Importantly, however, social facilitation did not represent the emergence of new group properties; individual behavior did not change qualitatively in groups, it was merely 'enhanced' so to speak" (Turner et al. 1987, 11). The fellow members, in this respect, function as a "reference group" (Merton and Kitt 1950), providing the members with cues about how to construct and possibly transform their own value patterns.

SELF-CATEGORIZATION THEORY

A recent attempt to build this line of research into a coherent theoretical framework can be found in the social identity, or self-categorization, theory as it was developed by Henri Tajfel (1981) and John Turner et al. (1987). They assume that individuals tend to avoid cognitive dissonance but that at the same time by themselves they are not capable of developing a coherent value pattern, which is congruent with the complexity of observations from the outside world. To counter that potential source of insecurity, individuals are dependent upon the interaction and the dialogue with significant others. Turner especially stresses the fact that processes of self-categorization can reduce complexity: Individuals learn to see themselves as members of a socially defined category, and therefore they also gain access to the corresponding role and value pattern.

Within this process of value congruence, one can distinguish two different levels (Turner et al. 1987, 35; Turner and Oakes 1989). With regard to information, group members are dependent upon the information they retrieve from other group members to construct their own worldviews and value patterns. This information has already been selected and this can lead to a certain congruence in the value patterns of the members. Secondly, one can distinguish a normative influence, causing group members to adopt, at least to some extent, the normative positions of their fellow group members.

This does not mean that the consequences of group interaction remain limited to facilitating a convergence toward a pre-existing average position, which would imply that group membership does not have an additive effect. Because of tendencies toward group polarization, the convergence will occur on a more extreme position, thus strengthening already existing values: "Uniformities in intra-group behavior result from the members' opinions becoming more extreme in the socially favored direction rather than from convergence on the average of their initial position" (Turner 1982, 35). It is assumed, and to some extent also documented, that the presence of like-minded others serves as a stimulus for the individual actor to further develop socially desired traits and values (Fraser and Foster 1984).

Turner's self-categorization theory implies that socialization will be most successful when the individual is integrated in a group with a relatively homogeneous value pattern. Homogeneity within the group allows the reinforcement of the influence of the various group members, or at least means that these various sources of influence will operate in the same direction. As Verba (1961, 40) already noted: "The greater the homogeneity of primary group contacts, the greater the intensity of political participation . . . it was found that voters with friends of various political persuasions were less strong in their voting intentions than those whose friends were all of the same persuasion."

If we confront the results of this body of empirical research with the assumptions of social capital theory, a clear problem arises. Authors stressing socialization within organizations assume that the interaction within groups leads to the introduction of qualitatively new values, like tolerance or generalized trust. The results of the research using social identity or self-categorization theory indicate that no new value patterns are introduced because of the interaction but that pre-existing value patterns are made more salient or are reinforced.

This insight could be important for the further development of social capital theory. Levi (1996) has called attention to the fact that if voluntary associations really have such beneficial effects, it is difficult to explain how criminal organizations could produce forms of "unsocial" capital, a point that has been acknowledged in some of the more recent writings on social capital (Putnam 2000, 350–363). Levi's remark indeed presents a dilemma for social capital theory, but not for social identity theory. Criminal organizations will recruit members attracted to a criminal way of life, and it will further socialize them into this value pattern, just as religious organizations will recruit members who are interested in spiritual matters and will further socialize them into a more religious value pattern.

The Belgian survey on participation in voluntary associations offers a unique opportunity to put these assumptions to the test. Because the survey contains numerous questions on participation, it is possible to distinguish various kinds of organizations. Of course, other authors, too, have already pointed out that not all voluntary associations will have the same beneficial effects. Sorting out what kind of interaction is associated with what specific kind of effect, however, should allow us to uncover the causal mechanism that could be responsible for the association between the structural and attitudinal components of social capital.

STUDYING ETHNOCENTRISM

In building the argument, we will rely on the results of a face-to-face survey our research unit conducted during the spring of 1998 ($n=$ 1,341) and that proved to be representative of the Dutch-speaking population of the Flemish autonomous region in Belgium (see appendix for technical details). In our analysis we will use a five-item balanced measurement scale on ethnocentrism as the main dependent variable. All of the items in this scale refer to negative prejudices toward migrant groups within Belgian society, with a typical item being "Generally speaking, migrants cannot be trusted."

There are four reasons why we have chosen to study ethnocentric prejudice. First of all, one has to keep in mind that racism has become a highly salient political issue in Belgium, as in most of the European Union countries. In the Flemish part of the country, an extreme right party with a very hostile view toward the presence of ethnic and cultural minorities in the country has taken 15 percent of the vote (Lubbers, Scheepers and Billiet 2000). Reducing ethnocentric prejudice therefore has become one of the main policy priorities, not only of the Belgian government but also for a lot of voluntary associations, and it seems worthwhile to investigate whether these associations actually succeed in reducing ethnocentrism among their members. Second, in the past decades Belgium, like most Western European countries, has evolved from an ethnically rather homogeneous nation into a multicultural society as a result of the influx of relatively large groups of migrants from the Mediterranean, Eastern Europe and Africa (Hooghe 2001). This heterogeneity implies that Belgian society will have to develop new citizenship concepts in order to allow full citizen participation of these ethnic minorities (Soysal 1994). One can argue, therefore, that reducing ethnocentric prejudice is of crucial importance for the future development and stability of a democratic political culture in Belgium and other Western countries. A third reason to study ethnocentrism is that this attitude is strongly correlated with other attitudinal scales, all of them related to the concept of an "authoritarian personality" that contrasts sharply with contemporary conceptions of what democratic civic attitudes should be. In our survey, we observed a marked affinity between ethnocentrism and a utilitarian conception of individualism, feelings of authoritarianism, feelings of insecurity, and also with a vote for the extreme right party in Belgium. No other single attitude is as strongly related to all these other indicators of a lack of support for democratic values. Therefore, it seems safe to consider ethnocentrism as the core of a complex of culturally conservative values, as it has indeed been used in the literature on cultural conservatism (Lipset 1959). A fourth reason to study ethnocentrism is technical: The concept can be measured by a solid scale that was developed by Billiet, Carton and Eisinga (1995). Because it has been used extensively in previous surveys, we know it to be a reliable instrument to register negative feelings toward outsider groups. Using solid attitudinal scales is more reliable than using just a single item as a dependent variable, which is often pursued in social capital research.

We know from earlier research that the feeling of ethnocentrism is not spread evenly across the Belgian population: Respondents with lower educational credentials support a more ethnocentric discourse than respondents with high educational credentials. In a standardized scale (that ranges from 0, which indicates no ethnocentrism, to 100, which indicates high ethnocentrism) the mean scores vary from 48.3 among the respondents who have only completed elementary education to 32.9 for those with higher education. The relation between education levels is not only very strong but also perfectly linear for all the various groups in the population. The fact that ethnocentrism is unevenly distributed throughout society and is more strongly present in the lower-educated strata allows us to contrast various groups in further analysis.[2] To fully test the proposition on self-selection, we would need data on the kind of values people adhere to when they enter associational life, and these data are not available for our research setting. This forces us to approach the problem of self-selection indirectly. Given the close relation between education and ethnocentrism, we can assume that if we know the educational level of a sufficiently large group of respondents, we at least have some indication about their initial feelings of ethnocentrism. The association between education and ethnocentrism is so strong that, if we have any group of a reasonable size of highly educated people it is very likely that their score on the ethnocentrism scale will be lower than that of a similar group with only elementary education, and vice versa, even if these groups are recruited through a process of self-selection.

SELF-SELECTION

The first step we have to take in the analysis, therefore, is to demonstrate that processes of self-selection are indeed occurring. To a large extent, this step is superfluous: We have access to a large body of participation research showing that the active population of any given society is not representative for the population as a whole (Verba and Nie 1972; Verba, Schlozman and Brady 1995; Dekker 1999). Education levels in particular explain an important part of the variation with regard to participation behavior. Nie, Junn and Stehlik-Barry (1996, 2) summarize the research quite neatly: "Formal education is almost without exception the strongest factor in explaining what citizens do in politics and how they think about politics."

In our survey, too, the traditional inequalities emerge: Active membership in voluntary associations is not spread evenly throughout society. In our survey, respondents were given a list of twenty-two different kinds of organizations, with five answering possibilities for each category: (1) never been a member; (2) has been a member; (3) passive member; (4) active member; (5) member of the board. If we perform a logistic regression analysis with the dichotomous variable "active member, or member of the board of at least one association/not an active member" as a dependent variable, the same picture emerges as in previous participation research. We see that gender, education and religion are strongly related to participation (Table 5.1). Men participate more intensely than women; churchgoers participate more than non-Christians or nonchurchgoing Christians. But again, as Nie et al. (1996) already wrote, education proves to be a very strong variable, with the higher-educated group participating almost twice as much as the lower-educated group. We learn from this regression that the higher-educated strata will be over-represented in voluntary associations, and given the strong relation between education and ethnocentrism, we can already expect that on average members of voluntary associations will be less ethnocentric than the rest of society.

Table 5.1   Logistic regression for active membership
in voluntary associations

	exp. (β)
Age	ns.
18–35 yr	
36–55 yr	1.19
56–75 yr	0.92
Sex	***
Male	
Female	.56
Education	***
Low	
Middle	1.29
High	1.92
Income	ns.
−750 euro/month	
750–1.500 euro/month	.64
1.500–2.500 euro/month	.95
+2.500 euro/month	1.07
Religion	***
Not religious	
Religious, not churchgoing	1.11
Churchgoing	2.16
Time on television	ns.
<14 h/wk	
14–20 h/wk	1.17
+20 h/wk	0.82
Family	ns.
Alone or with parents	
With partner	0.74
Divorced/widow(er)	0.59

Note: Entries are logistic regression coefficients (exp. β), representing difference from reference category (= 1).
* = $p < 0.05$; ** = $p < 0.01$; *** = $p < 0.001$.

Source: Flemish Citizen Survey 1998, $n = 1,341$.

EFFECTS OF MEMBERSHIP EXPERIENCE

The next step examines the relation between membership and feelings of ethnocentrism (Table 5.2). Our first regression model is a baseline model, simply integrating background variables as independent variables. In this model we also included the time spent on watching television, and the religious affiliation of the respondent, because we

Table 5.2   Explaining ethnocentrism

	Model 1 without associations		Model 2 associations included	
	B (SE B)	β	B (SE B)	β
Sex	−.82 (1.04)	−.02	−1.21 (1.03)	−.03
Age	.11 (0.04)***	.09	.14 (0.04)***	.12
Income	−.12 (0.19)	−.02	−.03 (0.19)	.00
Education	−1.17 (0.20)***	−.21	−.84 (0.20)***	−.15
Membership	—	—	−1.36 (0.22)***	−.19
Television time	.24 (0.04)***	.18	.21 (0.04)***	.16
Church involvement	1.68 (1.16)	.04	2.03 (1.14)	.05
Constant	45.50 (3.87)***		45.39 (3.80)***	
adj. r^2	.14		.17	

Note: Ordinary least squares regression; entries are nonstandardized (with standard deviation) and standardized regression coefficients.
* = $p<0.05$; ** = $p<0.01$; *** = $p<0.001$.
Source: Flemish Citizen Survey 1998, $n = 1,341$.

know from previous research that both these variables are significantly related with participation levels and with feelings of ethnocentrism (Hooghe 2002). We see that even this model can explain 14 percent of the variance, and again education proves to be the most influential factor.

While including the effect of associational membership in the regression (model 2), we have operationalized the variable as the sum of both current and previous memberships. This has been done because a previous analysis has shown that the effect of membership on civic attitudes is not dependent just on the current membership level but also on previous participation experiences of the respondent (Hooghe 2003). This finding can be easily explained: One of the things we expect from socialization experiences is that their effects remain discernible long after the experience itself has ended. Having been a member of a scouts group should have effects, even when the person involved has matured and is no longer a member (Stolle and Hooghe 2002). Furthermore, including previous memberships seems a more valid method for measuring participation habits, avoiding the risk of measuring momentary alternations of this behavior pattern, due, for example, to a recent relocation or to child-rearing responsibilities. Building on this analysis, we introduced "ever membership" as an independent variable in model 2, whereby "ever" is simply the sum of current and previous, that is, concluded, memberships.

The results of model 2 indicate that membership of voluntary associations indeed is negatively related to ethnocentrism. Explained variance rises from 14 to 17 percent, and membership becomes the most important variable, even more important than education.

THE COMPANY WE KEEP

We now come to the final piece of our argument, by assessing whether the negative relation with ethnocentrism is uniform for all kinds of associations or is dependent upon member and group characteristics (Stolle and Rochon 1998). Therefore we now leave the aggregate measurement level of membership to look at the figures for each kind of organization separately. Because a few categories were poorly represented in the survey, we had to regroup the original twenty-two categories into eighteen somewhat larger groups. For each kind of association, we can list the average number of years of schooling its members have completed (Table 5.3), and here one can observe distinct differences. Organizations involved with peace, human rights, environment, and school and neighborhood councils seem to attract highly educated members, with on average more than thirteen years of completed education. Cultural, political, social and sport associations seem to recruit mainly from a middle group, with on average something like twelve years of education. We also have some associations that seem to recruit mainly from lower-educated population groups, like trade unions or the Red Cross. Only organizations for women, pensioners and clubs affiliated with local cafés have members with lower educational credentials than those of the population as a whole. One can observe that the average education level is extremely low for the organizations of pensioners, and this is due to the fact that the educational system in Belgium has expanded enormously from the 1950s onwards. Given the fact that the average age of the members of this kind of organization is sixty-six years, they have received fewer educational opportunities during their youth phase than subsequent cohorts.

In the previous section we have argued that including "ever" membership (that is, current and previous combined) produces stronger socialization effects than limiting ourselves to a measurement of current memberships. Therefore, we also included in Table 5.3 the average education level of these "ever" members. There is very little difference with the current members: Only for environmental groups does the average drop, while for religious groups it goes up slightly. The next column shows the average score

Table 5.3 Characteristics of different kinds of organizations

	n	Years education current members	Years education members	Score ethnocentrism	Zero-order correlation	Partial correlation
Peace, human rights	64	13.82	13.98	26.4	−.24***	−.18***
Environment	82	13.47	13.00	31.7	−.18***	−.13***
Neighborhood, school	114	13.25	13.22	34.5	−.17***	−.11***
Family organization	183	12.78	12.46	35.3	−.14***	−.10**
Art, culture	111	12.75	13.02	37.5	−.14***	−.08*
Religion	52	12.74	13.24	32.4	−.14***	−.11***
Politics	72	12.62	12.56	35.5	−.08**	−.07*
Youth	49	12.46	12.41	40.7	−.19***	−.10**
Sports	323	12.26	12.21	39.6	−.15***	−.06
Caring, altruistic	102	12.18	12.58	35.2	−.11**	−.10**
Social/cultural	101	12.17	12.19	41.9	−.06*	−.05
Hobby	111	11.96	12.25	42.5	−.05	−.03
Red Cross etc.	126	11.66	11.80	37.9	−.07*	−.07*
Trade union	470	11.57	11.53	40.5	−.04	−.02
Women's organization	142	11.31	11.40	41.4	.00	.00
Local pub	79	10.94	10.88	42.9	.01	.00
Pensioners	81	9.06	9.03	45.1	.02	−.07*
Survey	*1341*	11.41		41.3		

Note: For each kind of organization, the columns represent: (a) number of "ever" members; (b) average years of schooling for current members; (c) average years of schooling for ever members; (d) average score on the scale for ethnocentrism (range 0–100); (e) zero-order correlation between ever membership and ethnocentrism; (f) partial correlation between ever membership and ethnocentrism, controlled for education, age, income and sex of the respondent.

* = $p < 0.05$; ** = $p < 0.01$; *** = $p < 0.001$.

Source: Flemish Citizen Survey 1998, $n = 1,341$.

on the scale for ethnocentrism, and here the relation confirms our expectations. The average is much lower for organizations with highly educated members than it is for organizations with less-educated members. Yet this relation is clearly not linear: The Red Cross, for example, has relatively lowly educated members, but the organization also displays low levels of ethnocentrism.

In the next column we present a simple zero-order correlation between membership in the organization and the score on ethnocentrism. Again, this column hardly presents any new information. Given the close link between ethnocentrism and education levels, it is evident that we are observing a close correlation between the average education level of members and the mean score on the ethnocentrism scale.

The final column of Table 5.3 is more surprising. In this column we have listed the partial correlation coefficients between membership of this kind of organization and ethnocentrism, but controlling for education, age, income and sex of the respondent. In this column, we no longer represent a bivariate relationship, but we list what can be considered a net effect of membership, and in this sense this partial correlation coefficient can be compared to the beta coefficients we would find in a regression analysis (see Table 5.4). One could expect that these partial correlation coefficients would be very low. After all, we know that education is the main determinant for ethnocentrism, and this variable is used here as a control variable. The most straightforward reasoning would be that the difference in the average scores for the various kinds of organizations is mainly caused by the fact that they attract members with different educational credentials. This is not the case: The partial correlation coefficients remain significant and powerful.

We can even observe that the partial correlation coefficients are more closely related to the education level of the members than the zero-order correlation coefficients. When plotting it in a figure, the relationship is clear: The higher the average education level of the members, the more efficient an organization suppresses ethnocentrism, even when controlling for the education level of the respondent. The overall correlation between the education level of the current members and the controlled effect on ethnocentrism is $-.69$ if a weighing factor is introduced for the number of members of the organization involved (i.e., the n reported in column 1 of Table 5.3).

In this analysis we are confronted with the same outlier: The organizations for old-age pensioners. Not only do they have an extremely low average education level, but they also seem to reduce ethnocentrism effectively, contrary to what we could expect from the low education level. If we exclude this obvious outlier from the analysis, the correlation

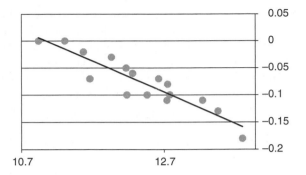

Figure 5.1   Years of schooling of members and partial correlation of membership with ethnocentrism

Note: Controls for education, income, age and gender, for seventeen kinds of organizations (excluding organizations for pensioners). X = average education level of the current members, in years of completed education; Y = partial correlation between membership and ethnocentrism, controlling for education, income, age and gender.

Source: Flemish Citizen Survey 1998, n = 1,341.

between education level and net reduction rises from −.69 to −.93, and as we see in Figure 5.1, the relation becomes almost linear. One can argue that these organizations for pensioners should be excluded from the analysis because for this older generation, the low level of education is not a good indicator for low schooling. Given the recent educational expansion in Belgium, it is very likely that nine years of schooling is in fact above-average for this cohort. Because we do not have good indicators allowing us to "weigh" the years of schooling to correct for the effects of the birth cohort of the respondent, the safest remedy is to exclude this kind of organization from the analysis.

The strong correlation between the average education level of the members and the ethnocentrism score (−.91 in the best design), does not come as a surprise: We know that ethnocentrism is determined mainly by education. But what we see is that after introducing controls for the education level of the members, the relation with the resulting partial correlations even becomes slightly stronger, up to −.93, while we reasonably could expect it to become much weaker.

This implies that not all kinds of organizations are equally effective in reducing ethnocentrism among their members. Organizations with highly educated members are especially effective in reducing ethnocentrism scores, even after controlling for the education level of the respondent. Given the very strong influence of education on ethnocentrism (see model 1 in Table 5.2), we have every reason to expect that the initial level of ethnocentrism of the members of these organizations is already very low. This implies that an ethnocentric discourse will have few chances of being tolerated, yet alone facilitated or encouraged in this kind of organizations. The fact that the partial correlation is just as strong as the zero-order correlation implies that the interaction within these organizations even further reduces the already low levels of ethnocentrism among its members, as one could expect from the literature on group polarization effects. The generalized socialization effect within associations, as it is invoked in parts of social capital theory, cannot explain this finding. Our findings are compatible, however, with social identity theory, postulating that socialization effects of associations are context dependent.

A MULTIVARIATE TEST

Because we are using eighteen different categories of organizations, thus far we have used simple correlations. When applying regression analysis, the results are the same. In order to reduce the number of independent variables, we have regrouped the eighteen kinds of organizations into four categories. The first category is composed of associations with highly educated members (> thirteen years of schooling), like peace, human rights, environment, school and neighborhood organizations. The second category includes organizations with members who have an upper-middle level of education (twelve and a half to thirteen years), like family, art, religious, political and youth organizations. Thirdly, we have organizations with a lower-middle level of education (twelve to twelve and a half years), like sports, caring and social/cultural organizations. The last category includes the organizations with a relatively low level of education (< twelve years) like hobby associations, clubs associated with a local pub, trade unions, the Red Cross and women's organizations. Again, the organizations for old age pensioners have been excluded from the analysis.

Membership in of one these four categories has been recoded as a dichotomous variable, and all four have been entered simultaneously. The regression reported in Table 5.4 confirms that, controlling for the education level of the respondent, only the organizations with high and upper-middle average education levels effectively reduce feelings of ethnocentrism. Organizations with lower-middle or low average education levels do not have a significant effect.

One could argue that this analysis does not offer sufficient proof for the claim that value effects of voluntary associations are dependent on member characteristics. Because ethnocentrism is such a politically

Table 5.4   Relation among membership, ethnocentrism and political powerlessness

	Ethnocentrism		Political powerlessness	
	B (SE B)	β	B (SE B)	β
Gender	−0.86 (1.06)	−.02	2.12 (1.07)*	.06
Age	0.11 (0.04)**	.09	0.04 (0.04)	.04
Income	0.03 (0.20)	.01	−0.22 (0.20)	−.04
Education	−0.82 (0.20)***	−.15	−0.64 (0.21)**	−.12
Member organization high education level (> 13.0 yr)	−6.35 (1.31)***	−.15	−4.64 (1.32)***	−.11
Member organization upper middle education level (12.5–13.0)	−3.83 (1.16)**	−.10	−3.14 (1.17)**	−.09
Member organization lower middle education level (12.0–12.5)	−1.53 (1.14)	−.04	−0.86 (1.15)	−.03
Member organization low education level (< 12.0 yr)	1.81 (1.11)	.05	−0.37 (1.12)	−.01
Television time	0.22 (0.04)***	.16	0.15 (0.04)***	.12
Church involvement	1.38 (1.15)	.04	−5.38 (1.17)***	−.14
Cte.	44.59 (3.92)***		71.70 (3.99)***	
adj. r^2	.18		.11	

Note: Entries are nonstandardized ordinary least squares regression coefficients (with standard deviation) and standardized regression coefficients.
* = $p < 0.05$; ** = $p < 0.01$; *** = $p < 0.001$.
Source: Flemish Citizen Survey 1998, $n = 1,341$.

salient issue in Belgium, the results presented thus far could be idio-syncratic. The way people talk about ethnic diversity is seen as politi-cally sensitive in Belgium, and therefore we might expect that this kind of discourse will be subjected to more social pressure than in other countries. Therefore we repeated the same analysis, but this time with a different attitudinal scale, measuring political powerless-ness (Table 5.4). Although it is often assumed that all kinds of asso-ciations boost feelings of political efficacy, here we observe the same pattern: Only the membership of associations with highly educated members is strongly and significantly related to the scale of political powerlessness.

CONCLUSION

Our analysis makes clear that not all voluntary associations auto-matically produce democratic attitudes, as some proponents of social capital theory would predict. At the aggregate level we observe a negative effect of participation in voluntary associations on ethno-centrism, but when we look at it more closely, we see that this effect is not uniform for all kinds of organizations. Only those organizations that, given the average education level of their members, create inter-action environments that are hostile to the expression of ethnocentric stereotypes effectively reduce ethnocentrism levels, even after intro-ducing controls for the education level of the respondent. This would indicate that the socialization effects of interaction within voluntary associations are not uniform but are context dependent, as we would expect following self-categorization theory. This implies that not all voluntary associations will actually contribute to the formation of social capital, but only those associations in which a democratic culture is present.

This finding also allows us to reconcile two of the main currents of thought within the debate on social capital. Too often it is assumed that processes of self-selection and socialization exclude one another. However, if social identity theory is correct, and if our findings would be confirmed in other research settings, this could imply that voluntary associations too are subject to a "selection and adaptation" dynamic. While members select themselves into an interaction set-ting, subsequently they adapt to the values that are being upheld in that setting. If socialization really occurs as part of a recursive relation between participation and attitudes, this does not imply that associa-tions do not *add* anything to a pre-existing average of attitudes and opinions and simply allow a convergence around this average. Research on group polarization processes demonstrates that conver-gence will occur not on a pre-given mean level but on a more extreme level. The selection and adaptation mechanism implies that actors make a deliberate choice to join an interaction sphere, but that sub-sequently they are influenced by that sphere. It therefore corresponds to the way de Tocqueville originally described the function of volun-tary associations as *"l'action lente et tranquille de la société sur elle-même"* (de Tocqueville 1835, 412). The effect of interaction within voluntary associations does not appear as a deus ex machina, as a result of exogenously induced changes, but as an enhancement of previously existing value patterns. Therefore, we have no reason to assume that all voluntary associations in all circumstances will con-tribute to the formation of the attitudinal components of social capi-tal. What makes voluntary associations an important source of social capital, however, is that in current Western liberal democracies there are many more associations producing social capital than there are producing "unsocial" capital, for example, intolerance, fanaticism or racism. Because of the fact that more civic-minded people are more easily organized than misanthropes, at the aggregate level, their norms will be spread more successfully within civil society than the values of misanthropes. This means that we should not expect each and every association to have a positive effect on the attitudinal components of social capital, but, within contemporary Western liberal democracies, associational life as a whole will be a vehicle to spread pro-social values and will thus function as a source of social capital.

APPENDIX

I. Description of the Survey

The survey was conducted during the spring of 1998 by the Free University of Brussels. The survey comprised 1,341 face-to-face interviews with inhabitants of the Flemish autonomous region. Respondents were drawn randomly from the official population registers, in the eighteen to seventy-five age bracket. Three lists of respondents were drawn, matching the three samples on age and gender. The response rate was 61 percent, which is average for these kinds of surveys in Belgium. The field work resulted in an overrepresentation of younger- and higher-educated respondents (as is usual in these kinds of surveys), which was remedied by introducing weight factors for education, age and gender.

II. Ethnocentrism Measurement Scale

We used a balanced scale developed by Jaak Billiet (Billiet, Carton and Eisinga 1995), consisting of five Likert items expressing negative feelings toward outsider groups. Factor analysis shows one factor, with an Eigen value of 2.65 and 53.0 percent explained variance. The scale is internally consistent: Cronbach's α is .78. Items: 1. Generally speaking, migrants cannot be trusted. 2. Migrants contribute to the economic prosperity of the country (reverse coding). 3. Migrants just try to profit from our social security system. 4. I am a racist. 5. The presence of different cultures is an enrichment (reverse coding).

III. Political Powerlessness Scale

We used a balanced scale of six Likert items. Factor analysis shows one factor with an Eigen value of 3.0 with 50.7 percent explained variance. The scale is internally consistent with a Cronbach's α of .80. Items: 1. Political parties are only interested in my vote, and not in my opinion. 2. If people like me communicate their opinion to politicians, they will take that into account (reverse coding). 3. Most politicians promise a lot, but they don't do a thing. 4. From the moment they are elected, most politicians feel way above people like me.

5. In fact, there is not a single politician I would trust. 6. In general, we can rely on our political leaders to make such decisions that are best for the population (reverse coding).

NOTES

1. Maybe the opposite effect is just as likely. One cannot help of thinking of the French political leader Jean Jaurès who, in 1898, after fifteen years in the socialist party (still a voluntary association at that time), exclaimed: "I don't have any trouble with my political opponents. But my political 'friends,' my fellow party men, they could eat me. *Ils me dévorent!*" (Harvey Goldberg 1970, 258).
2. A counterargument could of course be that what we are measuring with this scale is not ethnocentrism as such but rather cultural sophistication. Those with higher education "know" that it is culturally desirable to refrain from expressing hostile feelings toward foreigners. Although desirability certainly plays a role in answering patterns, the phenomenon cannot explain why these patterns are so consistent, both within the ethnocentrism scale and in the correlation with other scales. If respondents were giving a wrong representation of their true convictions, they at least do this in a very consistent manner, which makes it very improbable that this effect, by itself, could explain the strong correlation we observe with education levels. Furthermore, the desirability problem is present in all of the social capital-related questions used in this type of survey research. It is just as illegitimate to express hostile feelings toward foreigners as it is to say that people in general cannot be trusted. The social desirability problem is not crucial to our argument: We want to demonstrate convergence processes within groups, and it does not really matter whether these processes take place at the level of values or at the discourse level.

REFERENCES

Abrams, D. and M. Hogg (eds., 1991). *Social Identity Theory.* New York: Springer.

Adler, P. and P. Adler (1998). *Peer Power. Preadolescent Culture and Identity.* New Brunswick: Rutgers University Press.

Ajzen, I. and M. Fishbein (1980). *Understanding Attitudes and Predicting Social Behavior.* Englewood Cliffs: Prentice Hall.

Bankston, C. and S. Caldas (1996). "Majority African American Schools and Social Injustice." *Social Forces* 75(2), 535–555.

Berman, S. (1997). "Civil Society and Political Institutionalization." *American Behavioral Scientist* 40(5), 562–574.

Billiet, J., A. Carton and R. Eisinga (1995). "Contrasting Effects of Church Involvement on the Dimensions of Ethnocentrism." *Social Compass* 42(1), 97–108.

Brehm, J. and W. Rahn (1997). "Individual Level Evidence for the Causes and Consequences of Social Capital." *American Journal of Political Science* 41(3), 999–1023.

Claibourn, M. and Martin, P. (2000). "Trusting and Joining? An Empirical Test of the Reciprocal Nature of Social Capital." *Political Behavior* 22(4), 267–291.

Dekker, P. (ed., 1999). *Vrijwilligerswerk vergeleken. Civil Society en Vrijwilligerswerk III*. Den Haag: Sociaal en Cultureel Planbureau.

Duncan, S. and D. Fiske (1977). *Face to Face Interaction. Research, Methods and Theory*. Hillsdale: Erlbaum.

Forsyth, D. (1983). *An Introduction to Group Dynamics*. Monterey: Brooks and Cole.

Fraser, C. and D. Foster (1984). "Social Groups, Nonsense Groups and Group Polarization." pp. 473–497. In H. Tajfel (ed.), *The Social Dimension*, volume 2. Cambridge: Cambridge University Press.

Goldberg, H. (1970). *Jean Jaurès*. Paris: Fayard.

Goslin, D. (ed., 1969). *Handbook of Socialization Theory and Research*. New York: Rand McNally.

Haslam, S. A. et al. (1999). "Social Identity Salience and the Emergence of Stereotype Consensus." *Personality and Social Psychology Bulletin* 25(7), 809–818.

Hendrick, C. (ed., 1987). *Group Processes*. Newbury Park: Sage.

Hooghe, M. (ed., 2000). *Sociaal Kapitaal en Democratie. Verenigingsleven, Sociaal Kapitaal en Politieke Cultuur*. Leuven: Acco.

Hooghe, M. (2001). "Borders of Hospitality: The Difficult Birth of a Multicultural Society." *The Low Countries. Arts and Society in Flanders and the Netherlands* 9, 94–107.

Hooghe, M. (2002). "Watching Television and Civic Engagement: Disentangling the Effects of Time, Programs and Stations." *Harvard International Journal of Press/Politics* 7(2), 84–104.

Hooghe, M. (2003). "Participation in Voluntary Associations and Value Indicators. The Effect of Current and Previous Participation Experiences." *Nonprofit and Voluntary Sector Quarterly* 32(1), in press.

Katz, E. and P. Lazarsfeld (1955). *Personal Influence*. New York: Free Press.

Levi, M. (1996). "Social and Unsocial Capital." *Politics and Society* 24(1), 45–55.

Levine, J. and E. Russo (1987). "Majority and Minority Influence." pp. 13–54. In Clyde Hendrick (ed.), *Group Processes*. Newbury Park: Sage.

Lipset, S.M. (1959). "Democracy and Working-Class Authoritarianism." *American Sociological Review* 24, 482–502.

Lubbers, M., P. Scheepers and J. Billiet (2000). "Multilevel Modelling of Vlaams Blok Voting." *Acta Politica* 35(4), 363–398.

Merton, R. and A. Kitt (1950). "Contributions to the Theory of Reference Group Behavior." In R. Merton and P. Lazarsfeld (eds.), *Continuities in Social Research*. Glencoe: Free Press.

Mills, T. and S. Rosenberg (eds., 1970). *Readings on the Sociology of Small Groups*. Englewood Cliffs: Prentice Hall.

Mondak, J. and D. Mutz (1997). "What's so great about League Bowling?" Paper presented at the Annual Meeting of the Midwest Political Science Association, Chicago.

Newton, K. (1997). "Social Capital and Democracy." *American Behavioral Scientist* 40(5), 575–586.

Newton, K. (1999). "Social Capital and Democracy in Modern Europe." pp. 3–24. In J. van Deth et al. (eds.), *Social Capital and European Democracy*. London: Routledge.

Nie, N., J. Junn and K. Stehlik-Barry (1996). *Education and Democratic Citizenship in America*. Chicago: University of Chicago Press.

Paulus, P. (ed., 1989). *Psychology of Group Influence*. Hillsdale: Erlbaum.

Putnam, R. (1993). *Making Democracy Work*. Princeton: Princeton University Press.

Putnam, R. (1995). "Tuning In, Tuning Out. The Strange Disappearance of Social Capital in America." *PS: Political Science and Politics* 28(4), 664–683.

Putnam, R. (2000). *Bowling Alone. The Collapse and Revival of American Community*. New York: Simon and Schuster.

Robinson, W. P. (ed., 1996). *Social Groups and Identity*. Oxford: Butterworth-Heinemann.

Skinner, M. and G. Stephenson (1981). "The Effects of Intergroup Comparison on the Polarization of Opinions." *Current Psychological Research* 1(1), 49–61.

Soysal, Y. (1994). *Limits of Citizenship. Migrants and Postnational Membership in Europe*. Chicago: University of Chicago Press.

Stolle, D. (1998). "Bowling Alone, Bowling Together. Group Characteristics, Membership and Social Capital." *Political Psychology* 19(3), 497–526.

Stolle, D. (2000). *Communities of Trust. Public Action and Social Capital in Comparative Perspective*. Ph.D. Dissertation, Princeton University.

Stolle, D. (2002). "Social Capital—An Emerging Concept." In B. Hobson, J. Lewis and B. Siim (eds.), *Key Concepts in Gender and European Social Politics*. Cheltenham: Edward Elgar.

Stolle, D. and M. Hooghe (2002). "The Roots of Social Capital. The Effect of Youth Experiences on Participation and Value Patterns in Adult Life." Paper presented at the 98th Annual Meeting of the American Political Science Association, Boston, August 29–September 1, 2002.

Stolle, D. and T. Rochon (1998). "Are All Associations Alike?" *American Behavioral Scientist* 42(2), 47–65.

Tajfel, H. (1981). *Human Groups and Social Categories*. Cambridge: Cambridge University Press.

Tocqueville, A. de (1835). *De la Démocratie en Amérique*. Paris: Gallimard/ Pléiade, 1992.

Turner, J. (1982). "Toward a Cognitive Redefinition of the Social Group." pp. 15–40. In H. Tajfel (ed.), *Social Identity and Intergroup Relations*. Cambridge: Cambridge University Press.

Turner, J. (1984). "Social Identification and Psychological Group Formation." pp. 518–538. In H. Tajfel (ed.), *The Social Dimension*, volume 2. Cambridge: Cambridge University Press.

Turner, J. and P. Oakes (1989). "Self-Categorization Theory and Social Influence." pp. 233–275. In P. Paulus (ed.), *Psychology of Group Influence*. Hillsdale: Erlbaum.

Turner, J. et al. (1987). *Rediscovering the Social Group*. Oxford: Basil Blackwell.

Uslaner, E. (1998). "Social Capital, Television and the 'Mean World.'" *Political Psychology* 19(3), 441–467.

Uslaner, E. (2000). "Producing and Consuming Trust." *Political Science Quarterly* 115(4), 569–590.

Verba, S. (1961). *Small Groups and Political Behavior*. Princeton: Princeton University Press.

Verba, S. and N. Nie (1972). *Participation in America*. New York: Harper and Row.

Verba, S., K. L. Schlozman and H. Brady (1995). *Voice and Equality. Civic Voluntarism in American Politics*. Cambridge: Harvard University Press.

Whiteley, P. (1999). "The Origins of Social Capital." pp. 25–44. In J. van Deth et al. (eds.), *Social Capital and European Democracy*. London: Routledge.

Williams, T. (ed., 1975). *Socialization and Communication in Primary Groups*. The Hague: Mouton.

Yamagishi, T. and M. Yamagishi (1994). "Trust and Commitment in the United States and Japan." *Motivation and Emotion* 18(2), 129–166.

CHAPTER 6

ASSOCIATIONS OR INFORMAL NETWORKS? SOCIAL CAPITAL AND LOCAL DEVELOPMENT PRACTICES

Nadia Molenaers

CIVIL SOCIETY ORGANIZATIONS AND DEVELOPMENT POLICIES

In Western contexts, associational life is mostly thought of as the historical and almost natural outcome of the accumulated experiences of bottom-up, horizontal cooperation among citizens. The attitudinal disposition to trust, reciprocate and cooperate is closely linked to the existence of certain structures, like associations and associational membership, which exactly indicate the overcoming of the collective action dilemma. Both attitudes and structures, thus, form the two main components within the social capital debate. As such, large numbers of associations and elevated levels of associational membership tend to go hand in hand with high generalized trust scores. Taken together they point to the existence of a vibrant civil society with large social capital stocks (Putnam 1993). Social capital, understood as the presence of dense, horizontal networks of civic engagement and generalized norms of trust and reciprocity, seems to be the driving force for democratic performance and economic prosperity (Putnam 1993; Knack and Keefer 1997; Harrison and Huntington 2000).

The drive toward prosperity and democratic performance in non-Western contexts is a major concern, and development actors have acknowledged the potential role of social capital and a vibrant, strong civil society in development processes.[1] Especially since the 1990s, promoters of international development like the World Bank and the United Nations Development Program, but also the European Union and national governments in the West, explicitly chose to strengthen civil society in the developing world (UNDP 1993, 8; World Bank 1994, i). It is expected that the civil society approach can overcome the numerous exclusionary pitfalls of those development models that focused exclusively either on the state or the market (Nederveen Pieterse 1996; Hulme and Edwards 1997, 4–5; Brett 1998, 5–6). Civil society organizations thus became important instruments for increasing the effectiveness of poverty-reducing policies and for promoting social change, because their participative and bottom-up approach would empower the poor and vulnerable groups.

The belief in the important role of civil society has had some important side effects. Associations, civil society organizations and nongovernmental organizations have become important candidates for development funding. The donor-driven enthusiasm for civil society created opportunities for associations to start, grow, become larger and professionalize. The enlarged existence of associations and associational membership might say more about strategic choices, funding opportunities and "associational entrepreneurship" than about the bottom-up culmination of the horizontal cooperative spirit within a given population. This idea is supported by those scholars who point to the extremely low levels of trust and the predominance of clientelism in developing countries. Research shows that—on average—only 16 percent of Latin Americans trust their fellow citizens, while in Europe these scores reach up to 60 percent.[2] Transparency International states that a country like Nicaragua has entered in a situation of hypercorruption, only matched by the culture of tolerance toward noncompliance and defection.[3] The regional common heritage of distrust (Lagos 1997, 129) is reflected in social interaction patterns. The continent seems to be characterized and dominated by verticalism and clientelism, which basically indicates fragmentation and the incapacity to develop horizontal cooperation (Eisenstadt and Röniger 1984; Gambetta 1988).[4]

These insights seem to indicate that if we talk about social capital in non-Western contexts a possible disconnection, or even contradiction, might exist between the attitudinal aspects (trust and horizontality) and the structural components (associational vibrancy). On the policy level this might imply that the civil society approach is not necessarily linked to building, generating and enforcing trust, horizontal cooperation and participation. Therefore the main purpose of this chapter is to investigate whether in a Third World setting the same relationship between associational membership and the attitudinal components of social capital can be found, as is suggested in part of the literature.

In order to approach these issues, this chapter tries to answer the following questions: Is associational life linked to the attitudinal components of social capital, namely horizontal trust and cooperation (and does this horizontal cooperation exist?), or is associational life about verticalist and clientelist access? In other words: What do associations enforce? Do associations effectively play the role of "changers," or are they the fulminators of vertical and clientelist networks? As bearers of social change, it is expected that they work against the logic of the vertical and clientelist networks, because these maintain the poor and vulnerable in positions of dependency. In an ideal development context, aid channeled through associations should foster and stimulate horizontal, inclusive, trusting and cooperative social interaction patterns. Added to this, special attention should be given to the poor and vulnerable, as their position of exclusion has to be turned around. It is therefore imperative to analyze whether organizations are effectively reaching these poor groups.

The data presented in this chapter were collected in two Nicaraguan peasant villages (1998–1999). These villages were selected after intensive consulting with Nicaraguan development organizations. Although, due to lack of any reliable figures on social and economic characteristics of local communities in Nicaragua, we cannot ascertain whether these villages can be considered as representative for Nicaraguan society as a whole, during the fieldwork we did not find any indications that they should be considered as atypical. The associations, the membership structures and the recruitment mechanisms these organizations employ in the villages were analyzed in relation to the existing horizontal informal cooperation networks. We will see that associations heavily depend upon the local leaders and their informal networks, which indicates that the organizations are probably not changing the social interaction patterns in either village but are rather confirming them. The effectiveness of organizations in reaching the poor is also highly determined by the local networks. If these local networks are already including the poor, then the associations reach these groups; if not, the vulnerable groups remain outside the scope of the associations and their development interventions. It is important to mention here that the collected data do not allow discussion of the direction of the causality, so our ambitions are modest. The debate of whether a significant relation occurs among associations, trust and reciprocity proceeds the causality issue. Without a significant relation between both phenomena there is little point in debating the causality, and therefore it does seem worthwhile first to establish the existence and the strength of this relation.

THE ASSOCIATIONAL LANDSCAPE IN
BOTH VILLAGES

El Toro and La Danta are isolated peasant villages in Nicaragua, situated in the poorest region of the country, Chinandega, and very near
to the Honduran border.[5] Both villages represent a specific kind of
village. El Toro is a typical example of a land reform village. These
villages were organized in productive cooperatives and they received
large benefits during the Sandinist regime in the eighties. After the electoral defeat of the Sandinists in 1990, the cooperatives' assets (land
and cattle) were privatized and divided equally among the inhabitants
of the villages. These villages were frequently assisted by international
and national development organizations and nongovernmental organizations. Certain interviewees state that in spite of the large economic
benefits during at least a decade, land reform villages have a lot of difficulties in "getting ahead" because, according to several development
actors "they suffer from a 'culture of non-reciprocity,' they always
received a lot without having to do anything in return."[6] According
to these people, local bonds of solidarity have been negatively affected
by both the political presence in these villages and the relentless stream
of material and financial advantages that were distributed without
implementing monitoring systems, audits, control or accountability.
La Danta, on the other hand, did not receive this enhanced political
attention. No land reform benefits reached the village in the eighties,
and both Sandinist and nongovernmental organization attention was,
if not absent, at least very limited.

Both villages, however, also have a lot in common. More than
75 percent of the population in the villages is dependent upon agriculture and about 40 percent of the farmers do not own any land.[7] At
the associational level, similar numbers and kinds of organizations are
present in the villages. In total three interest groups, nine nongovernmental organizations and four government-related institutions were
found and each village had its own community committee. For the
distribution of these organizations in the villages, see Table 6.1.

It is important to mention that all the organizations and institutions
present in the villages have the participative development perspective
in common. A large majority of the organizations have been working
in the area since the beginning of the nineties. All these organizations
also have important links with the outside world as all of them are
connected to the municipal authorities or the central government,
national syndicates, regional development offices and international
and national nongovernmental organizations. The existence of these

links is fundamental for all actors involved as they channel tangible and intangible resources. The similarities among these organizations (participative approach, development discourse and bottom-up functioning) stand in stark contrast with the strict theoretical divide between state and civil society. Both governmental and nongovernmental actors play in the same field, organize the same kind of interventions and use similar approaches in these two villages. Nongovernmental actors can belong to governmental structures and vice versa. In this sense, the rigid division between state and civil society is difficult to maintain, and it becomes a challenge to catalogue all the different kinds of organizations and institutions in fixed compartments. The similarities between the organizations are of course strengthened by the fact that they all are heavily dependent upon and padding along the outlines as defined by donors.

In order to get a good view of the characteristics of the members of organizations, the families in the villages were divided according to their political preferences and socioeconomic class.[8] In Table 6.1, a summary of the most important results is shown. The large number of organizations and the extremely high (multiple) membership rates point to the idea that the inhabitants in both villages are quite organized. Furthermore, all local leaders are very much involved in the associational activities. The four local leaders in both villages are Sandinist and they function as the coordinators for the respective associations present in the villages. Each leader coordinated at least three organizations.

The participants in both villages seem to belong to a more privileged social class, as the elite and the landowning peasants are largely present within organizations. This finding runs parallel with the pattern we find in previous research: Associational activity tends to be connected to those that are not extremely poor. Membership, cooperation and trust seem to be particularly difficult for the poorest (Inglehart 1988; Newton 1999). From the development perspective however, associations should be reaching exactly these poor and vulnerable groups. In La Danta, the poorest group is effectively and largely included in the associations; in El Toro, however, only 20 percent participates.

In both villages, the participants seem to share a political preference for the Sandinists. This political membership characteristic remains present when multiple membership is analyzed. In both villages there were inhabitants accumulating up to five memberships, and most of them are Sandinists. The table below clearly shows that in both villages the average number of membership increases

Table 6.1   Associational structure in the villages

Organizations and membership	El Toro	La Danta
Interest groups	2	3
Nongovernmental organizations	7	6
Government institutions promoting development projects	3	2
Community committee	1	1
Total number of organizations in the villages	13	12
% of population with at least one membership	44%	60%
% of population with more than one membership	25%	32%
Average number of memberships per family	0.8	1.2
Participation of the local leaders (four leaders in each village)	all	all
Membership according to political preference and socioeconomic status		
Total population	44%	60%
Political preference		
Sandinist	79%	93%
Liberal	31%	36%
No political preference	27%	58%
Socioeconomic status		
Elite group (> 50 ha)	57%	80%
Landowning peasants (< 50 ha)	84%	68%
Landless peasants (no land)	20%	64%
Average memberships related to political preference		
Total population	0.8	1.2
Sandinists	1.7	2.2
Liberals	0.3	0.5

Source: Author's fieldwork, 1998–1999.

substantially when it concerns a Sandinist inhabitant, while it decreases when the inhabitant prefers the Liberal party. The absence of the Liberals is quite striking in both villages, but in El Toro the socioeconomic bias is even more impressive. Both villages suffer thus from a structural participation bias, even though a relatively large number of organizations are present in both villages, while the other organizations share the same goals and supposedly play according to the same rules. In order to understand the nonparticipation structure, we have to look at the associational recruitment mechanisms.

EXPLAINING THE BIASES

The Sandinist bias in membership is strongly related to the history of a large number of organizations in Nicaragua. In the 1980s the

Sandinist government promoted and welcomed all associational initiatives that were left wing–oriented. However, the 1990s were marked by an even bigger boom in numbers of associations, also mostly quite progressive.[9] Although most national left-wing organizations distanced themselves from the Sandinist party after the electoral defeat in 1989, these changes most probably have not caused a substantial difference in membership structures at the local level. So given the history of the country, the Sandinist overrepresentation within the membership structures is what we would expect.

Another extremely important, yet often overlooked, characteristic is that associations in developing countries always bring projects, and hence resources, into communities. Members seem to be the first beneficiaries of these tangible and intangible resources. Certain organizations in the villages use the food for work approach. Farmers are, for example, introduced to new methods and technologies in agriculture, and the ones that effectively implement those new techniques receive food supplies. Also materials, like wire netting, zinc, machetes and pumps to spray insecticides are offered. A few organizations have provided their members production materials and financial help, while others have made valuable market information on the prices of sesame available to their members, which strengthens the position of the farmers when they have to negotiate with the intermediate buyers. All the organizations offer education through workshops and seminars. The amounts of scarce resources these organizations carry are quite impressive and the benefits of joining are thus not imaginary. If we take into account that in both villages some inhabitants accumulate up to five memberships, the idea of multiple inclusion and exclusion suddenly receives an important economic weight. From the resources point of view, joining becomes a privilege.

Getting into associations is strongly influenced by the informal networks in the villages. Access to the resources is thus regulated through networks, through one's direct and indirect ties. This converts the resources into "social resources" as they are embedded in social networks (Lin 1982, 132).

> *Why don't you join one of the organizations?*
> Because they don't let me.
> *Who are they?*
> The leaders.
> *What do you mean?*
> When an organization comes and they want to do something in the village, like a project, they always end up with the local leaders and they say: "If you know any good people, hardworking people who

want to co-operate, get them together and we will start with the
project." And so the leaders decide who is going to be in the group
and they always pick the same ones [*siempre son los mismos*].
Would you like to join?
Of course...they are getting all the benefits and we never get
anything... (Farmer in La Danta)

This conversation reflects the more general view in the villages. Nonparticipants feel excluded from associational life, excluded from access
to resources. Membership is the strategy that guarantees access to
resources. In this respect, associations can create competition between
inhabitants because they want to get into the networks of local leaders
in order to get access to the resources. The interviews we conducted
with most of the inhabitants of these two villages revealed tensions
within the villages, as some people systematically are included while
others remain outside the associational structures. The organizations
and the local leaders confirmed the important role of the local
leaders in recruiting members:

Yes, I select the people that are going to be working in the project.
Sometimes the organization puts forward requirements like age or sex
or amount of land they have to have. Of course I follow their instruc-
tions and then I pick the people I know best, the people I can trust.
I cannot assume responsibility for people I do not know, because if they
"screw up," then the organization will blame me for it and I will lose
the connection. (Local leader in La Danta)

In Coleman's words (1990, 182), leaders occupy the position of
entrepreneurial intermediaries. These actors receive trust from several
trustors (the associations) to properly deploy the resources among the
trustees (the members) who then jointly produce the benefits of the
activity (project). This responsibility of selecting members by the local
leaders simultaneously decentralizes project performance and management to the local leaders. It seems, however, that this approach
offers advantages for the associations themselves: They lower their
transaction costs by relying on existing social networks of trust. This
tendency to use "social capital" to guarantee project performance can
be questioned, especially when it instrumentalizes existing networks
without questioning the composition, structure and content of those
networks. These networks can be verticalist, clientelist dependency
networks. Essentially this instrumental use of trust within the area
of development studies and development practice runs parallel with
and is a translation of the ideas of the pragmatic social capital school,

in which social capital is conceived as an instrument to mobilize resources. Networks are thus used to enhance effective control over the project performance through a group that is manageable (a few local leaders), and these leaders can be held responsible and sanctioned by withdrawing resources from the community. In order to avoid this, the leader will probably deploy all his power resources to guarantee the performance of the project. In other words, the power connected to his position as an entrepreneurial intermediary will most probably be added to the power he has as access-giver to his personally owned resources (like land, oxen, small amounts of money and food). The more resources an individual controls, the more hierarchical the position and the organization of access will become. If one wants to get access to those personal and social resources, one is obligated to compensate and behave in a reciprocal manner (Lin 1995, 687–688). Access receivers thus owe something to the access giver. This limits bottom-up control, accountability, empowerment and genuine participation (these being the exact goals of the civil society approach). The power differences between associations and local leaders, on the one hand, and local leaders versus inhabitants, on the other hand, are too large. Participation then becomes, at best, agreeing with the one above while sanctioning the one below. Confirmative participation in these cases bends toward clientelism rather than toward genuine participation. This indicates that getting into associational life is more connected to clientelist mechanisms than to the bottom-up culmination of cooperative spirit. It thus seems unlikely that, in this context, associations could be considered as a reflection or a source of the attitudinal components of social capital.

We already indicated that the strong Sandinist bias is explained by the historical evolution of the political opportunity structure, which shaped the character of associational life while creating and supporting mainly Sandinist leadership structures on the local level. The effect is that Liberals cannot fully take advantage of the associational opportunity structure. These mechanisms, however, do not explain why in La Danta local leaders do select poorer peasants for joining associations, while in El Toro this is not the case. Not selecting the poorer peasants could be viewed as quite rational because it is expected that noncompliance, distrust and defection will be found more frequently in the lower socioeconomic classes (Inglehart 1988, 1213; Newton 1999, 181). The poor tend to have a dimmer outlook on fellow citizens and the world in general (Newton 1999); they have more to lose and make narrow risk calculations because the pay-off is uncertain and the risk of defection is real. The recruitment behavior of the leaders in El Toro thus seems to respond to this rational logic, be it to the detriment of the development goals of the donor-driven civil society approach, as the resources do not reach the poorest groups. In La Danta the resources do reach a large part of the poorest strata, but the question is why local leaders risk an involvement with this seemingly "untrustworthy" group. The structure and content of the local informal networks might provide us with the answer to this question.

THE INFORMAL COOPERATIVE NETWORKS

According to Coleman (1990), the emergence and enforcement of norms is facilitated by the closure of networks. Closure furthermore enhances the trustworthiness of social structures, allowing the proliferation of obligations and expectations. A structure without closure has difficulties imposing sanctions. At best, the person to whom the obligation is owed can sanction defection. In closed networks sanctions can be collectively imposed and reputations can be lost or gained. So, closure creates trustworthiness of the social structure, while open networks lack these enforcement mechanisms. Therefore, we now turn to the study of the informal networks, found in the villages. Our aim here is to check whether horizontal forms of cooperation could be found in these generally verticalist societies, and how these relate to the more clientelist dimension of associational life. We wanted to investigate forms of cooperation that would approximate the horizontal, voluntary cooperation aspect of social capital. In both villages, such horizontal cooperation took the form of neighboring farmers exchanging labor force. This cooperative relation is called *cambio de mano* (in exchange for a hand). In its most simple form, this rural informal exchange mechanism means that farmer A helps farmer B a few days on the field and later on farmer B returns the favor by working a few days on the field of farmer A.

This mechanism is an important cash-saver, as money is extremely scarce and labor force extremely costly.[10] These kinds of cooperative networks are therefore of immense importance for the poorer peasants because they save them a lot of money. The rational thing to do is thus to engage in these forms of cooperation, unless there is a lack of trust. Trust is fundamental in these forms of cooperation because there is always a time lapse between the favor delivered and the favor returned. The risk of defection is thus real. The interviewed farmers explicitly stated that trust plays a major role in this mechanism. Especially when more complex forms of *cambio de mano* exist (involving more than two actors), trust is extremely essential. The trust mechanism involved in this kind of *cambio de mano* essentially runs like this: Person A, who delivers the service, trusts the beneficiary B (1) to acknowledge the fact that he owes something to A, (2) to execute one or more services in return (comparable in size and/or quality with the service delivered by A). It is important that A does not have to exercise pressure in order to receive a service in return. If A has to invest time and energy in insisting that B to return the favor, this might finally undermine the relation. In essence this mechanism is quite delicate. The involved actors spontaneously offer each other favors and services in return, thereby taking into account that they must not overload the counterpart with demands and/or obligations. If, after a certain amount of time, the involved parties feel that no one is trying to "have one's cake and eat it," these cooperative relations can eventually evolve into complex and multiple support mechanisms where all involved can deduct advantages from the talents, knowledge and relations of the other members of the cooperative community.

Furthermore, the respondents involved in *cambio de mano* relations argue that this work-for-work relation involves, in principle, equal exchange. Symmetry between the involved actors is fundamental in this relation. If one of both parties would start to nibble on the obligations inherent in the relation, both trust and reciprocity might in the end cripple. Not living up to the expectations can have direct consequences. The accountability mechanism in this kind of relation is informal and horizontal. In order to keep this relation alive the relation must be subjected to mechanisms that are enforcing horizontality: Equal rights and obligations must be maintained.

Table 6.2 shows that in El Toro only 35 percent of the respondents are involved in *cambio de mano* relations, wile in La Danta this amounts to up to 78 percent of the interviewed farmers. This already indicates that in La Danta a large majority of the people are cooperating horizontally with each other. An important characteristic of a network is whether or not it is connected. The actors in a disconnected network or graph may be grouped in two or more subnetworks or components that are not linked with each other. So, the more components a network counts, the more disconnected it is (Wasserman and Faust 1994, 109). We can see that in La Danta a very large group is organized in only five components. In El Toro, on the other hand, we see only a rather small number of farmers organized in ten disconnected components. Components, however, do not reveal specific information on the density of the networks. In a dense network, there is a path between every pair of actors, hence all actors are mutually reachable. All actors are mutually reachable when reachability equals

Table 6.2   Network structure and characteristics of the nodes

Network structure	El Toro	La Danta
% of the population involved	35%	78%
Number of network components in village	10	5
Reachability	0.12	0.59
Average *cambio de mano* relations per family	0.6	1.8
Participation of local leaders	None	All
Characteristics of network members		
Population	35%	78%
Political preference		
Sandinist	55%	89%
Liberal	31%	80%
No political preference	40%	63%
Socioeconomic status		
Elite (> 50 ha of land)	29%	80%
Landowning peasants (< 50 ha)	55%	88%
Landless peasants (no land)	40%	71%

Source: Author's fieldwork, 1998–1999.

one. One is thus the highest density score. La Danta scores high on this indicator: 59 percent of the actors in the network are mutually reachable. In El Toro only 12 percent of the actors are mutually reachable. The network analysis also showed that the average number of *cambio de mano* relations in La Danta lies significantly higher than in El Toro. This means that in La Danta, not only are more families involved in *cambio de mano*, but also that each family maintains more relations on average with other families. Furthermore, in La Danta all the associational leaders are integrated in *cambio de mano* relations, while in El Toro not one local leader maintains these cooperative relations with villagers.

Taken together, it seems that horizontal cooperation and trust is overwhelmingly present in La Danta. The high density indicates near closure of networks, and this makes them more effective in terms of norm compliance and reciprocity. Considering the number of involved families and the fact that the local leaders are subjected to these norms of accountability, La Danta seems less hierarchical, more inclusive and integrated, with more horizontal trust and reciprocity than El Toro. Furthermore, the presence of the local leaders in these networks in La Danta suggests that they are subjected to mechanisms of internal social control. The absence of associational leaders in El Toro might indicate that they escape the mechanisms of horizontal accountability, mutual equal exchange and mutual expectations and obligations. Social control and tracing deviant behavior will be much easier in La Danta than in El Toro.[11]

The profile of the involved nodes in both villages seems to be strongly Sandinist and landowning. These data coincide with the profile of the participants as displayed before. There is, however, a somewhat odd discrepancy. Where in La Danta the Liberals were very strongly underrepresented in the membership structure, in these cooperative networks not less than 80 percent of the Liberal group is involved. While in El Toro the landless peasants were almost totally absent from associational life, here we see that about 40 percent of the landless peasants are informally cooperating in *cambio de mano* structures.

After cross-checking the data on associational life with the data on cooperative relations, the following pattern emerged: In El Toro half of the formal nonparticipants are integrated in the *cambio de mano* relations and half of the organized families in the village are practicing *cambio de mano*. In La Danta, of the twenty-nine not-organized families, twenty are practicing *cambio de mano* (almost two-thirds) and of the forty-one organized families, thirty-four are organized in *cambio de mano* relations (which represents more than three-fourths). So, related to the question in the introduction, associational life is not necessarily linked to the attitudinal components of social capital. We saw that the groups that were underrepresented in the formal structures of participation in associational life are strongly present in the horizontal cooperative networks here. In both cases, it seems that formal participation in associational activities and development processes do not say all that much about cooperative spirit. Both the mechanisms behind recruitment and the data on membership-cooperation structures indicate the discrepancy between both phenomena.

More importantly, we also learn that, because of the expectations connected to associational activities, the strong integration of the poor in the networks in La Danta reduces the risk that they might defect. As the networks provide an environment in which reciprocity is generally expected, the leaders can include the poorest without running too much risk of suffering from large defection problems. The fact that large groups of poor are active in these horizontal networks (especially in La Danta and, to a lesser extent, in El Toro) seems to question the general picture of Latin America in which the poorest remain marginalized, isolated, unorganized, a bit fatalist and dependent on rich patrons (Huntington and Nelson 1976).

CONCLUSION

Large numbers of associations and elevated levels of associational membership are not necessarily linked to trust, reciprocity and horizontal cooperation. Associations can thus not automatically—not always and not everywhere—be seen as the structural embodiment of the attitudinal components of social capital. The villages we studied scored similarly on associational life, yet in El Toro there are only a few small groups cooperating in a horizontal manner, while in La Danta there are abundant numbers of people in the horizontal networks. In both villages, associational life is effectively linked to more clientelist interaction patterns, in which actors try to get access to social resources via the local leaders, who play the role of intermediaries between organizations and inhabitants. A very different picture emerged when the informal cooperative networks were studied. The network approach brought us much closer to the attitudinal components of social capital. Both villages scored quite differently on horizontal cooperation. If we had relied on the indicative link between associations and social capital, we would have concluded that both villages score more or less the same on social capital.

The "discovery" of the mechanisms related to *cambio de mano* networks reveals that this might be an alternative indicator for the horizontal and voluntary cooperation dimension of the social capital concept. It is necessary to find these kinds of indicators in order to deconstruct the complex social capital concept and its normative assumptions (Edwards and Foley 1998), especially in a non-Western context, because the policy implications can be significant.

In the introduction to this chapter, it was stated that the civil society approach in development cooperation is charged with high hopes. Donors hope that organizations can forge a social change, that they can work against the vertical and clientelist grain while stimulating the inclusion of poor and vulnerable groups. The cases show that these objectives are somewhat naive when held against the complex realities these developing countries face. We have seen that in the case of Nicaragua, the associational landscape is not as pluralist as often assumed. History and the evolution of the political opportunity structure color the actual composition of civil society and the membership structure within localities. We saw that in both villages, certain groups, in this case the Sandinist inhabitants, are better organized than others, get easier access to associations and have leadership structures that are externally supported. The leaders receive the power to select players and hence to distribute resources. Associations thus fall into networks and the effectiveness of their development efforts seem to be largely determined by the local structure of the informal networks. If these networks are relatively inclusive, horizontal, dense and ruled by mechanisms of accountability, if poor and rich, leaders and followers are situated in these networks (like in La Danta) then these associations are supporting, developing and stimulating exactly this kind of culture. In other words, important parts of the horizontal, inclusive networks of cooperation are strengthened, and the involved actors will effectively benefit from the resources introduced by associations. The insertion of the local leaders in the cooperative informal networks prevents them from abusing their power position, as they are subjected to internal mechanisms of social control through the dense networks. The networks in La Danta thus produce trustworthiness (Coleman 1988, 1990). In El Toro this is not the case. Local leaders do not participate in the horizontal cooperative networks. The networks themselves are quite fragmented, with small numbers of people involved, which, according to Coleman (1988, 1990), indicates the difficulty of creating a trustworthy environment where norm compliance and reciprocity is maintained. So, when associations have to deal with El Toro—like environments, they are effectively institutionalizing verticalism and clientelism and reinforcing the unchecked power position of the leaders. It is thus quite obvious that in these two villages, the horizontal and trusting relations can mainly be found in the informal networks and much less so in the formal associations. It is therefore quite unlikely that these associations can be seen as sources of trust. In both villages there are groups that are horizontally cooperating and trusting, yet they do not get access to the associations—because they have the wrong political preference (in La Danta) or because they are not connected with the local leaders (the latter were absent in the horizontal networks in El Toro). The bad news is that associations also strengthen and institutionalize this exclusion. The biased participation structure is most probably linked with biased informal networks, and therefore this indicates cleavages. Cleavages are (in and by themselves) not problematic, as long as all the groups can get access to scarce resources within their respective (pillarized) structures. This is, however, not the case in the villages studied, either because the associational landscape is not diversified enough or because associations lack the capacities, time or means to profoundly study the localities in which they will become active.

Local background studies can reveal important features. In the Nicaraguan context it seems relevant to distinguish whether a village has benefited largely form the land reform or not. By and large

El Toro responds to the characteristics that project managers, government officials and NGO coordinators had put forward as "quite typical land reform village features." In interviews these managers and officials heavily pointed to the idea that land reform villages in general seem to have more problems with cooperative and trustworthy behavior than traditional villages. They indicated that the strong presence of the Sandinist party and national and international solidarity organizations in the land reform villages has nurtured a culture of nonreciprocity. The abundant stream of advantages toward these villages without the expectation of anything in return, so state the interviewees, is in part responsible for the breakdown of local bonds of reciprocity, cooperation and the mechanisms of accountability. Most probably these explanations are only a part of the Nicaraguan story, and they need to be investigated empirically and in more detail rather than assumed. But it points to the idea that more research on the influence of political distribution mechanisms, both in the past and in the present, on local networks is needed, especially in developing areas.

To conclude, these insights bring us to some relevant policy recommendations. First of all, the civil society approach within development practice is in dire need of critical revision. The romantic and positive connotations that are linked with the role, function and effects of a large vibrant civil society for democracy and economic development are, in a developing context, somewhat naive, if not simply wrong. Put simply, the one-size-fits-all approaches that donors often impose denies the idea that contexts matter. It seems thus quite utopian to want to create social capital as if it were a simple resource, a fixed outcome resulting from the investment in a given instrument. Taking the context into account there are some relevant remarks to be made and questions to be posed. First of all, by stimulating civil society organizations we are not necessarily stimulating those attitudes we tend to connect to social capital. If strengthening civil society is vital, it seems just as vital to ask whether we need to support the diversification of civil society or whether we accept it as it comes. Is participation a good tool in any context. Reaching the poor in the fragmented, clientelist and distrusting villages will be more effective if leaders are not allowed to participate. If participation turns out to be strengthening clientelism, then imposing top-down transparent selection criteria, not necessarily involving participation, might actually work in favor of the weakest groups (Van der Linden 1997; Vandana 1996). The effective implementation of transparent mechanisms on the level of associations and development interventions (including sanctioning mechanisms in case of defection) institutionalizes trust and might as such even create trust and thus social capital. All these remarks call for more development-related research. It is important that ex-ante (locality) studies take place in order to assess the composition of a given community and establish a link with the different groups within the community. It seems imperative that the strengthening of monopolized leader positions is avoided, that sources of information are diversified and that the chances are increased that the poor and vulnerable groups will be actually reached. Finding out where the networks of leaders end might indicate where the real development work should start.

NOTES

1. See, for example, the website of the World Bank: www.worldbank.org/ poverty/scapital.
2. See http://www.latinobarometro.org.
3. See http://www.ibw.com.ni/~ien/c5-7.htm.
4. It has been argued that horizontal cooperation can be found in some developing countries, but it tends to be in-group oriented (bonding), between similar people, while dissimilar people and/or outsiders are rejected. Trust therefore thus seems to be particular, rather than generalized.
5. El Toro counted 103 families, La Danta 74. In each village, 65 families were interviewed.
6. All quotes in this chapter are taken from the 130 interviews which were conducted in El Toro and La Danta for the fieldwork of this research project in 1998 and 1999.
7. This means that in one decade El Toro has evolved from a more or less egalitarian landtenancy structure to a quite unequal socioeconomic situation. Due to a lack of space, this chapter will not go into the mechanisms related to this evolution.
8. Regarding their political preference, respondents could be catalogued as Sandinist (left-wing opposition), Liberal (right-wing party in power) or no preference. With regard to their socioeconomic class we catalogued the poorest as those that did not have land, the middle group as landowning farmers (less than 50 ha) and the elite as those farmers that owned more than 50 ha. This categorization was borrowed from the Ministry of Agriculture in Nicaragua.
9. For more information see Varela Hidalgo B. et al. (1998).
10. When a farmer has to prepare 1 ha for sowing, the weeding part by itself might take up to sixteen days of work if he works alone. If he would contract one agricultural worker, the labor time would be halved (eight days of work), but he would have to pay the worker ca. 1.25 U.S.$ per day. Eight days of labor would cost the farmer 10 U.S.$.

11. Obviously, the ideas of too much trust and social control are lined with the discussion on bonding and bridging social capital. Too much trust, especially on an in-group basis, can have quite a lot of negative effects (Woolcock 1998; Portes 1998; Granovetter 1982). Nevertheless, authors do seem to agree that whenever collective development is concerned, the existence of integrating networks is preferable over fragmentation and isolation. (Woolcock 1998) This chapter therefore mainly focuses on those aspect of social capital relating to integration, horizontality and trust, as necessary, but not sufficient, conditions for democracy and development.

REFERENCES

Brett, E. A. (1996). "The Participatory Principle in Development Projects: The Costs and Benefits of Cooperation." *Public Administration and Development* 16, 5–19.

Coleman, J. S. (1988). "Social Capital in the Creation of Human Capital." *American Journal of Sociology* 94, S95–S120.

Coleman, J. S. (1990). *Foundations of Social Theory.* Cambridge: Harvard University Press.

Dasgupta, P. and I. Serageldin (2000). *Social Capital: A Multifaceted Perspective.* Washington: The World Bank.

Edwards, B. and M. Foley (1998). "Social Capital and Civil Society beyond Putnam." *American Behavioral Scientist* 42(2), 124–139.

Eisenstadt, S. N. and L. Röniger (1984). *Patrons, Clients and Friends, Interpersonal Relations and the Structure of Trust in Society.* Cambridge: Cambridge University Press.

Gambetta, D. (1988). *Trust: Making and Breaking Cooperative Relations.* Oxford: Blackwell.

Granovetter, M. (1982). "The Strength of Weak Ties." pp. 105–130. In P. Marsden and N. Lin, *Social Structure and Network Analysis.* London: Sage.

Harrison, L. (1985, rev. ed. 2000). *Underdevelopment Is a State of Mind: The Latin American Case.* Lanham: Madison Books.

Harrison, L. (2000). "Why Culture Matters." pp. xvi–xxxiv. In L. Harrison and S. Huntington (eds.), *Culture Matters: How Values Shape Human Progress.* New York: Basic Books.

Harrison, L. and S. Huntington (eds., 2000). *Culture Matters: How Values Shape Human Progress.* New York: Basic Books.

Hulme, D. and M. Edwards (eds., 1997). *NGOs, States and Donors, Too Close for Comfort?* London: MacMillan.

Huntington, S. (2000), "Cultures Count." pp. xiii–xvi. In L. Harrison and S. Huntington (eds.), *Culture Matters: How Values Shape Human Progress.* New York: Basic Books.

Huntington, S. and J. Nelson (1976). *Political Participation in Developing Countries: No Easy Choice.* London: Harvard University Press.

Inglehart, R. (1988). "The Renaissance of Political Culture." *American Political Science Review* 82(4), 1203–1230.

Inglehart, R. (1997). *Modernization and Postmodernization, Cultural, Economic and Political Change in 43 Societies.* Princeton: Princeton University Press.

Inglehart, R. (2000). "Culture and Democracy." pp. 80–97. In L. Harrison and S. Huntington (eds.), *Culture Matters: How Values Shape Human Progress.* New York: Basic Books.

Knack, S. and P. Keefer (1997). "Does Social Capital Have an Economic Payoff? A Cross-Country Investigation." *Quarterly Journal of Economics* 112, 1251–1288.

Lagos M. (1997). "Latin America's Smiling Mask." *Journal of Democracy* 8(3), 125–138.

Lin, N. (1982). "Social Resources and Instrumental Action." pp. 131–145. In P. Marsden and N. Lin (eds.), *Social Structure and Network Analysis.* London: Sage.

Lin, N. (1995). "Social Resources: A Theory of Social Capital." *Revue Française de Sociologie* 36(4), 685–704.

Nederveen Pieterse, J. (1996). *My Paradigm or Yours? Alternative Development, Post-Development, Reflexive Development.* ISS Working Paper Nr. 229.

Newton, K. (1997). "Social Capital and Democracy." *American Behavioral Scientist* 40(5), 575–586.

Newton, K. (1999). "Social and Political Trust in Established Democracies." pp. 169–187. In P. Norris (ed.), *Critical Citizens.* Oxford: Oxford University Press.

Portes, A. (1998). "Social Capital. Its Origins and Applications in Modern Sociology." *Annual Review of Sociology* 24, 1–24.

Putnam, R. (1993). *Making Democracy Work. Civic Traditions in Modern Italy.* Princeton: Princeton University Press.

United Nations Development Program (1993). *Human Development Report 1993.* New York: Oxford University Press.

Vandana, D. (1996). "Access to Power and Participation." *Third World Planning Review* 18(2), 217–242.

Van der Linden, J. (1997). "On Popular Participation in a Culture of Patronage: Patrons and Grassroots Organizations in a Sites and Services Project in Hyderabad, Pakistan." *Environment and Urbanisation* 9(1), 81–89.

Varela Hidalgo, B. et al. (1998). *Los ONG en Nicaragua, Limitaciones y Tendencias en su Relación con la Cooperación Internacional.* Managua: C.N.O FONG-INIES.

Wasserman, S. and K. Faust (1994). *Social Network Analysis: Methods and Applications.* Cambridge: Cambridge University Press.

Woolcock, M. (1998). "Social Capital and Economic Development: Toward a Theoretical Synthesis and Policy Framework." *Theory and Society* 27(2), 151–208.

World Bank (1991). *World Development Report 1991.* New York: Oxford University Press.

World Bank (1994). *The World Bank and Participation.* Washington: The World Bank.

Chapter 7

Rain or Fog? An Empirical Examination of Social Capital's Rainmaker Effects

Job van der Meer

Introduction

Building on the work by Robert Putnam (1993, 2000) and others, most authors using the social capital concept assume that civic engagement and generalized trust influence each other and that jointly they influence the functioning of democracy and therefore trust in political institutions. Brehm and Rahn (1997) have examined this theory at the individual level. Their analysis finds reciprocal relationships between civic engagement and generalized trust as well as between these two elements of social capital and trust in political institutions. Other researchers, however, have challenged this conclusion (see Mayer this volume). Stolle (2001) shows that people who belong to voluntary associations for a longer period of time do not trust other people to a greater extent. According to Stolle, self-selection effects explain the observed relationship between civic engagement and generalized trust. Trusting people more often join voluntary associations, rather than the reverse, and she concludes that the main reason we find voluntary associations to accommodate more trusting, more open and more civicly engaged people has to be attributed to self-selection (Stolle 2001). Newton and Norris (2000) reach similar conclusions for the relationship between generalized trust and trust in political institutions. They argue that "people's confidence in public institutions is only weakly associated with generalized trust, and its associations with voluntary activism is even weaker" (Newton and Norris 2000, 64; cf. Newton 1999).

At the aggregate level Newton and Norris find more empirical support for Putnam's theory. In a comparative analysis of countries they report strong correlations between generalized trust and trust in political institutions. They therefore conclude that the societal effects of social capital are more important for trust in political institutions than the individual effects: "The overall pattern confirms our hypothesis that the relationship between generalized trust and institutional confidence operates largely at the societal rather than at the individual level" (Newton and Norris 2000, 71). In the introduction to the volume in which Newton and Norris's article is published, Putnam, Pharr, and Dalton (2000, 26) explain this finding by arguing that voluntary associations function as "rainmakers." Putnam et al. argue that the rain produced by civic engagement and generalized trust not only affects people who are active and trusting but also affects people who are neither active in voluntary associations nor trusting of other people. Generalized trust and civic engagement are, in other words, assumed to have societal consequences that cannot be reduced to individual effects.

In the literature we find several clues on how the occurrence of these societal effects might be explained. Most important is the argument that civic engagement can improve the performance of political institutions. Newton and Norris maintain that the cooperative culture of a trusting society "helps create strong, effective, and successful social organizations and institutions, including political groups and governmental institutions in which people can invest their confidence" (Newton and Norris 2000, 60). In this respect, voluntary associations can be an important asset for the functioning of a political system. Lipset summarizes the main effects of voluntary associations: "they inhibit the state or any single source of private power from dominating all political resources, they are a source of new opinions, they can be the means of communicating ideas, particularly opposition ideas, to a large section of the citizenry, they train men in political skills and so help to increase the level of interest and participation in politics" (Lipset 1959, 52; Boix and Posner 1996). If voluntary associations really function this way, this would imply that in areas with more dense social networks, increased government performance will give citizens more reason to trust their political institutions, whether they themselves are members or not. Following this reasoning, this would imply that voluntary associations do create generalized trust and other attitudes, but that they do so as a pure collective good, to the benefit of both members and nonmembers alike.

The aim of this chapter is to examine this theory more thoroughly than was the case in the macrolevel analysis by Newton and Norris (2000).

Their method does not allow them to disentangle individual and aggregate effects of voluntary associations and civic engagement. Robinson (1950) argues that aggregate correlations cannot be interpreted as evidence for the existence of an individual level effect. Robinson's work on ecological fallacy suggests that if a correlation is found between aggregate levels of generalized and political trust, this does not necessarily mean that on an individual level, the same relation will be found between political and generalized trust. The observation of aggregate level effects does not allow us any interference about the occurrence of microlevel effects: "an ecological correlation is almost certainly not equal to its corresponding individual correlation" (Robinson 1950, 357). This implies that just analyzing aggregate data sets and correlations on an aggregate level does not provide us with any information about the microlinkages between, for example, generalized and political trust and civic engagement. This can be highly problematic since most variance in attitudinal variables is found at the individual rather than at the societal level. My earlier research showed that not more than ten percent of the total variance of trust in political institutions can be attributed to aggregate effects (Van der Meer 2000). Consequently, if at the individual level within all or most macro-units the members of voluntary associations are slightly more trusting, this may lead to an impressive correlation between membership of voluntary associations and generalized trust at the aggregate level. In this case, however, in reality the relation would run purely through the individual level and would not be produced by aggregate level effects.

Therefore we cannot rely on a simple aggregate level analysis to disentangle individual and societal relations between generalized trust, civic engagement and trust in political institutions. In our effort to verify whether a rainmaker effect actually occurs, we will also perform an aggregate analysis but will limit our analyses to respondents who are not active in voluntary associations themselves or who do not trust other people. If even among nonmembers a significant relation is found between the density of networks in their region and their trust levels, this points in the direction of the occurrence of an aggregate "rainmaker" effect. Individual level effects are ruled out in this type of analysis, because the respondents themselves are not even members of these associations; we only know that among the neighbors of these nonmembers more people will be a member of a voluntary association. If Putnam's rainmaker indeed produces rain, aggregate levels of generalized trust and civic engagement should affect even people who do not join or trust themselves. If these effects are not found it should be concluded that Putnam's rainmaker produces fog rather than rain, which makes it more difficult to see the weaknesses in the concept of social capital. These weaknesses would explain why strong correlations are observed at the aggregate level only.

This chapter seeks to examine Putnam's rainmaker theory. The first section outlines the theoretical model that is examined, while in the second section the research design is developed. Afterward the operationalization of the relevant variables is explained, and the final section discusses the results of the analyses.

SOCIAL CAPITAL THEORY

The theoretical model of the analysis is presented in Figure 7.1. The model shows that, according to social capital theory, reciprocal relations exist between civic engagement, generalized trust and trust in political institutions (see also Stolle this volume). Each of these relations will be discussed in this section. First, it is hypothesized that civic engagement influences the level of generalized trust. Putnam maintains that knowledge of the trustworthiness of other people will be more easily available if civic engagement is more intense, because networks of civic engagement can spread reputations of people. Consequently, Putnam argues, networks of civic engagement increase the costs of defecting in a cooperative transaction. As he puts it: "Networks of civic engagement increase the potential costs to a defector in any individual transaction. Opportunism puts at risk the benefits he expects to receive from all the other transactions in which he is currently engaged" (Putnam 1993, 173).

On the other hand, Putnam also argues that generalized trust may increase the level of civic engagement, since in a trusting society people will join voluntary associations more often (Putnam 2000, 136). It can therefore be assumed that the relationship between civic engagement and generalized trust is reciprocal. Since trust and civic engagement are related to each other in this way, Putnam claims that vicious and virtuous circles exist. In the vicious circle both generalized trust and civic engagement decline, which is the feature of a society with low levels of social capital. In the virtuous circle generalized trust and civic engagement increase, which is the characteristic of societies with high levels of social capital.

Second, Putnam's theory implies that both generalized trust and civic engagement influence government performance. The argument is that associations and generalized trust improve the articulation and aggregation of interests. In a democratic society politicians will attempt to realize popular demands as much as possible to maximize their votes; therefore, the extent to which interests are articulated and aggregated partly determines the extent to which government is responsive (Boix and Posner 1996). Moreover, a strong and independent civil society can put pressure on government not only to implement responsive policies but also to work effectively.

Third, civic engagement may improve the functioning of society in general. Associations may provide all kind of services to help people. These societal effects ensure that people, regardless of the extent to which they actually are involved in associations, will trust their institutions to a greater extent if they live in a democracy with a large number of associations.

It can be assumed that the relation between social capital and trust in political institutions also is reciprocal. Levi stresses that social capital not only influences political institutions, but that political institutions may also influence the level of social capital: "governments also may be a source of social capital" (Levi 1996, 50, see also Uslaner as well as Rothstein and Stolle this volume). First, Levi maintains that government may influence the level of generalized trust. By protecting property and the importance of merit (rather than nepotism and favoritism) governments may give people more reason to trust each other. Brehm and Rahn (1997, 1014) hypothesize that institutions may provide "reassurance that defectors will not go unpunished." This would imply that because of the presence of an effective third-party enforcement (the state apparatus), citizens indeed have more reason to develop trust in their fellow citizens.

Second, Levi stresses that government may influence the level of civic engagement. As a negative example, she points to the fact that "today's politicians are more likely to target particular populations than encourage large-scale doorbelling and organization" (Levi 1996, 49), and therefore they may be responsible for a decline in civic engagement. Kriesi et al. (1995) also link civic engagement to political factors. They argue that the political opportunity structure of a country determines the extent to which citizens will engage in voluntary associations and social movements.

RESEARCH DESIGN

In this chapter the rainmaker effects of social capital are examined. The theory under scrutiny focuses upon the rainmaker effect of two aspects of social capital (civic engagement and generalized trust) upon trust in political institutions. Attention is also paid to the relation within the concept of social capital, namely between civic

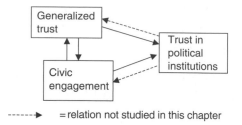

Figure 7.1 Theoretical model

engagement and generalized trust. The rainmaker effect of trust in political institutions upon the two elements of social capital is not examined as this is not crucial to Putnam's rainmaker theory. Putnam's theory focuses on the effects of social capital upon democracy rather than the other way around. Therefore, only four of the six causal arrows from Figure 7.1 will be examined: (1) the impact of civic engagement upon generalized trust, (2) the impact of generalized trust upon civic engagement, (3) the impact of civic engagement upon trust in political institutions and (4) the impact of trust in political institutions upon generalized trust.

Since aggregate effects are examined, we will rely on aggregated and individual level data for our analysis. A selection of data from the large database of the World Values Survey of 1990 is examined. In order to ensure comparativeness, only Western democracies are selected. It can be expected that comparisons could be hampered by the fact that Eastern and Central Europe, and the countries of the former Soviet Union, face the challenge of installing democratic government after a long period of autocratic rule, while many developing countries have to deal with ethnic conflicts and endemic poverty. Therefore one should expect different effects of social capital in these contexts (Letki 2001), and only Western countries were taken into account (see Appendix 1).

Within nations many differences exist as well. Regions, towns and even neighborhoods are known to have their own culture. To examine relations between aspects of cultures, some of these differences are also taken into account by examining regions from different countries, thus allowing us to examine the regional level of government, often referred to as "meso government" (Larsson et al. 1999; Sharpe et al. 1993). To ensure comparativeness, only European regions were selected. Our effort to examine regions was hampered by some practical problems. First, for some regions a sufficient number of respondents was not available. This is particularly problematic since most samples from the World Values Survey are door-to-door cluster samples. This means that a sample may be representative for a certain country, but that it is not a random sample on a regional level. No information about sampling techniques on the regional level is available, and in order to be on the safe side, I decided to include only regions for which more than forty respondents are available. Second, for some countries the regional code is either missing or does not correspond to the level of mesogovernment. Regions from these countries are not taken into account either. In spite of these omissions this selection still results in a database of sixty-four regions and covers respondents from a diverse group of regions in European democracies. The regions are listed in Appendix 2.

The aim of the analysis is to examine the aggregate effects of generalized trust and civic engagement. However, an ordinary analysis of aggregated data is not sufficient to examine these effects because relations that are found in such analyses could also be caused by individual-level effects. If, for example, within all countries or within all regions members of voluntary associations trust each other to a greater extent, one will also find a strong correlation between membership and generalized trust at the aggregate level. Therefore the analysis should control for individual-level effects. In the case of the impact of civic engagement upon generalized trust, this is done by examining the impact of aggregate levels of civic engagement upon generalized trust only among people who do not belong to any voluntary association themselves. The same logic is applied when the other effects are examined, where we examine only the respondents giving a negative answer to the generalized trust question. The empirical questions are, therefore:

(1) Are nonmembers more trusting when they live in areas with dense associational networks?
(2) Are nontrusters more involved in associations when they live in high-trusting areas?
(3) Are nonmembers more trusting in institutions when they live in regions with dense associational networks?
(4) Are nontrusters more trusting in institutions when they live in areas with high generalized trust?

MEASUREMENT ISSUES

Before the results of the analyses can be presented, the different concepts should be operationalized. Descriptive statistics for the different variables and the scales of the operationalizations are presented in Appendix 3.

Trust in Political Institutions

Trust in political institutions is measured as the extent to which the legal system, parliament and the civil service are trusted. These institutions cover the important political institutions of a democratic society. In order to make the interpretation clearer, the scale is recoded so that it ranges from 0 to 100. This four-item scale can be considered as reliable, with a Cronbach's alpha of .76.

Generalized Trust

Levi (1996) argues that generalized trust applies to situations in which there is reason to doubt the trustworthiness of other people. In this situation, Levi maintains, people with high levels of trust will show a tendency to invest less in an effort to scrutinize the trustworthiness of people with whom they cooperate: "a trusting individual is one who makes a low personal investment in monitoring and enforcing the compliance of the individual(s) with whom she has made a contract from which she believes she will benefit" (Levi 1996, 47). According to Putnam this confidence can have various sources. First, it can be based upon one's own experience with people with whom one cooperates. However, more important is the case in which people trust other people who they did not know before, what is known as generalized trust (Putnam 2000, 136; Yamagishi and Yamagishi 1994).

To measure this form of trust, the traditional generalized trust question is being used, asking whether "generally speaking most people can be trusted." Generalized trust is defined as the percentage of the population agreeing with the statement that most people can be trusted. On an individual level, the nontrusters in our analyses are the respondents who have given a negative answer to this question, stating that you can't be too careful in dealing with strangers. Putnam argues that this indicator measures the experiences people have in dealing with other people: "It is reasonable to assume that in each case these patterns reflect actual experience rather than different psychic predispositions to distrust" (Putnam 2000, 138). However, other authors see generalized trust more as a moral value or belief, regardless of the actual behavior of other people (Uslaner this volume).

Civic Engagement

Within Western societies, a great variety of voluntary associations can be found. Examples are sport organizations, interest groups, NGOs, religious associations, political parties and trade unions. It is to be expected, however, that not all kinds of associations will have the same effect on social capital (Mayer, Wollebæk and Selle, Hooghe this volume), and therefore a distinction has to be introduced between various kinds of associations. Some authors have introduced a distinction between informal and more formal associations and between associations of which people are only "checkbook members" and associations in which people interact more closely with each other (Van Deth 1998; Maloney 1999). In this analysis, however, we will use the distinction that has been made by Van Deth and Kreuter (1998). They differentiate between membership of new political movements, organizations for welfare and traditional interest groups. New political movements are organizations working for the environment, for animal rights, for the Third World and for peace. Organizations for social welfare are religious groups, women's groups and organizations for social welfare. Finally, interest groups are professional organizations and political parties and groups. For each of these groups the average number of memberships is calculated. In our operationalization both the notion of "belonging to," as the notion of "doing unpaid work for" were coded as memberships. We collapsed these two dimensions into one membership variable in order to ensure that different understandings of volunteering and membership do not distort the analysis.

OTHER RELEVANT VARIABLES

Besides the theoretical variables, several other variables may influence the different components of social capital theory and may distort the analysis, and therefore they should also be taken into account. In the analysis of countries these control variables could not be included, because not enough observations are available. However, in the analysis of regions these variables can and will be included in the analysis. Three variables are examined. First of all, economic factors are expected to be relevant. According to Lipset: "The more well to do a nation the greater the chances that it will sustain democracy" (Lipset 1959, 49–50; 1993; Diamond 1992). Lipset's argument is that economic modernization enlarges the middle class, diminishes class differences, increases the level of education and strengthens civil society. These consequences of economic modernization may influence the different aspects of social capital. Therefore an economic variable is included in the analysis. This variable is income per head of the population as reported by Eurostat for 1990 for each region separately.

Cultural theories assume that some cultures consist of enduring beliefs that are conducive to good government (La Porta et al. 1998). An important aspect of culture is the difference between Catholic and Protestant cultures. The argument is that a Protestant culture is favorable for democratic government. Putnam argues for example that in Italy the Catholic Church has adverse effects on trust (Putnam 1993). A quantitative analysis of La Porta and his colleagues (1998) suggests that countries with a Catholic culture have on average less efficient and more corrupt governments, smaller government consumption, smaller public sector employment and less democracy (La Porta et al. 1998, 32). These factors may influence both the level of social capital and trust in political institutions. Therefore, a dummy variable is included to distinguish between dominant Catholic and other countries or regions. Regions with more than 50 percent Catholics received a score of 1, all others were coded 0.

Finally, it could be argued that the research design influences the analysis. The fact that some regions come from federalist states, while others come from more unitary states may distort the analysis. It may for example be argued that German "Länder" are different, because they have their own and rather strong government. To control for the effect of federalism Lijphart's (1999, 189) measure of federalism was included in the analysis. This index ranges from 1 in unitary and centralized countries like Ireland or Portugal to 5 in federal and decentralized countries like Switzerland and Germany.

All of these variables were introduced in regression analyses, with first the countries and second the regions as units. The analysis was limited to, respectively, the respondents who are not a member of any of these associations and those who have given a negative answer to the generalized trust question.

RESULTS OF THE ANALYSIS

Social Capital: Civic Engagement and Generalized Trust

The operationalization of the variables enables us to examine the rainmaker effects within the different aspects of social capital (civic engagement and generalized trust). First, the effects of civic engagement upon generalized trust are examined. Does the presence of new political movements, welfare organizations or interest groups have an effect on the trust levels of those who are not members? (Table 7.1).

It appears that in European regions participation in new political movements and welfare organizations is related to generalized trust among people who do not belong to these associations. In regions where more people are active in these associations, generalized trust levels are higher, also among people who do not belong to these associations. Interest groups have a comparable rainmaker effect, which is also observed in the analysis of countries. Although we are estimating rather limited models, these results would lead us to the conclusion that participation in at least some kinds of voluntary associations indeed has some rainmaker effects on the generalized trust levels of nonmembers.

The second question we want to investigate is whether generalized trust has a rainmaker effect on civic engagement. Are the respondents who say that you can't be too careful in dealing with others more likely to participate in associations if more of their neighbors and fellow citizens do have high trust levels? The answer to this question is again positive, at least for some voluntary associations (Table 7.2). In the analysis of countries it appears that people who do not trust other people are more likely to join interest groups if they live in a country where generalized trust is higher. In the analysis of European regions it can be concluded that people without generalized trust join more new political movements and more welfare organizations if they live in a region where generalized trust is greater.

Social Capital and Trust in Political Institutions

After examining the rainmaker effects between the two aspects of social capital, the rainmaker effects of civic engagement and generalized trust on trust in political institutions is examined. The third relation we investigate is the effect of civic engagement on trust in political institutions, each time for respondents who themselves do not belong to any of the associations (Table 7.1). Here too, we find significant results: On the level of the regions, organizations for welfare and interest groups influence trust in political institutions among nonmembers. On the other hand, it also appears that membership of new political movements is not related to the level of trust in political institutions among nonmembers. Both within regions as within

Table 7.1 Generalized trust and trust in political institutions of nonmembers

	Generalized trust						Trust in political institutions					
	Countries (n = 19)			Regions (n = 64)			Countries (n = 19)			Regions (n = 64)		
	1	2	3	1	2	3	1	2	3	1	2	3
New political movements	.26			.40**			−.04			.18		
Organizations for welfare		.01			.52**			.24			.41**	
Interest groups			.48*			.27*			.35			.29*
Trust in political institutions	.56*	.63*	.32	.05	−.14	.03						
Generalized trust							.62**	.51*	.36	.03	−.14	.01
Income				.06	.02	.08				−.27*	−.28*	−.34**
Catholic culture				−.11	−.14	−.20				−.29*	−.19	−.28*
Federalism				−.09	−.01	−.13				.51**	.46**	.42**
Adjusted r²	.45	.33	.46	.16	.22	.10	.28	.31	.36	.33	.38	.33

Note: Regression analysis of the generalized trust level of nonmembers, for countries and regions. Entries are standardized coefficients. *: p < .05, **: p < .01 (one-tailed for theoretical variables, two-tailed for other variables).
Column 1: New political movements.
Column 2: Organizations for welfare.
Column 3: Interest groups.
Source: World Values Survey, 1990.

Table 7.2 Civic engagement and trust in political institutions among distrusters

	Civic engagement						Trust in political institutions					
	Countries (n = 19)			Regions (n = 64)			Countries (n = 19)			Regions (n = 64)		
	1	2	3	1	2	3	1	2	3	1	2	3
Generalized trust	.45	.02	.50**	.30**	.39**	.02	.57*	.42*	.21	-.12	-.27**	-.11
Trust in political institutions	-.04	.41	.28	.18	.46**	.25*						
New political movements	-.12						-.12			.22		
Organizations for welfare								.32			.53**	
Interest groups									.42			.32**
Income				.20	.09	.36				-.31*	-.28**	-.35**
Catholic culture				-.22	-.10	-.23				-.23	-.16	-.22
Federalism				.03	-.05	.10				.52**	.46**	.47**
Adjusted r^2	.08	.07	.44	.32	.46	.35	.18	.28	.26	.30	.46	.34

Note: Regression analysis of the membership of three types of voluntary associations, among respondents with a negative score on generalized trust. Entries are standardized coefficients. *: $p < .05$, **: $p < .01$ (one-tailed for theoretical variables, two-tailed for other variables).

Column 1: New political movements.

Column 2: Organizations for welfare.

Column 3: Interest groups.

Source: World Values Survey, 1990.

countries the coefficient for new political movements is not statistically significant.

Finally, it is examined whether generalized trust influences the level of trust in political institutions among people who are not trusting themselves (Table 7.2). In the analysis of countries, aggregate generalized trust levels do influence the level of trust in political institutions of people who are not trusting themselves, except when the density of interest organizations is taken into account. In the analysis of regions, generalized trust influences the level of trust in political institutions of people who do not trust other people, only if memberships of organizations for welfare are also taken into account. This would imply that this fourth relation is considerably weaker than the three relations we studied earlier.

DISCUSSION

In this chapter the rainmaker theory of social capital was examined. Our main research question was whether civic engagement has aggregate effects on generalized trust and trust in political institutions that cannot be explained by the sum of individual level effects of these variables. On the country level, most of the expected relations between civic engagement and generalized trust did not materialize or were not significant. Only the density of some kinds of associations is associated with higher generalized trust levels among people who are not members of these associations. At the level of the regions, we did encounter more conclusive evidence. Here, the density of all three types of associations was positively associated with generalized trust among nonmembers. Furthermore, in high-trust regions, even the distrusters are more likely to join an association.

Second, we turn to the rainmaker effect of civic engagement and social trust on trust in political institutions. The rainmaker effect of social trust on trust in political institutions was not found in all analyses. The presence of welfare associations and interest groups however, seems to be linked to higher levels of trust in political institutions among nonmembers. For most of the relations we examined, on the regional level, we indeed found some evidence for the occurrence of a rainmaker effect. We have to include a warning with our findings, nevertheless: The number of cases is relatively limited, and the models we estimated remain rather thin. Therefore, we have to consider the possibility that any correlation we have found does not point in the direction of a direct causal link (i.e., a rainmaker effect) but could also be the consequence of another factor that was not included in the analysis. Some regions, for some reason yet unknown to us, or at least not detected in this analysis, might simply be higher on trust and participation, without the two necessarily reinforcing one another.

In the introduction of this chapter we asked ourselves why voluntary associations would have this rainmaker effect on generalized trust and trust in political institutions. Our suggestion was that civic engagement improves the performance of government and therefore gives people more reason to trust their political institutions. Therefore the effect of civic engagement upon trust in political institutions does not work directly, but indirectly. Not only people who join associations profit from the improvement of government performance, but also people who do not join voluntary associations: Voluntary associations lead to more responsive governments, but this responsiveness is a collective good. Earlier research seems to suggest that civic engagement is strongly related to less corruption, while no correlation is found between civic engagement and government expenditure (Van der Meer 2001). This finding only leads us to numerous new questions. Most importantly, the question is: What aspects of government performance are influenced by what kind of voluntary associations and why? Moreover, it is also suggested that different associations may have different effects upon government. However, if the occurrence of a rainmaker effect should be confirmed in other analyses, this would mean that the relationship between structural and attitudinal components of social capital should not be studied at the individual level. We do not expect to find significant differences between members and nonmembers, who benefit alike from the collective goods produced by voluntary associations and networks of civic engagements. This is an important insight, because the evidence presented by Putnam (1993) in his study on civic traditions in modern Italy, is situated mostly on an aggregate level. Thus far, however, most of his critics have tried to put his theory to the test using microlevel data. If, however, the governments of the northern Italian regions are really as responsive as he claims because of the presence of dense associational networks, the inhabitants of that region have every reason to trust their regional governments, whether they are integrated into these networks or not.

APPENDIX 1.   THE COUNTRIES

Austria
Belgium
Canada
Denmark
France
Iceland
Ireland
Italy

Japan
Netherlands
Norway
Portugal
Spain
Sweden
Switzerland
United Kingdom

APPENDIX 2.   THE REGIONS

Austria
Burgenland
Lower Austria
Upper Austria
Salzburg
Styria
Tyrol
Voralberg
Vienna

Belgium
Brussels
Flanders
Wallonia

Germany
Baden-Württemberg
Bayern
Berlin
Bremen
Hamburg
Hessen
Niedersachsen
Nordrhein-Westfalen
Rheinland Pfalz
Saarland
Schleswig
Holstein

Italy
Piemonte
Liguria
Lombardia

Trentino-Alto
Adige
Veneto
Friuli-Venezia
Giulia
Emilia Romagna
Toscana
Umbria
Marche
Lazio
Abruzzo
Campania
Puglia
Calabria
Sicilia

Netherlands
Groningen
Overijsel
Gelderland
Utrecht
Noord-Holland
Zuid-Holland
Zeeland
Noord-Brabant
Limburg

Portugal
Continental Portugal
Acores
Madeira

Spain
Andalucia
Aragon
Asturias
Baleares
Basque Country
Canary Islands
Cantabria
Castilla Leon
Castilla la Mancha
Catalonia
Extremadura
Galicia
Madrid region
Murcia
Navarra
Rioja
Valencia

United Kingdom
England
Northern Ireland
Wales
Scotland

APPENDIX 3. DESCRIPTIVE STATISTICS AND SCALES

	Scale	Mean	Standard deviation	Range
Countries				
Trust in political institutions	Average score on a scale that ranges from zero to one hundred	52	5	41–59
Generalized trust	Percentage of population that says that most people can be trusted	44	13	22–66
Memberships of new political movements	Average number of organizations people belong to or do voluntary work for	.15	.12	.03–.56
Memberships of organizations for social welfare	Average number of organizations people belong to or do voluntary work for	.30	.19	.09–.74
Memberships of interest groups	Average number of organizations people belong to or do voluntary work for	.18	.09	.05–.30
Regions				
Trust in political institutions	Average score on a scale that ranges from zero to hundred	48	6	36–66
Generalized trust	Percentage of population that says that most people can be trusted	38	12	18–66
Memberships of new political movements	Average number of organizations people belong to or do voluntary work for	.14	.17	.00–.75
Memberships of organizations for social welfare	Average number of organizations people belong to or do voluntary work for	.24	.19	.03–.87
Memberships of interest groups	Average number of organizations people belong to or do voluntary work for	.12	.08	.02–.38

Source: World Values Survey, 1990.

REFERENCES

Boix, C. and D. Posner (1996). "Making Social Capital Work: A Review of Robert Putnam's *Making Democracy Work: Civic Traditions in Modern Italy.*" Working Paper Series 96(4). Cambridge: Harvard University.

Brehm, J. and W. Rahn (1997). "Individual-level Evidence for the Causes and Consequences of Social Capital." *American Journal of Political Science* 41(3), 999–1023.

Diamond, L. (1992). "Economic Development and Democracy Reconsidered." *American Behavioral Scientist* 35(4–5), 450–499.

Kim, U. (1994). "Individualism and Collectivism. Conceptual Clarification and Elaboration." In U. Kim et al. (ed.), *Individualism and Collectivism. Theory, Method and Applications.* London: Sage.

Kriesi, H., R. Koopmans, J. W. Duyvendak and M. Giugni (1995). *New Social Movements in Western Europe.* Minneapolis: University of Minnesota Press.

Larsson, T., K. Nomden and F. Petiteville (eds., 1999). *The Intermediate Level of Government in European States.* Maastricht: European Institute of Public Administration.

Letki, N. (2001). "Explaining Political Participation in East-Central Europe: The Role of Social Capital." Paper presented at the 97th Annual Meeting of the American Political Science Associations, San Francisco, August 30–September 2, 2001.

Levi, M. (1996). "Social and Unsocial Capital: A Review Essay of Robert Putnam's *Making Democracy Work.*" *Politics and Society* 24(1), 45–55.

Lijphart, A. (1999). *Patterns of Democracy.* New Haven: Yale University Press.

Lipset, S. M. (1959). *Political Man. The Social Bases of Politics.* New York: Doubleday.

Lipset, S. M. (1993). "A Comparative Analysis of the Social Requisites of Democracy." *International Social Sciences Journal* 45(2), 149–175.

Maloney, W. (1999). "Contracting Out the Participation Function: Social Capital and Checkbook Participation." pp. 108–199. In J. Van Deth et al. (eds.), *Social Capital and European Democracy.* London: Routledge.

Newton, K. (1999). "Social and Political Trust in Established Democracies." pp. 169–197. In P. Norris (ed.), *Critical Citizens. Global Support for Democratic Governance.* Oxford: Oxford University Press.

Newton, K. and P. Norris (2000). "Confidence in Public Institutions: Faith, Culture or Performance?" pp. 52–72. In S. Pharr and R. Putnam (eds.), *Disaffected Democracies.* Princeton: Princeton University Press.

Porta, R. La et al. (1998). *The Quality of Government.* NBER Working papers series 6727.

Putnam, R. (1993). *Making Democracy Work.* Princeton: Princeton University Press

Putnam, R. (2000). *Bowling Alone.* New York: Simon and Schuster.

Putnam, R., S. Pharr and R. J. Dalton (2000). "Introduction: What's Troubling the Trilateral Democracies?" pp. 3–30. In S. Pharr and R. Putnam (eds.), *Disaffected Democracies*. Princeton: Princeton University Press.

Robinson, W. (1950). "Ecological Correlations and the Behavior of Individuals." *American Sociological Review* 15, 351–357.

Sharpe, L. (ed., 1993). *The Rise of Meso Government in Europe*. London: Sage.

Stolle, D. (2001). "Clubs and Congregations: The Benefits of Joining an Association." pp. 202–244. In K. Cook (ed.), *Trust in Society*. New York: Russell Sage Foundation.

Van der Meer, J. (2000). "Communitarian Political Thought and Political Confidence. A Multilevel Analysis." Paper presented at the ECPR joint sessions, Copenhagen, April 14–19, 2000.

Van der Meer, J. (2001). "Interveniërende Variabelen voor het Verband tussen Maatschappelijke Participatie en Evaluaties van het Politieke Systeem." Conference paper presented at the SISWO conference, Antwerp, May 18, 2001.

Van Deth, J. (1998). "Political Involvement and Social Capital." Paper presented at the 94th Annual Meeting of the American Political Science Association, Boston, September 3–6, 1998.

Van Deth, J. and F. Kreuter (1998). "Membership of Voluntary Associations." pp. 135–155. In J. Van Deth (ed.), *Comparative Politics: The Problem of Equivalence*. London: Routledge.

Yamagishi, T. and M. Yamagishi (1994). "Trust and Commitment in the United States and Japan." *Motivation and Emotion* 18(2), 129–166.

CHAPTER 8

A TALE OF TWO CITIES: LOCAL PATTERNS OF SOCIAL CAPITAL

Joep de Hart and Paul Dekker

INTRODUCTION

An outsider entering the village of Asten in the south of the Netherlands has a good chance of not being treated with suspicion. The majority of the local population believe that "in general, most people can be trusted." By contrast, a visitor traveling to the districts of Wielwijk or Crabbehof in the town of Dordrecht (to the south of Rotterdam) will have to overcome more in the way of social barriers. Two-thirds of the inhabitants of these districts have formed the opinion that "you can't be too careful in dealing with other people." And there are other differences between Asten and these Dordrecht districts. In Asten, for example, people seek contact with other local residents easily and generally regard them as helpful. In Dordrecht this is true for only a minority of the inhabitants. Two-thirds of the inhabitants of Asten are members of an association, compared with just one-third of Dordrecht inhabitants. Attitudes to politics differ as well: In Asten the government is regarded as a reliable source of information on important social and political issues by half of the population, compared with a quarter of the population of Dordrecht. According to the survey from which we take these data, 16 percent of the citizens of Asten and 38 percent of those of Dordrecht think that whatever decisions the government makes, they are of no use for everyday life.

Perceptions of local community also differ between the two places. Eighty-four percent of the respondents in Asten feel that everybody who lives there is a member of the local community, compared to 66 percent in the Dordrecht districts. In Asten nearly 75 percent of the respondents state they feel a bond with the people of their street or district and another 75 percent disagree with the proposition that it is difficult to make contact with these; this is compared to 45 percent and 48 percent in Dordrecht.

The fact that such local differences of social solidarity (Putnam 1993, 107) exist within a small and densely populated country like the Netherlands might come as a surprise. At least most political scientists prefer to concentrate on analyses of representative national samples of individuals, and they tend to leave the local diversity to journalists, even though lots of research on social capital is inspired by the regional comparisons Putnam (1993) drew in *Making Democracy Work*. In recent years "social capital" has become a golden blend of positive attitudes, prosocial behavior, civic norms and cooperative networks. This is particularly true for political scientists, who see "social capital" as a modern version of a "civic culture" (i.e., an aggregation of individual attitudes). Our aim in this chapter is to align with the original (sociological) notion, which spells out that social capital is embedded in social contexts (Foley et al. 2001). Different social settings might imply different restrictions and possibilities for developing and maintaining bonds of solidarity, forms of cooperation and mutual helping behavior (reciprocity), voluntary organizations and mutual trust. As in the other contributions in this volume, we focus on specific societal interaction settings to learn more about the generation of social capital and the interrelatedness of social capital and political and social institutions (cf. the introductory chapter of Hooghe and Stolle in this volume). To get a grip on the complexities and effects of social capital, we focus on two "most different" localities with roughly the same population size in one country. We hope this will prove a fruitful way to investigate social capital under different cultural and institutional conditions. Our selection of two places is not based on a conviction that delineated localization of the residential setting is self-evidently the most important social setting for the study of social capital. Limiting the study to the local level does, however, have the advantage that a society's social capital can be linked to the local social institutions.

The empirical exploration of local settings and sources of social capital is the main undertaking in this chapter. For that reason we comply here with the approach of social capital that Robert Putnam took, without long theoretical considerations or listing caveats. Putnam's social capital refers to "features of social organization, such as trust, norms, and networks, that can improve the efficiency of society by facilitating coordinated actions" (Putnam 1993, 167) or to "connections among individuals, social networks and the norms of reciprocity and trustworthiness that arise from them" (Putnam 2000, 19). Social capital is about capacities for cooperation that are embedded in social relations. Although negative forms and "dark sides" of social capital are acknowledged, Putnam's empirical analyses focus on "forms of social capital that, generally speaking, serve civic ends" (Putnam 1995, 665) and that have benefits for all members of communities, the larger society and for politics. This social capital is primarily found in "networks of civic engagement" (1993, 171) and is closely related to what some have called "civic virtue" (2000, 19).

For the purposes of this chapter we will admit a wide range of indicators for this conception of social capital. Our first interest is to explore the relationships between these various indicators: Do they suggest one social capital complex or several clusters of variables? Are the patterns similar in the two localities? For example, we might expect that cultural and structural aspects of social capital build a grand syndrome that we find in various localities, at varying degrees. If this was true, we could distinguish localities purely on the basis of different levels of social capital: Some localities have high and others have low social capital, but there are no qualitative differences in the composition of social capital. Another scenario would be that localities can be distinguished more on the basis of the specific character of social capital. The local social composition or local characteristics might either relate to a participatory versus passive or trusting versus distrusting culture.

Second, the two locations analyzed in our study differ not only in terms of their social capital but also in terms of the composition of the population as regards relevant personal and background characteristics, such as age structure and the average level of education and prosperity. The social, political and moral perceptions of people also matter. Ross et al. (2001) find that mistrust develops among individuals with few resources who live in disadvantaged neighborhoods, and that the living conditions in these neighborhoods increase residents' perceptions of powerlessness, which in turn amplify the effect of neighborhood disorder on mistrust. For a better understanding of the character of local differences in social capital, it is important to investigate how much of the local diversity remains after adjusting for effects of individual backgrounds and beliefs.

Third, social and cultural factors do not only have an impact on social capital via composition or aggregation effects (a large number of individuals with low levels of efficacy results in a low level of social capital in the neighborhood) but also through interaction and contextual effects (the large number of individuals and the environment as such may generate a culture of fatalism etc.). Our data do not allow for multilevel analyses or other statistical investigations into the cultural factors, but we can try to explore them by listening to what citizens tell about their neighborhood. Summarizing, our aim is to investigate

• local patterns and levels of social capital;
• the impact of individual differences on local social capital; and
• contextual and cultural correlates of differences in local social capital.

The main source of individual data is the survey "Civil Society and Volunteering 1997," conducted in 1996–97 (De Hart 2002), with a national sample ($n = 2,320$) and samples in four localities, two of which are used in this chapter: the two Dordrecht neighborhoods ($n = 135$) and the municipality of Asten ($n = 138$). Besides survey data, we have other sources of information about the two locations at our disposal: statistical municipal and neighborhood data, observations during the local council election campaigns of 1998, and follow-up interviews and focus group discussions with some survey respondents and active citizens. In this chapter, we concentrate on individual and small group data from our survey and focus groups. However, our respondents do not act in a social vacuum. We first give an impression of the local social setting, on the basis of additional data: the location of the two places; some population characteristics; the facilities, clubs and associations that are available; and the level of political commitment.

ASTEN AND DORDRECHT: FIRST PICTURES OF THE SCENE

This section characterizes Asten and Dordrecht (where we investigated two neighborhoods, but which we will henceforth simply refer to "Dordrecht") on the basis of expert interviews, observations, municipal statistics and some survey results. Asten lies in the southeast of the Netherlands, in the province of Noord-Brabant. The three church towers of Asten and its two parish villages Heusden and Ommel are visible from afar in the flat landscape. A church stands in the center of each of the three villages. These centers form a hub for social activities and are also the places where the supermarkets and bars are situated. The Catholic religion dominates in this part of the Netherlands. The percentage of nonchurch members in the municipality, like the percentage of people who never go to church, is far below the national average.

Asten is a rural municipality covering an area of approximately 7,000 hectares, with a population of 16,000 in 1998.[1] The traditional single breadwinner household with children dominates here. There are few single people living alone and few members of ethnic minorities (3 percent). The level of basic amenities (primary schools, grocery stores, public transport stops) is more than adequate. Nearly 70 percent of all houses are owner occupied. Most accommodations have been built after the seventies and feature detached houses, duplex houses or row houses. Over one-third of the population has an income level above average (which corresponds with the national figure).

The inhabitants of the three villages appear content with their neighborhood and their home-loving existence. The vast majority have no desire whatsoever to move, and the turnover rate of residents is low. There is a reasonable level of employment. Young people from all over the region partake in the Asten nightlife over the weekends. Associations play an important role in all three villages making up the municipality of Asten. It seems that almost everyone is a member of at least one association.

The municipality of Dordrecht has a population of almost 200,000 and is divided into ten districts. Two adjacent districts, Wielwijk and Crabbehof, form the subject of our study. They are situated close to the old center of the town and house a total of 13,000 inhabitants. Wielwijk lies next to the large industrial and port area that surrounds the northwestern side of the town. It is regularly in the news, in a negative sense: drug nuisance, crime, vandalism, lack of safety. The residents of the post-war neighborhood of Wielwijk come from all parts of the country, including the far north and east of the Netherlands.

A relatively large number of people of foreign origin live in the district (23 percent).[2] The unemployment rate has risen steeply in recent years. Low-income categories are over-represented in both districts; nearly half the population has a level of income below average. Wielwijk and Crabbehof have a substantial lower proportion of families with children than Asten (33 percent compared to 55 percent); the proportion of singles is twice as high. Over three-quarters of the residents live in rented accommodations, which predominantly date from the sixties or before. Most of these are blocks of flats. Policy documents talk of social isolation. The overall recorded crime rate in Wielwijk has risen by over 10 percent in recent years.[3] Local surveys point to an increase in perceived lack of safety, and also reflect the growing degeneration of the neighborhood, which the residents of both districts experience. The level of basic amenities in the two districts is not high. According to the local Roman

Catholic priest, his church still plays a role in the local community, but this role is not as great as in the past and the rate of active church participation is very low. The ministers of the local Protestant churches indicate the same appraisal. There are a number of associations in both Dordrecht neighborhoods where people in principle could meet. In both districts, however, membership of these associations is fairly low.

In Asten and its parish villages, politics is closely interwoven with the associations, strongly personal and fairly local in orientation. The turnout percentages in the local council elections of 1994, 1998 and 2002 were well above the national average in the municipality of Asten. In the Dordrecht districts (especially Wielwijk), by contrast, the turnout percentages at all three local elections were substantially below that for the town as a whole and far below the national average. There are several indications that the local council elections in Asten were a much more pertinent issue for residents of Asten than for the population of Dordrecht. One way of expressing a political preference is to place a poster supporting a political party in the window of one's home. In the Dordrecht districts studied, a journalist doing field research for us counted only four such posters, with an additional seven posters affixed to lampposts. Compare this with the situation in Asten: In the parish villages of Heusden (2,300 inhabitants) and Ommel (just under 900 residents) alone, forty-six families declared their political colors by placing a poster in their window, and there were a further 243 posters attached to lampposts. In both parish villages, going to vote is regarded as much more the norm than in Dordrecht (as is also shown by the much higher turnout percentages). There is also an impression that, to a much greater extent than in Dordrecht, the personality of the candidates plays a decisive role in the political preferences of the electorate. The villagers also have a much stronger feeling than voters in Dordrecht that politics affects them directly and that important issues can be raised through the medium of politics.

Summarizing, it may be concluded that the physical and social circumstances (in terms of quality of life, structure of the living environment and local community life) are clearly different for people in Dordrecht, compared to their Dutch fellows in Asten. These differences in living conditions taken into account, we shall focus on the effects of demographic characteristics and perceptions of the residents on the various elements of social capital. But let us first take a look at the local pattern of relations between these elements.

THE MEASUREMENT AND LOCAL PATTERNS OF SOCIAL CAPITAL

Table 8.1 shows nine indicators of local social capital: two focusing on the individual's informal networks (visit, ask), two on his or her participation in face-to-face and locally oriented organizations (social, local), three on perceptions of social capital in the neighborhood (help1, help 2, nice), and two on social trust in general (trust1, trust2).[4] This selection is meant to cover the general idea of social capital as a social, network-based capacity to cooperate. Together with the two trust indicators we intended to arrive at a more or less balanced series of social capital indicators. All indicators are dichotomies, usually based on a single item. Most "don't know" responses are treated as 0 scores: People who do not know if they participate do not participate; those who do not know if they trust do not trust, etc.

In the first columns with figures, we see substantial differences between the localities. The neighborhoods of Dordrecht (DO) always show the lowest scores, the village of Asten (AS) often the highest. In some cases the differences between Dordrecht and Asten are quite substantial: 14 percent versus 47 percent expect neighborly help (help1), 30 percent versus 53 percent show social trust. The inhabitants of Asten are more involved in associational life than the entire Dutch population is.[5]

Judged from the percentages, Dordrecht seems mired in civic disarray, whereas Asten represents a rather community friendly place. Yet how do the relationships between the various aspects of social capital differ in these localities? Exploratory analyses of the correlations between the nine social capital indicators do not suggest the kind of strong interrelationship one would expect from talking about a "social solidarity syndrome" of social connectedness, trust and community involvement. The first component of a principal component analysis explains 21–22 percent of the variance in the national sample as well as the Asten and Dordrecht samples. These percentages confirm the weakness of the overall interrelationships of the social capital indicators. Moreover, as can be seen from the different loadings, the character of the first component differs. In Asten it is more or less the associational involvement and trust dimension Putnam *cum suis* might expect, but in the national sample and in Dordrecht the common factor is mainly a neighborhood networks dimension. The analysis with two orthogonal-rotated principal components reveals that in all three cases a distinction can be made between a network dimension and a trust dimension.[6] With a strong negative loading of neighborly help in

Table 8.1 Social capital indicators

		%			First principal component			1 of 2 varimax rotated components: "networks"			2 of 2 varimax rotated components: "trust"		
		NL	AS	DO	NL	AS	DO	NL	AS	DO	NL	AS	DO
Visit	has visited or has been visited by neighbors in the last 7 days	39	38	34	**.48**	.23	**.67**	**.54**	**.46**	**.68**	-.02	-.03	.13
Ask	would call on neighbors to do the shopping in the event of illness	64	69	53	**.57**	.37	**.65**	**.63**	**.58**	**.64**	.01	.06	-.17
Social	member/volunteer of a sports, hobby, cultural or women's organization, attends church or religious activities at least once a month or volunteers for a religious or philosophical organization	45	54	30	.32	**.54**	.02	.14	.10	.01	.45	**.58**	-.23
Local	member/volunteer of a neighborhood or local group or organization, or joined a local collective action in last 2 years	28	47	21	.38	**.59**	.41	.27	.47	.43	.33	.40	.34
Help1	thinks that people in the neighborhood would definitely help a neighbor without a car to transport newly purchased furniture	33	47	14	**.63**	.24	**.73**	**.66**	**.63**	**.73**	.06	-.12	.01
Help2	thinks that people in the neighborhood would definitely join a protest initiated by some of them to stop local government from implementing a plan that is bad for the neighborhood	31	39	27	.48	-.06	.37	**.52**	.39	.34	.01	-.33	-.57
Nice	agrees with "people here in general are very kind and willing to help"	74	83	55	**.62**	**.55**	.36	**.60**	**.58**	.34	.20	.27	-.34
Trust1	"most people can be trusted" (versus "you can't be too careful" or "don't know")	56	53	30	.31	**.66**	.03	-.03	.02	.07	**.78**	**.78**	**.59**
Trust2	disagrees with "nowadays you hardly know who can really be trusted"	42	45	30	.21	**.56**	.13	-.14	-.08	.17	**.79**	**.72**	**.69**
% of variance explained				22	22	21	21	19	21	18	20	17	

Note: Entries are percentage with a positive score, and loadings on first and on rotated principal components.

Source: National (NL = Netherlands) and two local samples (AS = Asten, DO = Dordrecht) from "Civil Society and Volunteering in the Netherlands Survey 1997."

collective action and a weaker negative loading of social associational involvement on the trust dimension, Dordrecht differs from Asten and the national sample. Trust and networks seem to be more separate aspects of social capital here than elsewhere.

INDIVIDUAL SOURCES OF SOCIAL CAPITAL

For further analyses of Asten and Dordrecht, we will use the networks and trust dimension as derived from a principal components analysis of the combined national and local samples (because the national sample is about ten times as large as the local samples together, the solution is similar to the national results in Table 8.1). In Table 8.2 we try to explain the differences between Asten and Dordrecht by introducing small selections of demographical and attitudinal variables that show a difference between the two localities and are relevant from a theoretical point of view.

The first columns for both dimensions show lower levels of social capital in Dordrecht. The second columns add three demographic factors that can be seen as personal advantages: dichotomies for educational level, household income and length of residence. Educational levels turn out to be empirically relevant for both dimensions, but in an *opposite* direction. As we already know from much research, people with more education show higher levels of social trust; it is unclear, however, whether this is because of their cognitive experience, their broader worldview, their more trustworthy networks; because they better know it is good to show trust; because they are treated better; or because they can defend themselves easier against cheating. But education is *negatively* related to the network dimension of social capital.[7] Less surprising is that length of residence is positively related with the network dimension of social capital, but slightly negatively with the trust dimension, and that a higher income has, in addition to a higher education, a positive impact on the trust dimension.

In the third columns we add three indicators for personal efficacy and moral confidence, more or less the opposite of the "sense of powerlessness" of Ross et al. (2001) and anomie. These variables have no effect on the network dimension but a positive effect on the trust dimension. Including these variables makes the original difference between Asten and Dordrecht insignificant. This in clear opposition to the results for the network dimension for which our individual variables do not reduce the difference between the localities at all. To get a better idea of these kinds of neighborhood differences, we will now turn to other data from our project.

Table 8.2 Individual backgrounds of differences of two dimensions of local social capital

	(% in Asten)	(% in Dordrecht)	Network dimension			Trust dimension		
			Locality	+Demographics	+Attitudes	Locality	+Demographics	+Attitudes
Dordrecht			-.36***			-.30***	-.17***	-.11
Educational level: high	(42)	(17)		-.20***	-.18***		.32***	.19***
Net household income: high	(51)	(22)		-.07	-.08		.19***	.17***
Length of residence >3 years (or moved inside neighborhood)	(81)	(73)		.19***	.19***		-.09	-.10*
Moral confidence: disagrees with "change is so fast now, that you hardly know what is good and bad"	(50)	(28)			-.06			.12*
Political efficacy: disagrees with "people like me have no influence on government"	(58)	(38)			-.01			.21***
Local political trust: disagrees with "members of municipal council are not interested in opinions of people like me"	(44)	(25)			.06			.19***
% of variance explained (adjusted r^2)			12	20	19	9	22	33

Note: Scores*100 on the two rotated principal components of Table 8.1; significance: * <.05, ** <.01 and *** <.005 (two-tailed). Entries are standardized regression coefficients.

Source: Two local samples from "Civil Society and Volunteering in the Netherlands Survey 1997."

A CLOSER LOOK AT CONTEXT AND CULTURE: EVIDENCE FROM FOCUS GROUPS

Additional information about the creation and experience of social capital was collected in interviews with residents, local activists and policy makers, and in observation studies during the local council elections of 1998. We also collected data via focus groups. In Asten and the two Dordrecht districts, in total four group discussions were organized, in each of which ten respondents, with diverse demographic characteristics (sex, age, education), participated for about two hours. Nearly all participants had lived for more than ten years in their present place of residence. Topics of conversation were, among other things: the social climate in the district, one's personal involvement with it, social contacts between residents, changes in the district, and the participation in voluntary organizations and informal groups. In this chapter we are confining ourselves to some results from the focus groups concerning Asten and Dordrecht.

First of all, not only in our survey but also in the focus groups the Dordrecht participants took more pessimistic views on their district than those in the other places. They talked about run-down streets, feelings of insecurity, language barriers among ethnic groups, and reservation against foreigners. They were also more critical about the youngest generation of residents and far more critical about the social commitment of their fellow residents. The bad reputation of the districts plays a part in their stories. They felt people from Crabbehof sometimes did not get jobs or positions because they were from there; some intend to move because they do not want their children to grow up in the area. In the focus groups in Asten (and the other communities we investigated) a bad image of foreigners hardly ever came up for discussion.

Via the focus groups and interviews with residents, local activists and policy makers, we collected some information about how people see connections between environmental characteristics and the elements of social capital we dealt with in the preceding sections. Our respondents often appeared to have strong opinions about these relationships. In the respondents' view the pattern and degree of social involvement in a district has its origin in three factors: population characteristics, features of the physical environment and actions of authorities (e.g., against vandalism, drugs dealing).

Neighborhood and Informal Networks, Social Participation

In Asten as well as in Dordrecht, many had the impression that the mutual commitment of residents is far stronger in the rural villages than in the cities, that people live their lives less anonymously and are less lonely there. That people in the country take more care of the well being of their fellow citizens and the physical quality of their environment is also a common opinion. Aspects we mentioned before return in the stories and opinions of the respondents. According to them, differences among communities (neighborhoods, municipalities, regions) in available social capital are related to the number of inhabitants and population characteristics (diversity as for ethnic background, age, education, income; number of partners who both have a job; average level of age; residential stability), but also to the building structure of the living environment and the way people treat public spaces. The presence of many apartment houses or drive-in homes for instance, is considered to be unfavorable to social contacts. This also applies to an environment that shows many signs of decay. Neighborhood associations flourish when many young families live in a district, and such associations enter difficult times when a district ages. Partners who both have a job can invest little time in social contacts and spend much time outside their residential area. Contacts between ethnic groups are complicated by cultural differences and language problems.

The history of a region and its dominant religion is also seen as an important factor. Stronger traditions of mutual aid have been cultivated in regions in which people have long depended on each other (such as the northern parts of the Netherlands) because of their very poor living circumstances, the isolation of the areas and the low level of formal facilities. In the Catholic regions in the southern part of the country, clubs and associations have a long and strong tradition; in the orthodox Calvinistic regions (mid and midwest) people have a very strong identification with their fellow believers.

Culture of Social Capital

Participants of the focus groups also reacted to the famous social trust question ("in general, most people can be trusted" versus "you can't be too careful in dealing with other people"). The strong difference between Dordrecht and Asten from the survey data, mentioned before, returns in the group discussions. In Asten eight out of ten participants choose the first proposition, as opposed to less than half of the participants from Dordrecht. The way respondents substantiate their choice however, is everywhere the same. Trusters appear to see their trust as a sort of principle of their life, a basic value they hardly validate from experiences (cf. Uslaner 2002).[8] If they do mention bad experiences, they stay optimistic about others: "Trust has to grow and sometimes you have to make a bet, and everyone learns from his mistakes" (female, eighteen, secondary education); "Because I am very open to people, I get openness in return. Whether I should be cautious is something I only think about later" (female, sixty, primary education); "When you have a positive attitude towards others, than the effects are usually positive" (female, sixty-eight, primary education).

On the other hand, respondents who prefer cautiousness in their contacts with others predominantly refer to experiences. They tell about people they trusted and who betrayed their confidence; they say that they have learned to be not too trustful because of their living environment, or they refer to what they read in the papers or saw on television (about violence, drug dealers, etc.). "Because I was inclined to trust people very quickly, I came into trouble. I had debts, because of others" (male, fifty-four, secondary education); "My daughter talks and laughs with everyone, but she should see that times have changed. You cannot do that any longer. I am living in the notorious Colijnstreet. People there cannot be trusted any longer; it has been several times now, that there was a burglary in my shed" (female, fifty-one, primary education). A second difference between trusters and nontrusters is that the latter are inclined to make a stronger distinction between groups: personal acquaintances (they say they trust) and strangers (who first have to prove worthy of their trust).

In the view of the nontrusters environmental aspects are also important for the readiness of people to trust strangers. In general people feel most safe in their own district (even when police statistics show that their district has an above-average level of crime!) (Maas-de Waal 2002). Where feelings prevail that one has lost control over the environment or is unable to affect that environment, others are received with less trust (Ross et al. 2001). Lack of control goes with feelings of insecurity. In such an environment people are more on their guard in their contacts with strangers. Respondents speak of feelings of insecurity because of crime and youth hanging out on the streets.

CONCLUSIONS AND DISCUSSION

In some places there is quite a great deal of social capital, while in other places this is a scarce commodity. Social capital is not an abstract entity; it is not something that distributes itself equally and diffusely over the entire social arena, like a sort of rain (see van der Meer this volume). Social capital is just as concrete as human society and it is clearly localized in social contexts. It is distributed unevenly—not just in Italy, as in the often-quoted study by Putnam (1993), but in the Netherlands as well. Satellite pictures at night show the Netherlands as one big conurbation, with here and there a good-sized public garden. However, even in such a small, exceptionally urbanized and socially tied-together country, we found substantial differences in terms of social capital.

The municipality of Asten presents an average picture in terms of the informal social networks of its inhabitants, the trust they have in others and the extent to which they are politically active. A proportionately large number of inhabitants of Asten are, it should be said, members of an organization or active as volunteers. The districts of Dordrecht studied here occupy an unfavorable position in all these respects seen from the perspective of social capital. The social contacts there are much less intensive, associations do not play a prominent role and both trust in others and political involvement are lower. It appears that in Dordrecht we could speak of a "nonaffiliation syndrome."

Local differences in levels and relationships of elements of social capital have been statistically elaborated in the preceding sections, but not all of the results are easy to interpret. The differences persisted even when controlling for demographic factors and for subjective and cultural correlates of social capital. Clearly, we might not have included all relevant elements of the composition of the population, but this is probably a minor problem compared to our incapacity to include characteristics of the local setting. This setting is not only constituted by the personal characteristics and ambitions of the residents, but it is also influenced by the physical environment and the social infrastructure. A systematic analysis of these factors is beyond the scope of this text—as it is limited by the small number of cases—but we tried to get some additional insight from municipal and police statistics and from the observation studies, in-depth interviews and focus groups we did in the localities.

This additional research suggests that in Dordrecht, as compared to Asten, there is a complex of complicating factors in the building of social capital. These factors relate to housing conditions, the structure of public space and level of collective facilities; to the composition of the population; to residential stability, the crime rate and feelings of insecurity. Some of these aspects are covered by our surveys and have been included as individual background variables of respondents, but they are probably more relevant as contextual factors about the setting than as individual traits. A study that includes multiple localities might overcome this problem by including various contextual characteristics in addition to important individual traits that explain local social and political differences.

Inhabitants of Dordrecht are less likely than residents of Asten to call on their neighbors, and they identify less with local residents and have a narrower basis for mutual trust. This applies to both the higher and the lower status groups. Subjective conditions for social integration and a positive perception of social contacts may appear to be present, but they are probably blocked (partly) by environmental factors. Such environmental (contextual) factors can be found in the publications of social scientists, but they also recur in the statements of our respondents. They refer to the stability of neighborhoods, to the degree in which residents have the same cultural background, to a decay of public spaces (as related to a decreasing identification of residents with the common good), and to the quality of the formal and informal social infrastructure that, in their view, can facilitate the formation of social capital and mutual trust.

Returning to the idea of social capital, it can be noticed that the existing literature is dominated by a view in which all characteristics are deemed to display a clear correlation: contacts between people, the strength of informal networks, the vitality of local associations and trust, the interaction between these aspects of community life with political activism and trust in the government, etc. Our data qualify this assumption of a coherent complex of characteristics. At the macrolevel of differences between localities we find much evidence for the general idea of social capital, but there is much reason to be skeptical about a uniform social capital syndrome of "networks, trust and norms" at the individual level. There we found not one syndrome but two dimensions, one referring to networks and one referring to trust in others, each with its own background, correlates and local pattern of characteristics. More education, for instance, is positively related to the trust dimension and negatively to the network dimension, while the opposite applies to residential stability. Personal efficacy and moral confidence have no effect on the network aspect of social capital, but they are positively related to trust. Substantial local differences remain for the network aspect of social capital, irrespective of the residents' demographic or psychological characteristics, while the trust aspect is clearly affected by both.

Thus, our distinction between two dimensions of social capital and the analyses of their individual backgrounds suggest an intriguing pattern: on the one hand the "generalized" social capital of the well to do, manifested in social trust and independent of locality, on the other hand the network capital of the less lucky ones who are more dependent on their neighborhood.

NOTES

1. The municipality of Asten comprises the village of the same name (12,750 inhabitants) and the parish villages of Heusden (2,300) and Ommel (900).
2. This is high compared to the 3 percent of Asten but low compared to the majorities found in some districts of larger cities such as Amsterdam, Rotterdam and The Hague.
3. The crime rate measure refers to various sorts of crimes: threat/ intimidation, maltreatment/assault, vandalism, burglary or attempted burglary, theft, etc.
4. As a core variable of the present social capital debate, we include the illustrious generalized trust question and add a proxy from an anomie scale, although there are good reasons to consider this kind of trust more as an indicator of personality strength than of social capital (Dekker 2003).
5. Our social participation measure is a simple dichotomy for a combination of face-to-face organizations, but the more frequent membership in Asten is not attributable to a specific organization type. The inhabitants of Asten are also more often members of interest and advocacy groups.
6. The selection of two and not more components is somewhat arbitrary (in the case of a three-components solution, the associational involvement falls apart). Results of oblique rotation are similar to those of orthogonal rotation. See Dekker (2003) for further analyses of the relationships between trust and other social capital indicators.
7. Although the slightly negative loading of the trust indicators on the network dimension contribute to this result, it is not an artifact of orthogonal rotation: There are negative bivariate correlations of educational level with visit, ask, help1, help2 and nice.
8. The dominant reasoning in our focus groups fits into the third of three frames of reasoning Wuthnow (1999, 215–221) found in qualitative interviews about what it means to trust: (1) belief in own trustworthiness, capacity to judge other people and belief in one's efficacy to control other people and situations; (2) the result of growing up in positive circumstances; and (3) as a "leap of faith": It may not be rational to trust, but it is morally better or a pragmatically best assumption for a happier life.

REFERENCES

Bulmer, M. (1984). *The Chicago School of Sociology*. Chicago: University of Chicago Press.
Campbell, K. E. and B. A. Lee (1991). "Sources of Personal Neighbor Networks." *Social Forces* 70, 1077–1100.

De Hart, J. (ed., 2002). *Zekere Banden.* Den Haag: SCP.

Dekker, P. (2003). "Social Capital of Individuals." In P. Selle and S. Prakash (eds.), *Investigating Social Capital.* London: Sage.

Fischer, C. S. et al. (1977). *Networks and Places.* New York: Free Press.

Foley, M., B. Edwards and M. Diani (2001). "Social Capital Revisited." pp. 266–280. In B. Edwards, M. Foley and M. Diani (eds.), *Beyond Tocqueville.* Hanover, NH: Tufts University.

Gans, H. J. (1967). *The Levittowners.* New York: Columbia University Press.

Jacobs, J. (1961). *The Death and Life of Great American Cities.* New York: Random House.

Maas-de Waal, C. (2002). "Veiligheid." pp. 245–278. In J. de Hart (ed.), *Zekere Banden.* Den Haag: SCP.

Putnam, R. (1993). *Making Democracy Work.* Princeton: Princeton University Press.

Putnam, R. (1995). "Tuning in, Tuning out." *PS: Political Science and Politics* 28(4), 664–683.

Putnam, R. (2000). *Bowling Alone.* New York: Simon and Schuster.

Ross, C., J. Mirowsky and S. Pribesh (2001). "Powerlessness and the Amplification of Threat." *American Sociological Review* 66, 568–591.

Uslaner, E. M. (2002). *The Moral Foundations of Trust.* Cambridge: Cambridge University Press.

Van der Poel, M. (1993). *Personal Networks.* Lisse: Swets and Zeitlinger.

Wuthnow, R. (1999). "The Role of Trust in Civic Renewal." pp. 209–230. In R. Fullinwider (ed.), *Civil Society, Democracy, and Civic Renewal.* Lanham: Rowman and Littlefield.

CHAPTER 9

TRUST, DEMOCRACY AND GOVERNANCE: CAN GOVERNMENT POLICIES INFLUENCE GENERALIZED TRUST?[1]

Eric M. Uslaner

INTRODUCTION

Some years ago the noted novelist E. M. Forster (1965, 70) gave "Two Cheers for Democracy": "...one because it admits variety and two because it permits criticism. Two cheers are quite enough: there is no occasion to give three. Only Love the Beloved Republic deserves that." Perhaps there is a reason for a third cheer. Democratic societies are trusting societies. The big pay-off from generalized trust, most contemporary observers say, is that it leads to "better" government and to a public that is happier with government performance. Or maybe good government makes people more likely to trust each other. Or perhaps both.

Can the state produce trust—and, if so, are certain types of state structures more likely to be associated with high levels of trust? Most who have written on trust and the state assert that governments can produce trust (Levi 1998; Rothstein 2000). But I disagree. Democracy does not make people become more trusting. Trust across nations without a legacy of Communism depends largely on long-term culture (specifically religious traditions) and on economic equality. Trusting publics will also produce more responsive governments and are more likely to adopt policies that will promote economic equality—and thus create more trust.

I shall argue that state structures cannot produce trust, but state policies can. Mostly, trust has cultural roots that are resistant to change. However, trust does not depend upon culture alone. The level of economic equality in a country has a powerful effect on the level of generalized trust—and here, government policies that foster a more equal distribution of resources can have a powerful effect on trust.

Trust matters: Societies with higher levels of trust in turn have institutions that function better. Trust leads to better institutions— not the other way around. It also produces higher spending for the sorts of policies that foster equality (more redistribution, more funding for education). So the countries with the lowest levels of trust are those with the most unequal distributions of wealth. But they are also the countries that are least likely to redistribute wealth to create the sort of trust that will breed institutions that function better.

THE CLAIMS ABOUT TRUST

Political life and trust have an uneasy relationship with each other. Some people say that the state can build trust. By ensuring that people cannot get away with cheating each other and flouting the law, the state can create respect for authority. People will ultimately come to accept legal dictates as moral stipulation. The state enforces property rights and contracts. A strong legal system will reduce transaction costs, making trust less risky. The more experience people have with compliance, the more likely they are to have confidence in others' good will (Brehm and Rahn 1997, 1008; Levi 1998; Offe 1999).

The state has a particularly important role in protecting the rights of minorities and in providing for the welfare of those who have fewer resources. The most vulnerable have the most to lose by trusting others— and thus will be more reluctant to place their faith in their fellow citizens. A strong state can lower the bar by empowering those with less power through legalizing trade unions or enforcing child labor laws (Levi 1998). States can build trust in three other ways. First, honesty in government may promote generalized, or interpersonal, trust. Corrupt governments set bad examples for the types of behavior that will be tolerated from the citizenry. The correlation between societal corruption and generalized trust across fifty-two countries is −.61.[2] The most corrupt countries have the least trusting citizens. This is hardly surprising, since "kleptocracies" send clear messages to the people that crime does pay.[3] Citizens feel free to flout the legal system, producing firmer crackdowns by authorities and leading to what Putnam (1993, 115) calls "interlocking vicious circles" of corruption and mistrust.

Second—and strongly related to the first claim—democracy promotes trust (Brehm and Rahn 1997, 1008). Democratic regimes, Levi (1998, 96) argues, may be prerequisites for generalized trust (cf. Muller and Seligson 1994). Such polities can actually change preferences by structuring the range of acceptable choices in a society, Levi argues. She does not specify how these changes occur, but seems to argue that democracy empowers people who do not control many resources. When political leaders need to rely upon the mass citizenry for political support, they are not free to adopt policies that enrich themselves (corruption) or the dominant interests in a society (economic stratification).

Third, strong government performance makes people feel better about government—and ultimately more willing to cooperate with each other (Brehm and Rahn 1997, 1008; Misztal 1996, 198). There is a direct link between trust in government and faith in other people. Rahn, Brehm and Carlson (1997, 24) argue that when people trust their government, they are more likely to believe that they can influence it. This growing sense of efficacy makes people more likely to trust each other.

Each of these claims is plausible. But most are disputable—and I shall challenge many of them in this chapter. The roots of trust are *not* institutional. They lie in the deeper values societies hold—and in the distribution of resources. Yes, democracies *are* more trusting. But a wide variety of structural variables fall by the wayside to the level of economic inequality in a society. Societies *do not* become trusting because they are more democratic. They become trusting because they distribute their resources more equally. Perhaps the logic works the other way around—more trusting countries work to redress economic inequality (Knack 1999). That would be nice—but it does not seem to happen. Societies with many trusters are more pleasant places to live. Not only are they more equal, but they also have better performing governments (less red tape and more responsive judiciaries). Their governments pursue policies that lead to even more equality: a larger public sector, more transfers from the rich to the poor, and more spending on education.

DEMOCRACY AND TRUST

Levi (1998), Offe (1999), and others (Cohen 1997, 19–20; Misztal 1996, 198; Pagden 1988, 139) argue that a state, and particularly a democratic state, can produce generalized trust in people. Levi (1999, 82) maintains that states build trust through "the use of coercion" and that "democratic states may be even better at producing generalized trust than are nondemocratic institutions... because they are better at restricting the use of coercion to tasks that enhance rather than undermine trust." Rothstein (2000) elaborates the link between trust and coercion: "If people believe that the institutions that are responsible for handling 'treacherous' behavior act in fair, just and effective manner, and if they also believe that other people think the same of these institutions, then they will also trust other people." Levi (1998, 87) holds that "[t]he trustworthiness of the state influences its capacity to generate interpersonal trust ..." Rothstein (2000) elaborates on this linkage: "...if you think...that these...institutions [of law and order] do what they are supposed to do in a fair and effective manner, then you also have reason to believe that the chance people have of getting away with such treacherous behavior is small. If so, you will believe that that people will have very good reason to refrain from acting in a treacherous manner, and you will therefore believe that 'most people can be trusted.'"

There is plenty of evidence that people are more likely to obey laws and pay taxes if they believe that laws are enforced fairly and if people trust government (Tyler 1990; Scholz and Pinney 1995). But the link between government and trust in people is tenuous. Across forty-two nations, there is but a modest correlation ($r = .154$) between trust in people and confidence in the legislative branch of government.[4]

If trust in people is a long-standing value that changes but slowly *and* if trust in people is not largely based upon our experiences (Uslaner 2002, chs. 3–4), then it is hard to see how government can generate faith in strangers. If we withheld trust in people until we had confidence that they were in fact trustworthy, then government might be able to generate faith in others. Levi and others are certainly right when they argue that trust in government is contingent upon our evaluations of how well our leaders have done their jobs.[5] And they are just as assuredly wrong when they argue that trust in people rests primarily upon demonstrations of trustworthiness (see Uslaner 2002, ch. 4). There is little reason to presume that government enforcement of laws will build trust. Yes, coercion can increase compliance with the law. Obeying the law because you fear the wrath of government will not make you more trusting—no matter how equally the heavy hand of the state is applied. People who trust others are less likely than mistrusters to endorse unconditional compliance. In the General Social Survey in the United States, just 35 percent of trusters say that you should always obey the law, even if it is unjust, compared to 48 percent of mistrusters (phi $= -.128$, Yule's $Q = -.269$).[6]

Simply getting people to obey laws will not produce trust. Perhaps this is a caricature of the argument on building trust, but it is easy to confuse compliance with voluntary acceptance, to confuse the law-abiding people of Singapore with those of Sweden (cf. Rothstein 2002). Even in high trusting countries such as Sweden, the linkage between confidence in the legal system and the police and trust in people is not very strong (Rothstein 2002).[7]

Courts can save us from rascals only if there are few rascals (cf. Sitkin and Roth 1993). Law-abiding citizens, not rogue outlaws, create constitutions that work. You may write any type of constitution that you wish, but statutes alone will not create either compliance or trust. Macaulay (1963, 58, 61–63) argues that business executives and lawyers prefer transactions based upon trust—and handshakes to seal the deal—to those based upon contracts and threats of legal sanctions. Most executives and even lawyers have faith that other people will keep their end of a bargain. Resorting to formal documents might undo the goodwill that undergirds business relationships (Macaulay 1963, 63). Coercion, Gambetta (1988, 220) argues, "falls short of being an adequate alternative to trust...It introduces an asymmetry which disposes of *mutual* trust and promotes instead power and resentment" (cf. Baier 1986, 234).

Yet, democracies are more trusting. A wide range of measures of democratization show that the more democratic the constitutional structure, the more trusting citizens are. I show correlations between trust and measures of democracy in Table 9.1. The indicators of democratization I use are the measures of political freedoms, civil liberties, and the overall freedom score developed by Freedom House and reported in Gastil (1991); updated Freedom House measures for 1993–94 and 1998–99;[8] a summary measure of Freedom House scores that assign each country a democratization measure from the year closest to the trust measure in the World Values Survey (WVS) (see Table 9.1); Coppedge and Reinicke's (1991) indicator of polyarchy; and measures of democratization reported in Bollen (1991); Gurr, Jaggers, and Moore (1991); Vanhanen (1997), and updated scores for the Gurr measure from La Porta et al. (1997). The measures of trust are the most recent available figures from the World Values Survey for 63 countries over the course of the three waves of the WVS.[9]

The correlations for these measures of democratization and trust range from the modest to the more robust. Particularly telling, however, are the many negative correlations between levels of democracy and trust for the formerly Communist countries in Central and

Table 9.1 Correlations between measures of democracy and generalized trust

Measure	All countries	Non-communist	Formerly communist*
Bollen democracy score	.375 (62)	.530 (29)	.114 (21)
Vanhanen democracy score	.439 (57)	.578 (37)	.139 (19)
Gastil civil liberties score (1988)**	.501 (58)	.617 (40)	−.029 (17)
Gastil political rights score (1988)**	.361 (58)	.369 (40)	−.100 (17)
Gastil composite freedom score (1988)**	.424 (58)	.497 (40)	−.070 (17)
Freedom House composite freedom score (1993–94)**	.377 (65)	.600 (41)	−.188 (18)
Freedom House composite freedom score (1998–99)**	.357 (69)	.639 (41)	−.402 (21)
Freedom House composite freedom score (year closest to survey)***	.393 (67)	.655 (41)	−.466 (19)
Gurr et al. democratization score (1978)	.604 (50)	.530 (29)	.000 (21)****
Gurr et al. democratization score (1994)*****	.439 (57)	.578 (37)	.130 (19)
Coppedge polyarchy score*	.311 (62)	.328 (40)	−.009 (21)
La Porta et al. property rights score	.530 (55)	.627 (36)	−.053 (19)

Note: * China is excluded.
** Scores reflected from original coding.
*** Scores reflected from original coding; when survey is from 1990, 1988 Freedom House scores used; when survey is from 1995 or 1996, 1993–94, Freedom House scores are used.
**** Correlation is zero because there is no variation in the coding of democratization.
***** Taken from La Porta, R., F. Lopez-Silanes, A. Schleifer and R. Vishney (1997). "Trust in Large Organizations." *American Economic Review Papers and Proceedings* 87, 333–338.

Source: World Values Survey, see note 2.

Eastern Europe. There is at best moderate support for the argument that democracy and trust go together—and very little evidence for the thesis that democratization leads to greater trust (Inglehart 1999). Authoritarian governments that set people against each other, such as the former Communist regimes in Eastern and Central Europe,[10] can make trust hazardous. When people feel compelled to turn on their friends lest the state turn on them, generalized trust may become too risky. In such a world, you really cannot be too careful in dealing with people, even if everyone would strongly prefer to treat others as if they were trustworthy. Even with democratic institutions in place, people living in countries with legacies of oppression will neither trust their fellow citizens nor participate in civic life.

Democracies may be trusting or mistrusting. In countries with no legacy of Communist rule, the mean proportion of trusters in highly democratic regimes is .41, compared to .22 in the least democratic countries. (I shall also refer to countries with no legacy of Communist rule as "democracies" for short, fully recognizing that many of these nations have not always respected the rights and freedoms associated with democratic regimes.) Democracies are all over the place in trust, ranging from .03 (Brazil) to .65 (Norway). Formerly Communist regimes also vary in trust, but only from .06 to .34. Half of all democracies have more than 34 percent trusters. The standard deviation for democracies is .15. It is less than half that value (.06) for authoritarian states. Democracies make trust possible. They do not necessarily produce it.

There is certainly little evidence that democratization increases trust. The correlation between change in trust in twenty-two nations from 1981 to the early 1990s (according to the World Values Survey) and variations in Freedom House scores from 1978 to 1988 is modestly negative ($-.38$). Yet, even this result turns out to be largely an illusion. Without the outlying cases of Argentina and South Korea, the correlation drops the correlation to $-.08$. Inglehart (1997, 1999) finds that trust does not depend upon democratization, once cultural heritages (Protestantism and Confucianism) and wealth are controlled.[11]

An Indian journalist commented on the sharp cleavages that led to a cycle of unstable coalitions, none of which could form a government: "We have the hardware of democracy, but not the software, and that cannot be borrowed or mimicked" (Constable 1999, A19). So is a third cheer for democracy misplaced? Maybe not. There is some evidence that democracy matters. According to Inglehart's measure of the years of continuous democracy, we see a powerful correlation between generalized trust and democratization (cf. Inglehart

1997, 172). Across forty-one countries the correlation between the number of years of continuous democracy and trust is .77. And no set of controls or simultaneous equation estimation makes the linkage go away. One could, of course, agree with Inglehart's (1997, 180–188) reasonable argument that stable democracy depends upon a trusting public. Regimes that merely give constitutional protections against state interference do not need an underbelly of civic responsibility (Mueller 1996, 118).

Generalized trust is quite stable over time across countries (the aggregate correlation from the 1981 to 1990 is .91, $n = 22$). We can predict levels of democratization over long periods of time by contemporary measures of trust. So Inglehart (1997, 186–188) infers that trust is a key component of prodemocratic attitudes that lay the foundation for popular constitutions. Yet, institutionalists might argue that the logic goes the other way: Long-standing democratic regimes can promote contemporary high levels of trust. Perhaps they are correct, but if so, their case is still weak. The democratic march to trust is a long and winding road. It takes forty-six years of continuous democracy to move a country from well below the mean on trust to above it. Countries with less than forty-six years of continuous democracy are no more likely to have trusting citizens than authoritarian states ($r = .056$, $n = 22$, $p < .237$, one-tailed test). If institutions matter, their effects are very slow and difficult to disentangle from other changes occurring in societies.

Trust is neither a prerequisite for nor a consequence of democracy. The democratic revolution that swept Eastern and Central Europe a decade ago—and quickly spread through many of the world's remaining autocracies—did not depend upon social trust. Eastern bloc countries with more trusting citizenries did not become democratic sooner than nations whose populations had less faith in others. Formerly Communist countries with higher levels of trust did not create polities with more political or property rights. Thus, whatever effects democracy has on trust occurs within countries without long legacies of authoritarianism. Yes, many democracies in the sample have experienced authoritarian rule from time to time (and more than from time to time): Ghana, Nigeria, India, Spain, Portugal, Greece, Turkey, Peru, and Bangladesh are notable examples. And many "democracies" in form have not been quite so "free": South Africa, South Korea, Mexico, Taiwan and the Dominican Republic (among others) fit this pattern.

Democracy's benefits seem confined to long-standing democracies. The correlations between levels of democracy and generalized trust are almost always higher for countries with no legacy of Communist rule than for all countries (see Table 9.1). The major exception is for the earlier Gurr et al. (1991) index, in which all Communist countries had identical scores at the bottom of the democratization scale. Democratization has no appreciable effect on trust for countries in Eastern and Central Europe that formerly were authoritarian regimes. In some cases the correlation between trust and democratization is even negative (though never significant). The long lag between democratization and trust in Inglehart's continuous democracy measure shows how difficult it is, if it can be done at all, to generate new values from structural changes.

TRUST ACROSS CULTURES

Why, then, are some nations more trusting than others? Inglehart (1999) argues that rich nations are trusting, poor countries more distrustful. Putnam's (1993) logic goes the other way around: Trust brings economic growth and prosperity. We can argue either way around, but there ought to be a connection between trust and wealth. Beyond simple measures of riches, there are several other reasonable correlates of trust: education levels, poverty rates, infant mortality,[12] life expectancy, the fertility rate, ethnic diversity, postmaterial values, and media exposure. Knack and Keefer (1997, 1278–1279) argue that ethnically diverse societies are more likely to develop sharp cleavages—which, in turn, destroy trust. I show elsewhere (Uslaner 2002, ch. 4) that parents who wanted their children to hold values that emphasize the welfare of others are more likely to trust other people. Inglehart (1999) extends this logic: People whose own values are less materialistic (or postmaterialistic) should also be more trusting.[13] He finds support for this argument only in the fifteen richest nations. Putnam (1995) tracks changes in trust in the United States to increased viewing of television and a drop in newspaper readership. Newspapers tie us to other people, while television keeps us inside our homes, away from civic engagement. We might also expect that countries that rank high on corruption will also have less trust (La Porta et al. 1997, 335). If others are untrustworthy, why should I play the fool, a reasonable person might ask.

All of these arguments are reasonable and none of them hold. Various measures of ethnic diversity, income, education, and well-being all fall to insignificance in multivariate analyses.[14] At bivariate levels, most of these variables (education, quality of life, infant mortality) matter at least in countries with no legacy of Communist rule.

Postmaterialist values, as determined by aggregate scores in the World Values Survey, are modestly associated with generalized trust. There are stronger relationships with newspaper readership in democracies ($r = .69$), television viewing ($r = .60$), and listening to the radio ($r = .55$). Corruption is more strongly related to trust in bivariate relationships ($r = -.75$). Yet again, none is a significant predictor in multivariate models.

What, then, makes some societies more trusting and others less so? The answer is neither structural (democratic institutions) nor ethnic (the diversity of groups). Nor is it simply wealth. It is, in part, how resources are distributed in society. The more equitable the distribution of wealth in a country, the more trusting its people will be. For countries without a legacy of Communism, the simple correlation of generalized trust and the Gini index for income equality is $-.68$. Economic inequality is strongly related to trust, and this connection does not vanish in multivariate tests. It does go away in the formerly Communist nations of Eastern and Central Europe (where the correlation falls to $-.24$). The dynamic of economic inequality and trust clearly works differently in democracies and authoritarian societies.

Knack (1999) argues that the causal arrow runs from trust to inequality in his crossnational analysis. To test this claim, I estimate simultaneous-equation models to see whether trust is both the cause and effect of economic inequality. Trust may flourish in Protestant societies because the Protestant Church has historically been more egalitarian than the Catholic Church (Lipset 1990, ch. 5; Putnam 1993, 175). More egalitarian societies are more likely to be trusting (see Uslaner 2002, chs. 2, 6, 8). Additionally, many Muslims find Western culture threatening and are thus less likely to trust people unlike themselves—especially since Westerners have colonized many Muslim nations and tried to convert Muslims to Christianity. Muslims also see themselves as a community apart: Non-Muslims, according to Islamic law, belong to a "second class" of citizens who must acknowledge the supremacy of Islam and who stand apart from the majority of Muslims (Esposito 1991, 291).

The equation for inequality includes trust, as well as a measure of corruption (the log of the black market currency value for 1985), the population growth rate (high rates of population growth make it more difficult to redistribute wealth), and the percentage of Muslims in a society. Countries with more Muslims may be less trusting, but they are more egalitarian (cf. Esposito and Voll 1996, 25). As Protestantism has stressed individual achievement, Islam has placed greater emphasis on collective goals, especially on one's economic responsibility to the larger community (as reflected in the prohibition on charging interest on loans). The model for trust and inequality is used on the larger sample with thirty-three cases and, using just the most recent measure of trust, offers less hope for a direct link between public policy and economic inequality. And it once more suggests that both cultural factors and real economic circumstances shape trust. I present the results in Table 9.2.

The Gini index has the greatest impact on trust of any independent variable. Moving from the least to the most equal nation in the sample, trust jumps thirty-five points. As expected, Protestant societies are more trusting and Muslim ones less so. A standard assumption people make in informal discussions about trust is that the Scandinavian countries rank highest on generalized trust (cf. Rice and Feldman 1997) because it is easy to trust other people in a homogenous society. The reasoning is, of course, that most people can be trusted if they look and think just like you do. And, yes, the Scandinavian countries are more homogenous,[15] but they are more egalitarian and especially more heavily Protestant.[16] And, overall, ethnic diversity does not shape trust—or, even, indirectly, economic inequality. So Scandinavian societies are so trusting because they are more equal and more Protestant, not just because they are all blond with blue eyes.

In democratic nations, the single biggest barrier to generalized trust is economic inequality. Both over time in the United States and across thirty-three democracies, trust goes down as inequality goes up (Uslaner 2002, ch. 6). Beyond its cultural foundations, trust reflects an optimistic view of the world—the expectation that tomorrow will be better than today. And this must have some foundation in reality. The measure that I have used in this study, whether you can count on success in life (from the World Values Study), expresses well optimistic assumptions about the future. Expectations for success do not track levels of inequality across cultures ($r = -.32$ for democracies, $-.25$ for all countries). But they are strongly related to the overall wealth of a society, as measured by the log of the gross national product ($r = .66$) and a measure of the "total quality of life" offered by Diener (1995) ($r = .68$). In addition to these measures, expectations of success also vary with the infant mortality rate ($r = -.66$, $n = 23$), how many years of school the average person has had ($r = .53$) and life expectancy ($r = .56$).

Clearly, there are a plethora of possible determinants of both trust and economic inequality. And these socioeconomic and political variables just as surely are related to each other. Sorting out what matters

Table 9.2 Two-stage least squares estimation of trust and economic inequality for countries with no communist legacy: model II

	Gini index equation including trust				Gini index equation excluding trust			
	Coefficient	Standard error	t Ratio	Bias	Coefficient	Standard error	t Ratio	Bias
Equation for trust	$r^2 = .733$		RMSE = .084					
Gini index of inequality	-.908****	.192	-4.735	.004				
Percent Muslim	-.004**	.002	-2.062	-.002				
Percent Protestant	.003****	.001	4.963	.00002				
Constant	.626****	.077	8.125					
Equation for Gini index	$r^2 = .619$		RMSE = .066		$r^2 = .642$		RMSE = .063	
Trust in people	.041	.166	.245	.062				
Log black market currency value	.516***	.148	3.491	.103	.490****	.100	4.914	.372
Percent Muslim	-.013*****	.003	-4.443	.00003	-.012*****	.002	-5.733	.0002
Population growth rate	.072***	.025	2.951	.006	.069***	.020	3.452	-.003
Constant	.271****	.076	3.569		.289****	.020	14.542	

Note: **** $p < .0001$, *** $p < .01$, ** $p < .05$, * $p < .10$, $n = 33$.

Source: World Values Survey, see note 2.

is mostly a theoretical concern, but there are plenty of competing theories that must also be given their due. Thirty-three cases are hardly sufficient to constitute a critical test of any argument, especially when many of the variables are related to each other. However, the final models seem very robust. Each model was tested including alternative specifications with the variables discussed above (as well as others). Theoretically important variables (ethnic diversity, levels of democracy and income) were tested in a variety of models and each model was subjected to bootstrapping (to ensure that the results did not depend upon the particular set of countries). So the final model not only is based on strong theoretical assumptions but also on extensive sensitivity testing. The only measure of democracy that remained significant in a simple ordinary least squares regression predicting trust was the number of years of consecutive democracy. But, as I argued above, the number of continuous years of democracy displays a highly nonlinear relationship to trust—and including this variable reduces the sample size to just twenty-five cases. The model I present here thus seems by far the best—and it is not at all plagued by multicollinearity among the predictors.

Trust is essentially cultural but, like culture itself, is shaped by our experiences. Whether specific individuals trust other people is largely divorced from their personal histories (Uslaner 2002, chs. 2–4). But whether a society is composed of many trusters depends upon its collective experiences. Knowing whether someone is rich or poor helps relatively little in predicting whether they will trust others. Knowing whether a society is rich or poor does not help that much either. But knowing how a society's resources are distributed—a collective outcome that cannot be reduced to any individual's fate—will tell you a lot about trust in that culture. In contrast to Inglehart's (1997, 1999) model, inequality matters more than simple wealth. Both are highly correlated with trust, but the partial correlation of trust with income (using the log of per capita gross domestic product adjusted for purchasing power in 1980, from the Penn World Tables) is lower (.44) than the partial correlation with inequality (−.61). Inequality and wealth are related, but they are hardly the same thing ($r = -.41$). There is a bit of good news here: Redistributing resources so people become more optimistic and feel a sense of common fate with others is within the capacity of state actors.

Does equality lead to trust or does trust promote more equality? The direction of causality is, of course, difficult to establish with cross-sectional data. And there are no good time series data on trust across nations. However, there is a clear connection between trust and equality

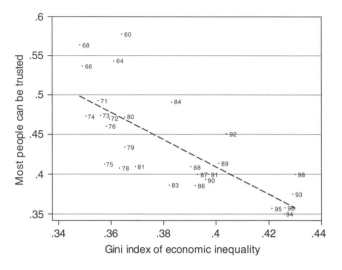

Figure 9.1　Trust and economic inequality for the United States, 1960–98
Source: General Social Survey, 1960–98.

in the one country for which there are good time series data on trust, the United States. There is a strong correlation between trust and inequality from 1960 to 1998. The bivariate r^2 is .54 (see Figure 9.1). As in this analysis, a simultaneous equation model shows that the relationship goes from inequality to less trust, not from trust to more equality (see Uslaner 2002, ch. 1 for a discussion of the sources of data on trust, and ch. 6 for the statistical models).

Reprise

Trusting societies have bigger governments that redistribute wealth from the rich to the poor, spend more on education, and pursue policies that will stimulate economic growth. Thus, while there is no direct connection from trust to economic equality, trusting societies in democratic regimes pursue programs that indirectly will boost faith in others. Trusting nations spend more of their total income on governmental programs in general and on education in particular. They also have a larger share of their total population employed by the government. In particular, trusting societies are more likely to devote a higher share of their national wealth to transfer programs that assist the poor. Finally, trusting societies are more willing to reach out to outsiders (Woolcock 1998, 158): High trust goes hand-in-hand with open economies and fewer restrictions on trade. And trade promotes economic growth.

Governments that redistribute income, spend money on education, transfer wealth from rich to poor, have large public sectors, and maintain open economies do not generate trust. Trust seems to come first. Well, almost. Economic equality is a strong determinant of trust. And trust leads to policies that create wealth and reduce inequalities. Here we find what Putnam would call a "virtuous circle." The equal become more equal. However, there is also a vicious circle: Misanthropy and inequality feed on themselves. One can increase trust indirectly by pursuing policies that reduce economic inequality: Each of the public policies I have considered leads to more economic equality, though the correlations are moderate (ranging from .4 to .5) except for one: How open the economy is (where the correlation approaches .7). And, yes, you can adopt these policies without a trusting citizenry. But a public that is public spirited gives some countries advantages over others in reducing inequality and boosting trust. It is easier to make the hard political decisions when there is trust in the land.

We thus come full circle to the nexus between trust in government and trust in people. People have confidence in their leaders when government is working well. Their judgements about government performance reflect their evaluations of specific personalities, institutions and policies. But each of these actors must work in, and perhaps contribute to, an atmosphere of compromise or confrontation. And political leaders are ultimately responsible and responsive to the public and its hopes and fears. Government cannot produce trust in people. People can provide government officials with the latitude to work on major social problems, and thereby indirectly increase trust in government. We need to be careful about the inferences we draw, since many people will look at the range of policy options that trust in people makes possible and decide that they would rather opt out. Such divisions are inevitable, because politics is all about choosing sides based upon ideas of what government should or should not do.

But whatever government does, a trusting environment makes it possible for government to act. Mueller (1996, 106) argues that we oversell the benefits of democratic government: "Democracy is ... an extremely disorderly muddle in which contending ideas and forces do unkempt, if peaceful, battle and in which ideas often are reduced to slogans, data to distorted fragments, evidence to gestures, and arguments to poses." However, if Inglehart (1997, 180–188) is correct, then democracies that are stable and that work well rest upon cultural foundations, especially social trust. Democratic structures cannot be dismissed, but overall they are generally less powerful determinants of inequality than trust and usually sink to insignificance in multivariate analyses. In the end, democracy is worth two cheers. Save the third for trust.

NOTES

1. I gratefully acknowledge the support of the General Research Board of the University of Maryland—College Park and the Everett McKinley Dirksen Center for the Study of Congressional Leadership. Most of the data I employ were obtained from the Inter-University Consortium for Political and Social Research, which is absolved from any responsibility for my claims. I owe debts of gratitude for comments and conversations to Gabriel Badescu, Dennis Chong, Karen Dawisha, Paul Dekker, Marc Hooghe, Ronald Inglehart, Margaret Levi, Jane Mansbridge, Jeffrey Mondak, John Mueller, Joe Oppenheimer, Robert Putnam, Bo Rothstein, Tara Santmire, Dietlind Stolle, Shibley Telhami, Mark Warren, and Yael Yishai. This chapter is adapted from parts of chapter 8 of Eric M. Uslaner (2002). *The Moral Foundations of Trust.* New York: Cambridge University Press.

2. The data base are the countries that have World Values Survey questions on generalized trust in either 1981–82 or 1990–93. For countries with surveys in both years, the figure for trust is the average. I eliminated China, since its trust score is suspiciously high. (The correlation is reflected, since higher scores on the corruption index indicate honesty in government.) Later in the chapter, I shall analyze trust data for countries without a legacy of Communism. I simply note here that the correlation rises to $-.749$ when I restrict the analysis to these thirty-four nations. The data on corruption (for 1998) come from the global organization Transparency International and are found on its web site, at http://www.transparency.de/documents/cpi/index.html.

3. The correlation between the measures of corruption and tax evasion in the La Porta et al. (1997) Quality of Government data set are .619.

4. I focus on the legislative rather than the executive branch since most democratic governments are parliamentary systems. The correlation is not much different for nations with and without a legacy of Communist rule ($r = .143$ and .189, respectively).

5. Fenno (1978) and Bianco (1994) provide compelling arguments that members of Congress must expend much effort to develop trust among their constituents.

6. The question was asked in 1985, 1990 and 1996.

7. The correlation between trust in people and confidence in the legal system in the World Values Survey is modest (tau-c = .069, gamma = .122). And the country by country correlations tend to be higher where trust in people is higher.

8. These updated measures were obtained from the web site: http://www.freedomhouse.org/rankings.pdf. The Freedom House web site contains scores for both political and civil liberties. They were very highly correlated, so I summed the two (cf. Inglehart 1997, 357).

9. I am grateful to Ronald Inglehart for providing updated data for the third wave (1995–96) of the World Values Survey, where available.

These figures are not averages. The nations and the years for which I have trust data are as follows. Countries marked with an asterisk either formerly had Communist governments or are still Communist regimes (China): Argentina (1996), Armenia (1995)*, Australia (1995)*, Austria (1990)*, Azerbaijan (1995)*, Bangladesh (1997)*, Belarus (1996)*, Belgium (1990), Brazil (1996), Bulgaria (1990)*, Canada (1990), Chile (1996), China (1995)*, Colombia (1996), Croatia (1996)*, Czech Republic (1990)*, Denmark (1990), Dominican Republic (1996), East Germany (1996)*, Estonia (1996)*, Finland (1996), Georgia (1996)*, Ghana (1995), Greece (1990), Hungary (1990)*, Iceland (1990), India (1996), Ireland (1990), Italy (1990), Japan (1995), Latvia (1996), Lithuania (1996)*, Luxembourg (1990), Mexico (1996), Moldova (1996)*, Montenegro (1996)*, Northern Ireland (1990), the Netherlands (1990), Nigeria (1995), Norway (1996), Peru (1996), the Philippines (1996), Poland (1996)*, Portugal (1990), Romania (1990)*, Russia (1995)*, South Africa (1996), South Korea (1996), Serbia (1996), Slovakia (1990)*, Slovenia (1995)*, Spain (1996), Sweden (1996), Switzerland (1996), Taiwan (1995), Turkey (1996), the United Kingdom (1990), the United States (1996), the Ukraine (1996)*, Uruguay (1996), Venezuela (1995) and West Germany (1996). I generated some aggregate results directly from the World Values Survey and in other cases used the compendium by Inglehart et al. (1998).

10. Communist governments still existing elsewhere, as well as other tyrannical regimes, fit the pattern as well. However, I omit China from all discussions. It has a very high percentage (52 percent) of generalized trusters. Inglehart (1999) attributes this to its Confucian culture, comparing it with Taiwan (where 42 percent of people say most people can be trusted) rather than with other countries with legacies of Communist rule. However, I see the Chinese figure as a likely outlier that might reflect the hazards of conducting survey research in a country that Freedom House puts at the bottom of its rankings on both political and civil liberties.

11. My model for trust also includes Protestantism. But it does not include Confucianism; to get a significant coefficient for Confucianism, one has to include China in the equation. China's very high trust score (.52) is abnormally high. Wang Shaoguang (now of the Chinese University of Hong Kong, then of Yale University) said that his surveys indicate that trust is no higher than 33 percent (private e-mail, December 6, 1999).

12. I owe this suggestion to my colleague Ted Robert Gurr.

13. Postmaterial values include putting more emphasis on freedom of speech and having more say on the job (and in government) rather than maintaining order and fighting price rises (Inglehart 1997, ch. 4).

14. To conserve space, I do not report the data sources in this chapter, nor do I present the full specifications of some of the regression equations. For details, see Uslaner (2002, ch. 8).

15. The mean score for the Scandinavian nations on the Easterly-Levine (1997) measure of ethnic fractionalization is .067, compared to .220 for other countries with no legacy of Communism (which only reaches significance at $p < .12$, one-tailed test).

16. The average Gini index in Scandinavian countries is .383 compared to .313 for other countries with no legacy of Communism ($p < .10$). But the five Scandinavian countries have an average of 88.6 percent Protestants, compared to 18.7 percent in other countries ($p < .0001$).

REFERENCES

Baier, A. (1986). "Trust and Antitrust." *Ethics* 96, 231–260.

Bianco, W. (1994). *Trust: Representatives and Constituents.* Ann Arbor: University of Michigan Press.

Bollen, K. (1991). "Political Democracy: Conceptual and Measurement Traps," in A. Inkeles, ed., *On Measuring Democracy.* New Brunswick, NJ: Transaction.

Brehm, J. and W. Rahn (1997). "Individual Level Evidence for the Causes and Consequences of Social Capital." *American Journal of Political Science* 41, 888–1023.

Cohen, J. L. (1997). "American Civil Society Talk." College Park, MD: National Commission on Civic Renewal, Working Paper no. 6.

Constable, P. (1999). "India's Democracy in Uncertain Health." *Washington Post* 21 April, A17, A19.

Coppedge, M. and W. Reinicke (1991). "Measuring Polyarchy," in A. Inkeles (ed.), *On Measuring Democracy.* New Brunswick, NJ: Transaction.

Diener, E. (1995). "A Value Based Index for Measuring National Quality of Life." *Social Indicators Research* 36, 107–127.

Easterly, W. and R. Levine (1997). "Africa's Growth Tragedy: Policies and Ethnic Divisions." *Quarterly Journal of Economics* 112, 1203–1250.

The Economist (1990). *The Economist Book of Vital World Statistics.* New York: Times Books.

Esposito, J. (1991). *Islam and Politics*, third ed. Syracuse: Syracuse University Press.

Esposito, J. and J. Voll (1996). *Islam and Democracy.* Oxford: Oxford University Press.

Fenno, R. F. (1978). *Home Style.* Boston: Little, Brown.

Forster, E. M. (1965). "Two Cheers for Democracy," in E. M. Forster, *Two Cheers for Democracy.* New York: Harcourt, Brace.

Gambetta, D. (1988). "Can We Trust Trust?" pp. 213–237. In D. Gambetta (ed.), *Trust.* Oxford: Basil Blackwell.

Gastil, R. D. (1991). "The Comparative Survey of Freedom: Experience and Suggestions," in A. Inkeles (ed.), *On Measuring Democracy.* New Brunswick, NJ: Transaction.

Gurr, T. R., K. Jaggers and W. H. Moore (1991). "The Transformation of the Western State: The Growth of Democracy, Autocracy, and State Power

Since 1800," in A. Inkeles (ed.), *On Measuring Democracy*. New Brunswick, NJ: Transaction.

Inglehart, R. (1997). *Modernization and Postmodernization*. Princeton: Princeton University Press.

Inglehart, R. (1999). "Trust, Well-Being and Democracy," in M. Warren (ed.), *Democracy and Trust*. Cambridge: Cambridge University Press.

Inglehart, R., M. Basznez and A. Moreno (1998). *Human Values and Beliefs: A Cross-Cultural Sourcebook*. Ann Arbor: University of Michigan Press.

Knack, S. (1999). "Social Capital, Growth, and Poverty: A Survey of the Cross-Country Evidence." Center for Institutional Reform and the Informal Sector (IRIS), University of Maryland—College Park.

Knack, S. and P. Keefer (1997). "Does Social Capital Have An Economic Payoff? A Cross-Country Investigation." *Quarterly Journal of Economics* 112, 1251–1288.

La Porta, R. (1998). "The Quality of Government." Unpublished manuscript, Harvard University.

La Porta, R., F. Lopez-Silanes, A. Schleifer and R. Vishney (1997). "Trust in Large Organizations." *American Economic Review Papers and Proceedings* 87, 333–338.

Levi, M. (1998). "A State of Trust," pp. 77–101. In M. Levi and V. Braithwaite (eds.), *Trust and Governance*. New York: Russell Sage Foundation.

Levi, M. (1999). "When Good Defenses Make Good Neighbors: A Transaction Cost Approach to Trust and Distrust." New York: Russell Sage Foundation Working Paper no. 140.

Lipset, S. M. (1990). *Continental Divide*. New York: Routledge.

Macaulay, S. (1963). "Non-Contractual Relations in Business: A Preliminary Study." *American Sociological Review* 28, 55–67.

Misztal, B. (1996). *Trust in Modern Societies*. Cambridge, UK: Polity Press.

Mueller, J. (1996). "Democracy, Capitalism, and the End of Transition," In M. Mandlebaum, (ed.), *Post-Communism: Four Perspectives*. Washington: Council on Foreign Relations.

Muller, E. N. and M. A. Seligson (1994). "Civic Culture and Democracy: The Question of Causal Relationships." *American Political Science Review* 88, 635–652.

Offe, C. (1999). "Trust and Knowledge, Rules and Decisions: Exploring a Difficult Conceptual Terrain," in M. Warren (ed.), *Democracy and Trust*. Cambridge: Cambridge University Press.

Pagden, A. (1988). "The Destruction of Trust and its Economic Consequences in the Case of Eighteenth-century Naples," in D. Gambetta (ed.), *Trust*. Oxford: Basil Blackwell.

Putnam, R. (1993). *Making Democracy Work: Civic Traditions in Modern Italy*. Princeton: Princeton University Press.

Putnam, R. (1995). "Tuning In, Tuning Out: The Strange Disappearance of Social Capital in America." *PS: Political Science and Politics* (December): 664–683.

Rahn, W., J. Brehm and N. Carlson (1997). "National Elections as Institutions for Generating Social Capital." Paper presented at the Annual Meeting of the American Political Science Association, Washington, D.C., August–September.

Rice, T. and J. Feldman (1997). "Civic Culture and Democracy from Europe to America." *Journal of Politics* 59, 1143–1172.

Rothstein, B. (2000). "Trust, Social Dilemmas, and Collective Memories: On the Rise and Decline of the Swedish Model." *Journal of Theoretical Politics* 12(4), 477–503.

Rothstein, B. (2002). "Sweden: Social Capital in the Social Democratic State," pp. 289–331. In R. Putnam (ed.), *Democracies in Flux.* Oxford: Oxford University Press.

Sachs, J. and A. Warner (1997). "Natural Resource Abundance and Economic Growth." Unpublished manuscript, Center for International Development and Harvard Institute for International Development, Harvard University.

Scholz, J. and N. Pinney (1995). "Duty, Fear, and Tax Compliance: The Heuristic Basis of Citizenship Behavior." *American Journal of Political Science* 39, 490–512.

Sitkin, S. and N. Roth (1993). "Explaining the Limited Effectiveness of Legalistic 'Remedies' for Trust/Distrust." *Organization Science* 4, 367–392.

Tyler, T. (1990). *Why People Obey the Law.* New Haven: Yale University Press.

Uslaner, E. M. (2002). *The Moral Foundations of Trust.* New York: Cambridge University Press.

Vanhanen, T. (1997). *Prospects of Democracy.* New York: Routledge.

Weber, M. (1958 [1930]). *The Protestant Ethic and the Spirit of Capitalism.* New York: Charles Scribners' Sons.

Woolcock, M. (1998). "Social Capital and Economic Development: Toward a Theoretical Synthesis and Policy Framework." *Theory and Society* 27(2), 151–208.

CHAPTER 10

SOCIAL CAPITAL, IMPARTIALITY AND THE WELFARE STATE: AN INSTITUTIONAL APPROACH

Bo Rothstein and Dietlind Stolle

INTRODUCTION

This chapter sheds more light on the sources of one important aspect of social capital, namely generalized trust. Most discussions about the sources of social capital thus far have been focused on the realm of civil society. The more people are engaged in voluntary associations and informal networks, the more trusting toward other people they will become (Putnam 1993, 2000). This approach is problematic because there is no successful theory of social capital that links aspects of civic life and trust at the micro- and macrolevels. Previous chapters have shown that, at the microlevel, voluntary associations do not necessarily work as *producers* of civic values and attitudes, such as generalized trust (e.g., Mayer, Wollebæk and Selle this volume; see also Stolle 2001; Uslaner 2002). In addition, it is difficult to distinguish between networks that produce distrust toward others, for example criminal or racist organizations, and networks that potentially produce trust, such as Parent-Teacher Associations or the Boy Scouts (however, Hooghe tries to make this distinction in this volume).

The theoretical discussion and findings in our chapter are intended to situate the concept of social capital more squarely in the realm of public institutions. Specifically, we respond to the critique that the social capital literature does not pay enough attention to the link between government institutions and social capital. We intend to present an institutional theory of generalized trust that makes the connection between the individual level and the macrolevel. We will also present some preliminary empirical findings that test our theory.

The argument in this chapter is twofold. First, we argue that *contemporary* political institutions are important determinants of social capital. It might be true that generalized trust is shaped by sociocultural historic forces that can be traced back to the Middle Ages (Putnam 1993), but there are many problems with such an approach, not least of which being that it becomes deterministic (Tarrow 1996). Moreover, while social trust may be closely intertwined with various aspects of civil society, we argue that present-day political institutions are also able to have an impact on generalized trust. Second, we present a theoretical approach in which we specify the causal mechanisms of the relationship between government institutions and social capital. Based on this theory of institutional trust, we argue that it is the degree of perceived fairness and impartiality of the institutions responsible for the implementation of public policies that serves as an important foundation for the building and maintenance of high institutional trust levels, which, in its turn, spills over to influence generalized trust in others.

GENERALIZED TRUST: THE ROLE OF THE STATE

Most problematic in this discussion about the relationship between state institutions and social attitudes is the issue of the causal flow. Mixed interpretations have been developed in light of the strong correlation between political factors and institutional trust, on the one hand, and generalized trust, on the other. Whereas some authors claim that this correlation is based on the causal relationship from social to political forms of trust (Lipset and Schneider 1983; Newton and Norris 2000; Putnam 1993), others conclude exactly the opposite (Brehm and Rahn 1997; Rothstein 2001; Sides 1999; Stolle forthcoming). Although social scientists attempt to determine the causal flow of the relationship between institutions and generalized trust, the main problem is that the causal mechanism in both claims remains unclear. As many have argued, we need to understand the causal mechanisms between interpersonal trust, collective action, civil society, and trust in government institutions (Braithwaite 1998). Can political institutions be arranged so as to increase their legitimacy? Ronald Inglehart has argued that it seems likely that democratic institutions are conducive to generalized trust, as well as that trust is conducive to democracy (Inglehart 1999). The difficulty in this discussion is, according to Inglehart, how to specify the causal connection(s) between these variables at the individual level (Hedström and Swedberg 1998).

Our response to this challenge is twofold. First, no plausible causal mechanisms have been developed to explain the causal argument from trust and norms of reciprocity to institutional performance. Certainly, more trusting citizens are possibly more participatory, and might therefore have better access to government and might have more opportunities to hold governments accountable. Yet we claim that the reverse causal logic is just as plausible, namely, that the manner in which public services are delivered can influence the development of generalized trust (Levi 1998). Our caveat is that in the search for the sources of social capital, the focus on trust in politicians is misguided, or at least incomplete, as it is more connected to specific political and short-term economic considerations and is not sufficiently linked to the way we think about others. Instead we advance the argument here that more important for the development of generalized trust is the experience of impartial, just and fair political institutions, which are responsible for the implementation of public policies. In other words, we need to redirect our attention to the character of service delivery, the impartiality of the street-level bureaucrats, as well as the perceived opportunities to cheat the system. They cause differences in regional or national institutional trust, which in turn influence generalized trust.

DIMENSIONS OF INSTITUTIONAL TRUST: THE IMPORTANCE OF IMPARTIALITY

There is a variety of forms of institutional trust that we can identify in the study of advanced industrialized democracies, but it is often a problem that most of them are collapsed under one label. For example, we are certainly aware of concepts such as trust in politicians, trust in the functioning of democratic institutions, trust in people who run democratic institutions, trust in various agencies that implement public policies, trust in the overall democratic system, and trust in the procedures that make institutions work. Our point here is that the literature has not distinguished between confidence in the institutions on the representational side of the political system (parties, parliaments, cabinets) and confidence in the institutions on the implementation side of the system. The latter type of institution has especially been forgotten or neglected in the debate about social capital.

The theoretical reason for the difference in confidence that people place in these types of political institutions is the following. On the representational side, one of the main roles for political institutions is to be partisan. A political party that holds government power, or the majority in a parliament, is supposed to try to implement their ideology in a partisan way. Thus, people that support the ideology of the ruling party or parties are likely to have confidence in them, while people that oppose their ideology are likely to report a lack of confidence. For example, a city government run by the party one supports can be seen as one's political agent. In such a case, one is likely to have confidence in the government—as long as one supports its policies and it keeps its promises. But, of course, people who oppose the ruling party are more likely to distrust or to show a lack of confidence in that very same government, especially if the ruling party does what it has promised to do. This is why we usually find a strong correlation between political leanings and political trust (Hetherington 1999; Norén 2000), but a weak correlation between confidence in these types of political institutions and social trust.

Now we are interested here in a very different dimension of institutional trust or institutional perception. It is mostly connected to the legal branches of the state and to many government organizations responsible for implementing public policies. The issue here is not so much whether these institutions speak for one's interests but, more important for the citizen, whether these institutions represent the ideals of universalism, equality before the law, and impartiality. In these cases, a government institution that simply acts in my interest as my agent, no matter what, is one that I have bribed (or one that is run by my cousin). And if I can bribe judges or civil servants in general, so can someone else, including my adversaries.

We will provide empirical evidence for this distinction below. The idea is that despite different political leanings in government, people are able (or not) to trust that institutions responsible for the implementation of public policies are run and guided by the principles of impartiality and fairness. Being fair and impartial is very different from—in fact the opposite of—acting as an agent of someone or acting on behalf of someone. The argument here is that if we have reason to believe that the government institutions responsible for implementing laws and policies behave according to the principles of fairness and impartiality, we may trust them with our demands for education, social insurance, health care, protection from crime and other essentially private goods. This logic is easy enough to follow: It makes no sense to pay your taxes if you think that the tax authorities are discriminating against you or are heavily corrupt. You would not take your dispute to a court if you did not trust the judge to be impartial and to follow the universal rules such as equality before the law; or if you had to, you would maybe try to bribe a judge in your favor.

You would not send your children to a public school if you were convinced that the teachers would give special favors to other children from a different (ethnic, religious, etc.) group; or if you had to, you would maybe send your children to a school that discriminates against groups other than your own. Again, people are not likely to trust political institutions because they think that the officials will act in their interests as their agents. Instead, they will trust public institutions if they have reason to believe that they are fair, impartial and competent.

The principle of impartiality and fairness is, above all, a very strong principle against any form of discrimination, but it is also a principle working against the idea that government institutions should act as agents for someone's special interests. It is, of course, also a strong principle against all forms of direct or indirect corruption of government institutions. Still, states differ in the way the distant goal of impartiality is practiced, in the type of welfare system that is installed, in the actual government offices, such as street-level bureaucracies, and in the type of judicial system that is in place (Rothstein 1998). In short, citizens do have different experiences with the impartiality of the public institutions responsible for the implementation of public policies, depending on which country or in which region they have had their experience with state agencies.

In sum, we argue that the impartiality and fairness of political institutions that implement public policies are important dimensions of institutional trust and confidence that can be conceptually separated from conventional political trust in politicians, parties, and "the government" (see for example Hibbing and Theiss-Morse 2001; Nye, Zelikow and King 1997; Newton and Norris 2000). In fact, these dimensions of institutional trust are the ones that are beneficial for the development of generalized trust, as we will show below. Let us now examine one of the arenas in which impartiality and fairness play the most dominant role.

AN EXAMPLE OF EXPERIENCES WITH STREET-LEVEL BUREAUCRACY: THE WELFARE SYSTEM

Citizens have various experiences with impartiality or lack of impartiality in dealings with the police, the judicial system, and the welfare system, for example. We concentrate here on the arena of the welfare state, as an important example of citizens' experiences, though other arenas have a similar impact. Gøsta Esping-Andersen's well-known typology of different types of welfare states and their different institutional foundations, character, ideology, and consequences provides a useful scheme for distinguishing how the principles of fairness and impartiality are implemented differently (Esping-Andersen 1990). The basic principle of a universal welfare policy is not to discriminate between citizens on economic grounds, which means not to separate "the needy" and "the poor" from other citizens and to treat them differently (Rothstein 1998). Instead, services such as health care, day care and care for the elderly are organized by government for the whole population on the principle of equal access. Social insurances are also intended to cover income loss (due to unemployment, disability or sickness) for the whole population. Thus, in a universal welfare scheme, there is no need to leave room for bureaucratic discretion, such as a means-testing procedure. This stands in contrast to the situation under a selective and a conservative (mixed) system (Esping-Andersen 1990).

As shown in Table 10.1, the fundamental difference between the universal system and other potential systems of welfare distribution is

Table 10.1 The three worlds of social capital

	Type of welfare state		
	Universal	Selective	Conservative
Main characteristics	Universal programs dominate	Means-tested programs dominate	Programs are mixture between means-tested and universal
Important characteristics for societal divisions	Encompassing Includes ALL citizens Does not create or manifest societal divisions	Divisive Singles out the "needy" and "deserving"	Etatist Singles out the privileged from the unprivileged
Prone to fraud?	Easy rules, everyone gets the same	Desire to "cheat the system" Complicated rules and tests of eligibility (fraud is likely)	Complicated rules (fraud is possible)
Norm of impartiality?	Everyone is treated the same way	Citizens receive very different treatment Stigma	Citizens receive very different treatment
Consequences for trust	Can spread widely	Those singled out will trust less	Compartmentalized trust for one's group, prevents generalized trust

Source: Authors' summary.

its undivisive, encompassing and inclusionary character. There is no need for discussions about who are the "needy" or the "undeserving," and there is also no need to single out certain groups of the population who might need more or less, because everyone is considered entitled. Certainly, universal welfare states are not completely free of any form of stratification, as many scholars on gender and the welfare state have demonstrated (Sainsbury 1997, Hobson 2000). Yet the focus on overall inclusiveness functions as an important factor in the development and maintenance of generalized trust, as we will see below. Moreover, universal welfare programs are much easier to administer and enable fewer opportunities to cheat the system. Programs such as flat-rate pensions, universal health care or child allowances are a great deal simpler, cheaper and easier to implement than their selective or etatist counterparts. This is largely due to the fact that in a universal-type program there is no need for an administrative apparatus to undertake any kind of eligibility testing, which is a necessary concomitant of a selective program and, to a degree, of programs of a conservative welfare state. If everyone is entitled to have the same or a proportional share, there is hardly any possibility for welfare fraud (Rothstein 1998).

Both selective and conservative systems have a divisive character. In their essence these welfare states are designed to plot groups of the population against each other. This is the case because in welfare states with mostly selective programs the "needy" or the "others" are singled out, questioned and possibly blamed for their situation. In the selective model, the discussion often focuses on how to separate the "deserving" from the "undeserving" poor, which translates into a seemingly unending debate about how and where to draw boundaries. Leading politicians are therefore likely to find themselves in a situation where it becomes increasingly difficult to argue that the selective programs are normatively fair. Public consent to the system is undermined because the social policy debate comes to turn not on what is *generally fair* but rather on what is *specifically necessary for the "others."* In fact, citizens who pay for services that are targeted at selected groups of the population with whom they believe they do not have many similarities might also feel unfairly treated (Hetherington 2001). Friction is created between those who are in need of governmental services and those who are not. Obviously this friction might coincide with pre-existing divisions such as race and immigrant status in selective welfare states (Rothstein 1998).

Similar distinctions are made in conservative welfare states, which are highly hierarchical and status oriented (Esping-Andersen 1990, 59ff.).

In countries such as Austria, France and Germany, for example, civil servants are endowed with an extraordinarily high share of welfare privileges and "extras." In other words, privileged groups of the population are singled out to receive more than the rest of society, a benefit originally intended as an award for loyalty to the state. The status-oriented compartimentalized social insurance schemes in Germany, which are tailored to its specific clientele, are a case in point. Another example is the Italian pension scheme with its hundreds of occupationally distinct variants (see more evidence in Esping-Andersen 1990). Health care systems in such mixed conservative welfare states have unequal treatment outcomes, so that some groups of the population benefit from lavish public or excellent private insurance, and other groups of the population must be satisfied with waiting in line for the "average" public care. The result is exclusiveness and a greater barrier between the privileged and the workers, which is still reflected in today's legislation. In other words, in conservative welfare states, modern social policy manifests class distinctions and immigrant status.

The fact that both selective as well as conservative welfare states entail programs that single out groups for special benefits is accompanied by the necessity to establish rules and tests of eligibility in which it must be ascertained whether a given applicant is entitled to support, and if so, to how much. In addition, the needy are stigmatized and usually stamped as socially inferior or as "others" with other types of social characteristics and needs. Many authors have criticized the consequences of such a welfare system due to its impact on the recipients' self-respect and confidence (Walzer 1983, 227f.).

Welfare states with selective programs present further problems of administration, as local administrators enjoy a wide range of discretionary power. The consequences are that the bureaucratic power is easily abused, and that fraud on the part of clients is easily committed. For example, applicants in a selective system, if rational, will claim that their situation is worse than it actually is and might be more pessimistic about a self-reliant solution to the problem. The administrators in such a system often have incentives from their superiors to be suspicious of clients' claims. As a consequence, even if cases of cheating, fraud and the abuse of power are in fact relatively rare, the sensationalistic logic of mass media ensures that such cases will receive great attention, thereby influencing the population at large. All of our thoughts on the relationship between welfare states, its character, and generalized trust have been summarized in Table 10.1.

Institutional Impartiality and Generalized Trust: The Causal Mechanism

The question is how the differences in experiences and perceptions of impartiality of the welfare state institutions might influence and shape attitudes of generalized trust. Our argument is that generalized attitudes about others and generalized attitudes about the fairness and impartiality of institutions are inherently intertwined. The two types of attitudes are related through one indirect and two direct links. On the one hand, citizens make inferences about their system experiences and extend them to everyone else living under the same system. On the other hand, the character of the political system also influences the behavior and experiences of citizens directly.

The first link between system impartiality and generalized trust is purely based on cognitive inferences. We believe that citizens generalize from their experiences with the street-level bureaucrats and authorities. So, for example, if citizens have evidence that their public policy system is corrupt and that public school principals, social workers, etc. cannot be trusted, they will extend this perception of people to the "generalized other." If even government officials are not fair, then why should the rest of society be? If civil servants cannot act honestly, why would the rest of society be different (see Stolle forthcoming)? Conversely, if they perceive that the political system that implements public policies does act fairly, honestly and responsively, they feel more secure and encouraged to trust others. We have argued that universal welfare systems and uncorrupt legal systems are much more prone to exhibit impartiality. We suggest that this knowledge of impartiality and fairness will influence how citizens think about their fellow citizens as well because official authorities and their ethics are seen as exemplary for other people.

Second, people base their generalized attitudes on observations they make about other people and fellow citizens. We argued above that, in contrast to universal systems, selective and conservative welfare states are structured such that citizens who use the systems have more (perceived) incentives to try to cheat the system. As a result, it makes no sense to trust "most people" if they are generally known to cheat, bribe or in some other way try to corrupt the impartiality of government institutions in order to extract special favors—even if the actual occurrence of such frauds is much more rare than emphasized in the media or by political forces. One reason "most other people" may be trusted is that they are generally known to refrain from such forms of behavior.

Finally, we argue that the citizens' own experiences or those of closely related others (e.g., parents, friends, members of same identification groups, etc.) within the welfare and legal system has an impact on the way they think about others. If citizens feel that they are not treated fairly and respectfully by the authorities and politicians, their self-esteem will be negatively influenced, which in turn shapes how they deal with strangers or other people who are not known (Tyler 1990). If citizens experience systematic discrimination, as do many minority groups in Western democracies, and if citizens are singled out as special or "problem" cases, as in selective welfare systems, and perceive that their opinions are not heard, it seems plausible that the majority of citizens might not trust them. So then why should they be willing and open to engage with people not known to them? How can citizens with these experiences trust all people if they perceive the majority's interests to be different? Alternatively, citizens who feel that politicians and other official authorities take them seriously, listen to them and respect them may also develop a belief in other people or people in general, though the negative influence is probably more predominant here.

Our argument is certainly not that all forms of "generalized trust" are caused by experiences with and trust in the impartiality and honesty of certain government institutions. There are other important sources that are creating such social capital, for example the early childhood experiences of trust relationships in one's immediate family (Uslaner 2002). However, our model helps to identify some of the important dimensions of state institutions that are closely related to a significant aspect of social capital, generalized trust, and we thus present an institutional theory of generalized trust.[1]

EMPIRICAL ILLUSTRATIONS AND ANALYSIS

Our argument entails three aspects that specify the causal mechanism between institutional impartiality and generalized trust. In this section we test and present evidence for the microlevel causal mechanism with data from various sources. At the macrolevel, it is clear that the most universal, and therefore the most impartially structured and the most egalitarian, welfare states are the ones that accommodate citizens with the highest trust levels. It is widely known and has been shown that citizens in universal welfare states (e.g., Scandinavian countries) score much higher on generalized trust than citizens who are socialized in other institutional settings. This roughly confirms our theoretical insight about the relationship between the character

of state institutions and generalized trust. However, our goal here is
to test our theory at the microlevel.

MEASUREMENTS FOR EMPIRICAL ILLUSTRATIONS
AT THE MICROLEVEL

The theory we specified is, after all, a micro theory of trust development. As discussed above, most microtests of the social capital theory
have failed in the past (see Wollebæk and Selle this volume; Stolle
this volume and 2001; Uslaner 2002), so it is important that we
provide the micro evidence for our theoretical insights. For the analysis, we utilize the yearly Society-Opinion-Media (SOM) surveys
from 1996 to 2000, which have been conducted by the SOM institute at Göteborg University, Sweden.[2] The survey includes a variety
of indicators on social capital, political attitudes and demographic
data. However, since Sweden is a country that developed one of
the most universal welfare states, our test will indeed be a difficult
undertaking.

Our evidence here consists of three pieces, according to the three
causal mechanisms we specified. First, we argued that citizens generalize from knowledge about the honesty and impartiality of public
officials and the public welfare system to other people. If this causal
link is true, we should see a relatively strong relationship at the individual level between trust in the impartiality of institutions, on the
one hand, and generalized trust, on the other. However, we need to
distinguish various types of institutional trust, which the SOM data
allows us to do. Second, we argued that citizens observe others who
might be perceived as abusers of the system. In particular we argued
that in means-tested welfare states, for example, citizens are more
prone to be perceived as abusive of the system. In Sweden, we only
find a few selective welfare programs; however, if this insight about
the causal mechanism is correct, we should see that regions with
higher proportions of citizens in selective programs are also inhabited
by less trusting people. Our final argument was that citizens who
experience discrimination through the welfare system themselves
or through close others feel threatened and develop distrust for
outsiders. If this proposition is true, we should see that citizens who
participate in Swedish selective programs trust less. Here we utilize
indicators that measure contact with the very few selective and means-
tested welfare programs in the Swedish system, namely the handout
of social welfare benefits, as well as participation in selected labor
market schemes.

Results: Microlevel Analysis

We turn to the analysis of these causal mechanisms in a slightly modified order for better illustration. First, we examine our indicators of institutional trust. Our previous discussion demonstrated that there are at least two dimensions in which citizens judge political institutions: (1) they expect representatives of political, legal and social institutions to function as their agents; (2) citizens expect impartiality. Moreover, citizens expect more agency and potential political bias from political institutions with elected offices, whereas, we argue, citizens expect impartiality and an unbiased approach from order institutions. Our claim is, of course, that the lack of impartiality of certain institutions disturbs trust development within the population. Let us first have a look at the distinctions citizens draw between various institutions.

We subjected the pooled SOM data to a factor analysis. As the results in Table 10.2 indicate, citizens in Sweden make distinctions between different types of confidence in institutions in a list of ten. The factor analysis (principal component, with varimax rotation) reveals that three different dimensions of institutions emerge. Indeed most political institutions with elected offices fall under the first dimension, such as confidence in parliaments, regional governments and local governments. A second dimension reflects the group of impartial institutions that are expected to function with less political

Table 10.2   Varieties of institutional trust

	Component		
	1 Political trust (institutions with elected officials)	2 Trust in impartial institutions	3 Trust in control institutions (media)
Trust in government	**.876**	.161	.054
Trust in the Parliament	**.874**	.204	.100
Trust in the local government	**.672**	.254	.191
Trust in the police	.198	**.733**	.052
Trust in the health system	.088	**.743**	.034
Trust in the defense system	.159	**.625**	.071
Trust in schools	.130	**.527**	.287
Trust in the legal system	.353	**.531**	.156
Trust in newspapers	.145	.092	**.815**
Trust in TV	.090	.153	**.833**

Note: Rotated Component Matrix. Extraction method: Principal Component Analysis. Rotation method: Varimax with Kaiser Normalization. A rotation converged in 5 iterations.

Source: Pooled SOM surveys.

bias and in an impartial manner. They include the health system, school systems, the police, legal institutions and defense. A third dimension taps confidence in institutions that are mostly control institutions that check power of institutions with elected offices, and includes the media. These results are confirmed in an analysis of the World Values Survey (results not shown, but see Rothstein and Stolle 2002). In other words, citizens make distinctions between political institutions according to the theory we have presented; they do not view all institutions in a similar way but rather distinguish between the ones on the representation side and those on the implementation side of the political system.

What is even more interesting in light of our argument is the relationship between the three dimensions of institutional confidence and generalized trust. The correlation between confidence in political/biased institutions and generalized trust, as well as between confidence in power check institutions and generalized trust, is lower at the individual level ($r = .17$ and $r = .08$ respectively) than the relationship between generalized trust and trust in impartial institutions ($r = .20$). The results indicate that trust in impartial institutions is more important for the development of generalized trust than are other forms of institutional trust. This result is strengthened at the macrolevel in a larger cross-national sample including fifty countries, where confidence in impartial institutions and generalized trust correlate at $r = .54$ and the other correlations are insignificant (for results see Rothstein and Stolle 2002).

We now move to analyzing our third causal linkage proposition since this is the one that will later serve as our basic model for further analyses. The SOM 2000 survey allows us to determine which respondents participated in selective and means-tested programs, which is fairly rare in Sweden. If our causal mechanism is correct, we should see that respondents in selective programs are less trusting.

In a simple comparison, we see in Figure 10.1 that those who received benefits from Swedish selective welfare state institutions, such as means-tested social welfare benefits *(socialtjänst)* and early retirement benefits *(förtidspension)*, are less trusting. This is particularly clear in a comparison to others who did not receive such benefits and in comparison to those who received benefits from programs with a universal character (we used the example of the *sjukpenning*). The differences are significant between those with selective benefits and everyone else. This is indeed an important finding given the causal logic developed. The results also hold in a simple regression model in which we include important demographic and attitudinal predictors of generalized trust.

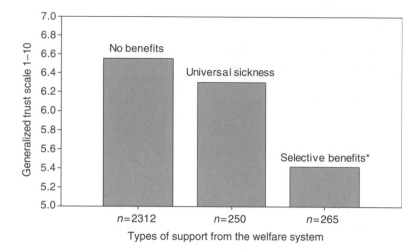

Figure 10.1 Universal versus selective benefits and generalized trust
Note: * Significant difference between selective benefits versus others.
Source: Swedish SOM survey 2000.

In the regression model in the first column, we include a wide variety of predictors of generalized trust that have been found to be important in the social capital literature, including associational membership. The inclusion of age, for example, is of course related to the argument about the civic generations in the United States (Putnam 2000); education has often been shown to be an important predictor of trust (Brehm and Rahn 1997; Putnam 2000), whereas marriage status is an embattled variable (Uslaner 2002). We also included employment status as a particularly important control variable in our test, as unemployment in itself could be the source of lower trust for people in special welfare programs. Also, immigrant status is an important experience that is related to generalized trust, as immigrants might experience more discrimination within various social and political institutions. Finally, we included an array of attitudinal correlates of trust, such as satisfaction with life, satisfaction with democracy in Sweden, trust in the parliament, and trust in impartial institutions, as well as a self-placement variable on the left-to-right political scale. Most importantly, we include a variable that measures membership in all associations as these are seen as producing trust in the societal approach to social capital theory.

The results in Table 10.3 show that even controlling for the above demographic and other indicators, citizens who have used selective

Table 10.3 The experience of impartial institutions and generalized trust: micro results

	Model 1		Model 2	
	Std. error	Standardized coefficients	Std. error	Standardized coefficients
Constant	.361		.570	
Demographic variables:				
Age	.003	−.087***	.003	−.086***
Education	.021	.114***	.021	.118***
Married or not	.094	.025	.095	.023
Being unemployed	.230	−.013	.231	−.013
Being an immigrant	.216	−.057***	.220	−.053***
Attitudinal correlates:				
Life satisfaction	.070	.212***	.070	.213***
Left-right self-placement	.040	−.064***	.040	−.058***
Trust in the parliament	.050	.120***	.051	.120***
Trust in impartial institutions	.024	.176***	.024	.170***
Social capital indicators:				
All association index	.245	.071***	.247	.072***
Welfare state experiences:				
Selective programs	.071	−.073***	.071	−.072***
Contextual county level characteristics:				
Membership in study circles			.001	.014
County participation in selective labor market schemes			.063	.046*
Proportion of foreign citizens per county (heterogeneity)			.016	−.022
Average income per county			.001	.034
Model indicators				
Number of cases	2465		2443	
Adjusted R square	.19		.20	

Note: * $p<.10$; ** $p<.05$; *** $p<.01$; **** $p<.001$.
Source: SOM Survey 2000.

welfare state services in Sweden are less trusting than the rest of the population. We argue that the experience of these selective programs is discriminatory in an otherwise universal welfare state. Admittedly, the coefficient is not very strong, however, in a universal system as the Swedish one, we would not expect the contact with the few selective services to have such a large impact. In fact, our theoretical insights are best proven in the Swedish context, if the effect of means-tested programs remains small. In addition, we see that contrary to some previous evidence, age negatively correlates with trust, so that older people in Sweden trust less. Being married and being unemployed, given all other explanatory variables, are not related to trust. All other variables are significantly correlated with trust. More education, not being an immigrant, a more positive outlook on life, satisfaction with democracy, left political placement, and trust in various political institutions are all positively correlated with trust. Trust in impartial institutions is a strong predictor of generalized trust, even controlling for various other influences. Interestingly, it also matters that the respondent is a member of associations (such as sports clubs and cultural groups, etc.).

Third, we argued that certain types of welfare states and legal systems are more prone to fraud and the perception of fraud, dishonesty and corruption. If our causal mechanism is true, Swedish areas in which there are particularly high proportions of people who are dependent on selective services should correspond with those areas inhabited by people with lower trust levels. Again, Sweden is a difficult case in this test, because of its universal system and the minor differences between regions. Yet, if we divide Sweden into over 280 counties *(kommuner)*, we can make distinctions between regions in which there are proportionally more or less citizens in selective labor market schemes. We additionally include regional characteristics, such as participation in selective welfare institutions, regional participation in study circles (one of Sweden's famous associations), regional heterogeneity in terms of proportions of immigrants, and median regional income in our regression model. We see that people in those counties with particularly high levels of people in selective welfare programs are also those with significantly lower trust, all controls provided (see Table 10.3). The result holds even if we control for the individual influence of being in selective welfare program schemes and for unemployment status.

These results confirm some of the macro effects that can be found in cross-national samples where trust levels are consistently higher in universal welfare states (Rothstein and Stolle 2002), though the difference is that we show here contextual effects on the individual, and we control for the other two causal mechanisms that operate as well: the individual experience of discrimination and the experience of political and impartial institutions. In other words, holding personal discrimination as well as perceptions of institutions and several other controls constant, we still find a small effect caused by the experience of observing other citizens in potential fraudulent situations, confirming the second causal mechanism we identified.

CONCLUSION

We have developed here an institutional theory of generalized trust. Our argument is that the structure of contemporary institutions is an important and overlooked factor that matters for the generation of generalized trust. In particular, we developed a causal mechanism that explains and specifies the causal flow from impartial, just, and inclusive institutions responsible for the implementation of public policies to generalized trust. The impartiality of these institutions influences: (1) how citizens make inferences from the system and public officials to other citizens; (2) how citizens observe the behavior of fellow citizens; and (3) how they experience discrimination against themselves or close others. In our empirical section we have shown that these three causal mechanisms are at work. Citizens do make strong connections between the impartiality of institutions and generalized trust at the micro- and macrolevels. Citizens develop different levels of trust dependent on their observations of their fellow citizens. And finally, citizens who have experienced discrimination are significantly less trusting.

These findings reveal important insights about social capital, as they suggest that the concept is not exclusively linked to the arena of civil society. The character of state institutions that might be responsible for some variation in social capital within a society or across several societies represents an important link between the state and civil society. Our research so far suggests two avenues for further scrutiny. First, our theory should be tested at the microlevel within and across other types of welfare systems outside the Swedish-style universal context. At the macrolevel, we already know that universality and impartiality of welfare states strongly relates to high levels of generalized trust, but our micro test performed here needs to travel to other welfare systems. Second, we should examine the norm of impartiality and its implementation in a wider variety of political and social institutions, for example in the legal system or in relation to contacts with the police (a first analysis can be found in Rothstein and Stolle 2002). Furthermore, we need to know more about the transmission mechanisms that link institutional norms, experiences and citizens' attitudes. It is plausible that citizens learn about such norms very early on, such as from their parents and in schools, which suggests that social capital research could learn a lot from the forgotten school of socialization research.

Notes

1. The question, of course, arises of how these aspects and structures of institutions can be implemented and built up. The answer to this important question, though obviously relevant, goes clearly beyond the scope of this chapter and builds on a vast literature about the rise of the welfare state (Esping-Andersen 1990, Rothstein 1998). However, it would be utterly dissatisfying if these institutional dimensions are purely a product of important historical constellations and critical junctures and could not be implemented any more in today's systems.

2. The institute is managed jointly by the Departments of Political Science, Public Administration and Journalism/Masscommunication at Göteborg University. For this project, questions about trust have been added to the five surveys of 1996 to 2000 with funding from the Swedish Council for Research in the Humanities and Social Sciences. For information about sampling, response rates, etc. please visit www.som.gu.se or contact som@jmg.gu.se.

References

Braithwaite, V. (1998). "Communal and Exchange Trust Norms: Their Value Base and Relevance to Institutional Trust." In V. Braithwaite and M. Levi (eds.), *Trust and Governance*. New York: Russell Sage Foundation.

Brehm, J. and W. Rahn (1997). "Individual Level Evidence for the Causes and Consequences of Social Capital." *American Journal of Political Science* 41, 999–1023.

Esping-Andersen, G. (1990). *The Three Worlds of Welfare Capitalism*. Princeton: Princeton University Press.

Hedström, P. and R. Swedberg (1998). "Social Mechanisms: An Introductory Essay." In P. Hedström and R. Swedberg (eds.), *Social Mechanisms: An Analytical Approach to Social Theory*. New York: Cambridge University Press.

Hetherington, M. (1999). "The Effect of Political Trust on the Presidential Vote, 1968–96." *American Political Science Review* 93, 311–326.

Hetherington, M. (2001). "Resurgent Mass Partisanship: The Role of Elite Polarization." *American Political Science Review* 95, 619–631.

Hibbing, J. and E. Theiss-Morse (2001). *What Is It about Government that Americans Dislike?* Cambridge: Cambridge University Press.

Hobson, B. (2000). *Gender and Citizenship in Transition*. New York: Routledge.

Inglehart, R. (1999). "Trust, Well-being and Democracy." In M. Warren (ed.), *Democracy and Trust*. New York: Cambridge University Press.

Levi, M. (1998). *Consent, Dissent, and Patriotism*. New York: Cambridge University Press.

Lipset, S. M. and W. Schneider (1983). *The Confidence Gap*. New York: Free Press.

Newton, K. (1997). "Social Capital and Democracy." *American Behavioral Scientist* 40, 575–586.

Newton, K. and P. Norris (2000). "Confidence in Public Institutions." pp. 52–72. In S. Pharr and R. Putnam (eds.), *Disaffected Democracies*. Princeton: Princeton University Press.

Norén, Y. (2000). "Explaining Variation in Political Trust in Sweden." Paper presented at the European Consortium for Political Research Joint Session of Workshops, Copenhagen, April 14–19.

Nye, J., P. Zelikow and D. King (eds., 1997). *Why People don't Trust Government*. Cambridge: Harvard University Press.

Putnam, R. (1993). *Making Democracy Work: Civic Traditions in Modern Italy*. Princeton: Princeton University Press.

Putnam, R. (2000). *Bowling Alone: The Collapse and Revival of American Community*. New York: Simon and Schuster.

Rothstein, B. (1998). *Just Institutions Matter: The Moral and Political Logic of the Universal Welfare State*. Cambridge: Cambridge University Press.

Rothstein, B. (2001). "Social Capital in the Social Democratic State. The Swedish Model and Civil Society." *Politics and Society* 29(2), 209–240.

Rothstein, B. and D. Stolle (2002). "How Political Institutions Create and Destroy Social Capital: An Institutional Theory of Generalized Trust." Paper prepared at the 98th Annual Meeting of the American Political Science Association, Boston, MA, August 29–September 2.

Sainsbury, D. (1997). *Gender and Welfare State Regimes, Gender and Politics*. Oxford: Oxford University Press.

Sides, J. (1999). "It Takes Two: The Reciprocal Relationship between Social Capital and Democracy." Paper presented at the 95th Annual Meeting of the American Political Science Association, Atlanta, September 2–5.

Stolle, D. (2001). "Clubs and Congregations: The Benefits of Joining an Association." pp. 202–244. In K. Cook (ed.), *Trust in Society*. New York: Russell Sage Foundation.

Stolle, D. (forthcoming). "Communities, Social Capital and Local Government—Generalized Trust in Regional Settings." In S. Prakash and P. Selle (eds.), *Investigating Social Capital: Comparative Perspectives on Civil Society, Participation and Governance*. Delhi: Sage India.

Tarrow, S. (1996). "Making Social Science Work Across Space and Time: A Critical Reflection on Robert Putnam's *Making Democracy Work*." *American Political Science Review* 90, 389–397.

Tyler, T. (1990). "Justice, Self-Interest, and the Legitimacy of Legal and Political Authority." In J. Mansbridge (ed.), *Beyond Self-Interest*. Chicago: University of Chicago Press.

Uslaner, E. M. (2002). *The Moral Foundations of Trust*. New York: Cambridge University Press.

Walzer, M. (1983). *Spheres of Justice. A Defense of Pluralism and Justice*. New York: Basic Books.

Chapter 11

Institutions and Their Impact on Social Capital and Civic Culture: The Case of Italy

Michel Huysseune

Introduction

Robert D. Putnam's *Making Democracy Work* has propelled the issue of social capital to the front stage of the social sciences. It argues that the difference in the efficiency of regional governments in Italy—the northern ones being much more efficient than those in the south—results from the differentiated presence of social capital in both parts of the country. Social capital, defined as the "features of social organization, such as trust, norms, and networks, that can improve the efficiency of society by facilitating co-ordinated actions" (Putnam 1993, 167), is, according to Putnam, much more present in northern than in southern Italy. As a consequence, northern Italy is characterized by its cooperative and civic culture sustained by a strongly rooted associative life, contrasting with the southern culture of "amoral familism," based on the exclusive defense of the interests of the nuclear family. The civic communities of the North are "bound together by horizontal relations of reciprocity and co-operation, not by vertical relations of authority and dependence," characteristic of the South. In a civic community, citizens develop attitudes that enhance cooperation. They are "helpful, respectful, and trustful toward one another" (Putnam 1993, 88), and they can hence count on reciprocal trust, even in the case of self-interested transactions. Southern Italy, on the contrary, is an individualist society, based on a Hobbesian equilibrium of "mutual distrust and defection, vertical dependence and exploitation, isolation and disorder, criminality and backwardness" (Putnam 1993, 181).

Putnam's reading of Italian society has caused a vast scholarly debate animated both by Italian scholars and Italianists abroad (for an overview of these debates see Tarrow 1996; Huysseune 1999). Because the publication of Putnam's book coincided with the challenge of the Italian state by the northern Italian separatist party Lega Nord and with scholarly reinterpretations of southern society, much of the debate concentrated on Putnam's interpretation of southern Italian society and history. While substantially agreeing with his evaluation of regional governments, critics have focused on what they perceive as Putnam's misinterpretation of southern culture. Relying on a stereotyped and negative vision of southern society, Putnam has neglected forms of social cooperation effectively present in the South.

In more theoretical terms, many scholars contest Putnam's explanation of the weakness of the South's civic culture. Putnam traces the origins of the South's individualist culture to the authoritarianism and feudalism of the absolutist monarchy of Frederick II in the thirteenth century, which inhibited the development of a civic culture at the grassroots level. Once consolidated, this individualist culture has been path dependently reproduced, hence constraining future choices. Putnam's critics, on the contrary, draw attention to the role the Italian state has played in reproducing the societal features of the South that have inhibited the development of civic culture and of good governance in this region. They have also drawn attention to the role of the communist (and to a lesser extent the Catholic) subculture in sustaining civic culture in northern Italy. This political reading of civic culture, highlighting the positive role of political mobilization and ideologies in northern Italy, and the negative role of institutions in the South, raises new questions. Does it reproduce in a different form Putnam's North–South dichotomy? Does it imply a positive role for ideologies, a negative one for institutions? And how has this negative role of Italian institutions to be interpreted, in light of the scholarship on social capital highlighting the positive role of institutions in generating social capital?

To answer these questions, I analyze in the first section the most controversial element of Putnam's book, his view of southern culture. I highlight how Putnam gives a unilaterally negative representation of southern Italy, neglecting the presence of social capital and civic culture. I argue that the institutionalist perspective, focusing on the role of the Italian state in producing clientelism and patronage, offers a more convincing explanation for uncivicness and bad governance in the South. In the second section, I propose an explanation of two issues raised by this institutionalist perspective: why the Italian state has had a negative impact on civic culture, and why this negative impact is stronger in the South. A third section analyzes the extent to which this institutionalist perspective is relevant for understanding the North and its civic culture. In a final section, I give an overview of how debates on the origin of Italian civic culture are relevant for our understanding of social capital.

EXPLANATIONS OF INSTITUTIONAL INEFFICIENCY IN SOUTHERN ITALY

In relating the inefficiency of southern institutions to the weakness of its civic culture, Putnam has identified an issue whose relevance is also acknowledged by his institutionalist critics. As a concerned party, southern intellectuals have themselves a long-standing tradition of critiquing the deleterious effects of clientelism and of denouncing the role of organized crime in several regions of the South. As Putnam, they highlight the inadequacies of southern institutions and critique their "particularism," that is, their defense of private interests and (often abusive) privileges, and their inability, or rather unwillingness, to guarantee collective rights and the rule of law. Identifying the causes of these phenomena is, however, much more controversial. In his explanation, Putnam concentrates on the culture of amoral familism, which, according to him, permeates southern society. Putnam borrows the concept of amoral familism from the American political scientist Edward Banfield. In his book *The Moral Basis of a Backward Society*, originally published in 1958, Banfield used this formula to explain the economic backwardness of the village of Chiaromonte (referred to as "Montegrano" in his book) in the southern Italian region of Basilicata. From his field research in this village, conducted in 1954–55, he deduced that its ethos of amoral familism was the cause of the organizational and political incapacity of its inhabitants. This ethos, summarized in the formula "Maximise the material, short-run advantage of the nuclear family; assume that all others will do likewise" (Banfield 1967, 83), produced, according to Banfield, a culture of mutual distrust that inhibited the cooperation of the citizens of Chiaromonte. Using a communitarian perspective inspired by de Tocqueville, he contrasted this culture with the rural communities in the United States, characterized by their cooperative culture sustained by a strong tissue of associative life.

Putnam's critics accept his diagnosis of southern problems, his observations on the deleterious effects of vertical networks of patronage on southern society and on the weakness of its civic culture. They argue, however, that his identification of southern culture with amoral familism is based on a unilateral vision of southern society (Lupo 1993; Sabetti 1996). Against Putnam's Hobbesian description of southern culture, they highlight the ample empirical evidence of neighborhood and community solidarity in the South, both in the past and in the present. Their scholarship retraces the presence of grassroots forms of cooperation and trust in the various social environments characteristic of the South: inland hill villages like Chiaromonte, large coastal towns like Naples, and the smaller towns in the coastal plains. Critics have thus highlighted how Banfield's research—Putnam's source—neglected the networks of community solidarity within Chiaromonte (Marselli 1963; Colombis 1992). Alessio Colombis has also proposed an alternative reading of Banfield's research findings, highlighting how Banfield's quotations of statements of Chiaromonte's inhabitants reveal in fact the norms and values ruling community life (Colombis 1997). From her historical and anthropological research of a city of the coastal plains of Campania, Eboli, Gabriella Gribaudi concludes that the predominance of nuclear families did not hinder the development of forms of solidarity and collective identity (Gribaudi 1990, 1993, 15–16). Descriptions of Naples highlight the pervading presence of social solidarity (Alcaro 1999, 32–33) and the richness of its social tissue, which cannot be reduced to the denominator of amoral familism (Gribaudi 1993). Scholarship on community life in southern Italy and its important impact on attitudes, norms and values of southern society undoubtedly disproves Putnam's identification of southern culture with amoral familism. Many descriptions of southern networks of neighborhood and community solidarity moreover prove the existence of exactly those grassroots forms of civic cooperation that Putnam considers to be important instruments for the accumulation of social capital, like networks for mutual economic support and labor sharing, relying on strongly entrenched social trust (Alcaro 1999, 30–31). These examples disprove Putnam's view that such informal forms of cooperation are characteristic of northern and central Italy but that they are absent in the South (Putnam 1993, 142–143).

Although revealing the inadequacy of Putnam's description of southern Italy, this scholarship does not necessarily contradict Putnam's research findings. As Mario Alcaro points out, cooperative attitudes in southern Italy have difficulties in transforming themselves in productive undertakings (e.g., cooperatives) and in civic engagement, and they remain outside of and alienated from public institutions (Alcaro 1999, 32). From this perspective, the weakness of a public civic culture and the problem of bad government remain as crucial as from Putnam's perspective, and scholars critiquing Putnam's vision of the South do not contest his data on its weak civic culture or on the inadequacy of its regional governments.[1] They only contest Putnam's identification of the cause of the South's problems in its culture of amoral familism allegedly dominating the whole of southern society.[2] The point is rather why a cooperative community culture at the grassroots level does not (or only marginally) lead to the development of a solid civic tissue sustaining good government and the creation of a virtuous public culture (Alcaro 1999, 11).

At this point, some scholars have in fact proposed an alternative interpretation of southern clientelism and the deleterious features of southern public life (Donzelli 1990, 38). They suggest understanding clientelism in light of the importance and strength of interpersonal and community networks in southern Italy, as an expression of a culture that is excessively attached to traditional interpersonal relations, instead of the impersonal relations of modernity.[3] The politicians in vertical networks of patronage and the exponents of organized crime instrumentalize southern cultural traditions and social networks, and the Mafia even explicitly presents its actions as expressing the values of Sicilian culture (Lupo 1993, 103–114). This interpretation is nevertheless also problematic, since it cannot prove the existence of a causal relation between southern community culture and clientelism. Its negative evaluation of community culture raises a theoretical issue, since the value of forms of community solidarity for sustaining democracy has in fact been highlighted by a whole tradition of political thought, to which Putnam's *Making Democracy Work* belongs. Forms of community solidarity should in fact be conceptually distinguished from clientelist networks (Alcaro 1999, 38), even when they may be related, as is the case in southern Italy.

THE ROLE OF THE ITALIAN STATE

To understand the role of "particularism" and "clientelism" in southern Italy, it is necessary to take into account the sociopolitical dynamics of Italian history after unification (which occurred in 1860–61) and their impact on southern society. The highly centralized Italian state intended to maintain a tight control over its newly acquired territories. The fragility of its authority in the South, where it was confronted with large-scale banditry, frequently motivated by hostility against the new state, obliged it to come to terms with local elites and to integrate them through networks of patronage.

These practices gave southern elites access to the spoils of government, offered its clients job opportunities in the state bureaucracy, and allowed the state and these elites to maintain social control over the South. Putnam himself describes the impact of such an institutional arrangement on society: "Vertical networks of patron–client ties became a means of allocating public works and softening administrative centralization. *Trasformismo* [the practice of supporting all governments, regardless of their political color, to obtain patronage, used especially by southern deputies] allowed local elites and national deputies to bargain for local interests against national directives in return for electoral and parliamentary support. Political channels to the center were more important than administrative channels, but in either case the link to the center remained crucial" (Putnam 1993, 19).

An understanding of the negative effects of this interaction between southern local elites and the state had already been put forward in 1876 by the young intellectual (and later prominent conservative politician) Sidney Sonnino. In a volume describing his journey to Sicily, undertaken together with Leopoldo Franchetti, he referred to the "iron circle of the oligarchy," that is, the cooperation between southern elites and the Italian state against any challenge of their dominant position, an alliance that moreover maintained equivocal relations with organized crime. The history of post-unification southern Italy is hence the history of the maintenance and continuity of this domination, embedded in society through clientelist networks. It characterized the prefascist liberal state and fascism and was reproduced after the restoration of democracy. The Italian postwar governments, and particularly the Christian Democrat party (Democrazia Cristiana, DC) uninterruptedly in power from 1945 to 1993, were successful in constructing new vertical networks of patronage, dominated by the DC.

Putnam and his institutionalist critics agree about highlighting the negative role of the state in southern Italy, particularly in producing networks of patronage in the South. However, while Putnam understands this role as a consequence of a strongly rooted uncivic culture path dependently reproduced since the Middle Ages, institutionalists emphasize the impact of the intervention of the Italian state. It should be noted that Putnam is careful to outline that the predominance of uncivic amoral familism does not express a preference of the citizens of southern Italy, whose dissatisfaction of southern institutions and contempt of the southern political class he repeatedly highlights (Putnam 1993, 5–6, 77, 80). He rather understands it as a rational survival strategy in adverse social circumstances (Putnam

1993, 177), an adaptation to the vertical networks of patronage that have dominated southern society since the Middle Ages. According to Putnam, the long predominance of this culture has nevertheless rendered southern Italians incapable of sustaining the long and patient work of constructing the social networks necessary to form a civic community (Putnam 1993, 146).

This judgment seems inadequate, because since its incorporation in the Italian state southern Italy has experienced many instances of collective political mobilization contesting its social order. Important prefascist experiences include the formation of agrarian leagues in Sicily (especially the movement of the so-called *fasci siciliani* in 1893–94), and of a trade union movement of landless laborers in Puglia. After fascism, the movement of land occupation in the late 1940s forms an impressive example of collective mobilization. These mobilizations, the equivalents of the political mobilizations in the North that are at the roots of much of its present civic tissue, belie Putnam's description of a South reduced to the choice between resignation and ephemeral anarchic rebellion (Putnam 1993, 146).

The example of the prefascist trade union of agricultural laborers in Puglia and Emilia, highlighted by Filippo Sabetti, is especially revealing. It shows the inadequacy of Putnam's image contrasting southern laborers of Puglia constrained to individual competition to their (northern) Emilian counterparts, which formed cooperatives. Turning upside down Putnam's metaphorical apparatus, Sabetti emphasizes moreover how the union in Puglia possessed a horizontal and participatory structure, against the vertical structure of its equivalents in Emilia. Sabetti highlights how the fascists easily dismantled the unions in Emilia by liquidating their leaders, while the union in Puglia was able to offer enduring and strenuous resistance to fascism (Sabetti 1996, 32–33).

Since Putnam emphasizes the importance of collective political mobilizations for the creation of social capital (Putnam 1993, 89), understanding the dynamics of these mobilizations in the South and their relation to the state is particularly relevant. Putnam seems to have underestimated their extent. In prefascist Italy, for example, the regions with the strongest development of associative life and political mobilization include southern Puglia and Sicily, together with the northern regions Emilia, Liguria, Lombardy, and Piedmont (Lupo 1993, 163–164).[4] Political mobilizations in southern regions dominated by the "iron circle of oligarchy" have nonetheless not resulted, unlike those in northern Italy, in the formation of a permanent and solid civic tissue. They more directly confronted the power of local elites and were therefore politically more antagonistic to the whole social order (Alcaro 1999, 36). They were either repressed (the prefascist liberal monarchy was notoriously more authoritarian in the South, as was exemplified by the fierce repression of the *fasci siciliani*) or integrated within the dominant clientelist networks. The latter tactic, characteristic of the post-war period, has played a particularly important role in neutralizing the civic potential of political mobilizations.

The most outstanding example of this process is the outcome of the important post-World War II southern mobilizations for an agrarian reform. The state and especially the Christian Democrat party then in power were obliged to respond to the claim for land of the *braccianti*, the landless agricultural laborers. The political elite ensured, however, that the agrarian reform they conceded would neutralize the potentialities toward cooperation and collective action the *braccianti*'s mobilizations had revealed. They allowed an important distribution of land but organized the reform in such ways that its beneficiaries would have minimal possibilities of mutual cooperation and would hence remain dependent on vertical networks, controlled by them (Ginsborg 1990, 122–140).

The contrast between grassroots networks of solidarity and a "particularistic" public culture, characteristic of southern Italian society, should thus be understood in the context of the structures of dominance of the Italian state and of southern elites. It is precisely the collusion between networks of patronage and the state apparatus and its effects on its social environment, that is, the active opposition to the creation of horizontal networks of cooperation and the formation of a civic culture that would threaten vested interests, that remain absent from Putnam's description of southern culture. Notwithstanding his interest in the early history of the Italian state, the impact of its institutions on society regresses into the background, to be replaced by an exclusive focus on amoral familism.

An institutional understanding of the weakness of southern civic culture does not exclude the impact of culture. It acknowledges the negative influence of clientelism and the vertical hierarchies of patronage on society. It highlights how it has produced a culture of particularism and how its inhibition of civic culture contributed to attitudes of fatalism and resignation widespread in the South. By relating this culture to the institutions of the Italian state, it proposes a more complex vision of southern culture than Putnam's reductionist assimilation with a path dependently reproduced amoral familism (or the opposite assimilation of community culture with clientelism). It understands "culture" in a less monolithic and determinist way and has more interest in its variations and internal contradictions. From such a viewpoint, southern society is less imprisoned by its culture than in Putnam's vision, and it has more cultural resources that offer perspectives for societal change.

The recent history of the South confirms the relevance of such an approach. Already in the 1980s, southern Italy experienced an important upsurge of associative life, generally independently of the dominant clientelist networks, a phenomenon that only acquired visibility after the publication of Putnam's book (Ramella 1995). Its participants soon became politically active, especially at the local level. The crisis of the party system in the 1990s, which caused a temporary breakdown of clientelist networks, frequently gave them the opportunity to acquire political influence, inaugurating in several municipalities, including some important ones, a virtuous circle between a resurgent associative life, civic culture and local good government. The negative inheritance of the clientelist past and of decades of bad government has by no means disappeared, and the impact of political abuse and organized crime on large parts of southern society remains important. The visibility this civic upsurge has acquired has nevertheless already made clear the limits of reductionist approaches that identify southern culture with amoral familism or "particularism."

EXPLAINING THE PARTICULARITIES OF THE ITALIAN STATE

Taking into account Italian politics and the negative effects of its institutions on civic culture, especially in the South, offers a more convincing explanation than Putnam's culturalist focus on amoral familism. At the same time, such an institutional approach itself raises new problems. It requires an analysis of the characteristics of the Italian state that explain the existence and persistence of such an "iron circle," and of the reasons why the effects of this phenomenon are concentrated in the South. Concerning the first issue, students of the Italian state have highlighted its oligarchic nature (Tarrow 1977, 1996; Romanelli 1995). It originated as an instrument of control from above—of newly incorporated territories and of democratic movements contesting the authority of an elite whose liberalism remained imbued with the values of a semi-absolutist culture. The central state thus actively neutralized instances of autonomy within the state, like oppositional municipal governments in the decades after unification, especially when guided by socialists.

The absolutist characteristics of the Italian state have never completely disappeared. The post-war republic inherited many of its features, especially its centralist state structure, and the cold war facilitated an authoritarian use of the Italian state by the ruling Christian Democrat party. The post-war republic nonetheless allowed more space than its predecessors for dissident experiences. Local and, after 1970, regional governments controlled by the opposition did acquire space for autonomous policy making, but they remained constrained by the absolutist logic of the central state bureaucracy. It is too early to assess in which direction the present wave of institutional reforms will evolve, but the centrality given to concerns for strong leadership would rather suggest continuity with this absolutist tradition.

Imposed as a foreign body (outside Piedmont) on a frequently reluctant society, the Italian state has at the same time suffered from crucial weaknesses. It has been obliged to negotiate its hegemony with peripheral elites, who have frequently been able to manipulate the state to their own advantage. The Italian state has in particular revealed its inability to impose a just authority on society, and in particular to guarantee an impartial and fair rule of law, which explains the distrust of Italian citizens toward it. Notwithstanding this, the Italian state has not inhibited economic development, and it has in fact encouraged local economic dynamism. However, it has generated a "disordered development" without respect for public interest (expressed in its strongest form in organized crime, but characteristic of much of Italy's economy).

Because of its particular history, its oligarchic structure and its reliance on vertical networks of patronage, the Italian state has incorporated a strong tendency to inhibit the accumulation of social capital, especially in the public sphere. The post-war development of the Italian welfare state is in this light particularly revealing. The Italian state has attempted as much as possible to attribute welfare allocations and social services on a personal basis, as privileges distributed through the channels of patronage. It was not uniformly successful in imposing clientelist solutions: The revolutionary impact of the fall of fascism, and trade union activism, especially in the 1960s and 1970s, did lead to, for example, the establishment of collective labor rights. The imposition of the *statuto del lavoratore* (the worker's statute) and the abolition of regional wage differences in the early 1970s extended these to the South. Because of its lesser degree of industrialization, and the larger presence of informal and clandestine economic activities, the impact of these measures has nevertheless remained more limited in the South. A reform implemented by the communist minister Gullo just after the war that gave agricultural laborers collective bargaining rights, particularly important for the South, was, for example, effectively neutralized once the communists had been expelled from the government (Ginsborg 1990, 60–63). Unemployment allocations are another characteristic example of how the Italian welfare state only partially guarantees universal rights: They are only attributed to previously officially employed people, through the *casse integrazione* (integration pay-desk), whose origins date from the 1970s. For those categories excluded from its benefits, invalidity pensions have functioned as its de facto substitutes. These pensions were frequently attributed according to arbitrary criteria, unrelated to real diseases—and hence the frequent tales about, for example, officially blind taxi drivers—and functioned as instruments of patronage, especially in the South.

The concentration of the negative consequences of clientelism and patronage in the South is frequently explained by relating them to cultural traditionalism and/or economic backwardness. The larger measure of dependence from public expenditure that less-developed regions experience undoubtedly enhanced clientelism. Its strongly entrenched presence cannot, however, be reduced to cultural traditionalism and/or lesser economic development, especially since the post-war economic modernization of the South was accompanied by a vast extension of practices of clientelism.

The more outspoken strength of clientelism in the South undoubtedly has strong historical roots. It is clearly related to the political dynamics of the process of Unification. The problems the Italian state was confronted with in incorporating the Kingdom of the Two Sicilies—which broadly corresponds with the South—especially the widespread wave of banditry supported by the peasantry, explain its close collaboration with local elites, its most likely allies in sustaining its authority. The support of southern deputies—ready to support any government for clientelistic reasons—became moreover instrumental to governments to maintain political control, both in the pre- and the post-fascist period, and the state soon became colonized by southern clients.

Southern elites themselves, however, also had a strong need for a strong authority, since southern Italy in the early nineteenth century was "one of the principal epicenters of political upheaval, revolution, and endemic rural unrest and protest in Europe" (Davis 1998, 217). As John Davis argues, these regions "can be seen as victims of Polanyi's Great Transformation, where the violence of change precluded the formation of those checks and controls that Polanyi identified as the keys to political and social stability" (Davis 1998, 211). Because of its contested hegemony, the southern elite of landowners also resorted to the state for protection and as an alternative resource of social and economic power, inaugurating the process of symbiosis between elites and state that would characterize the post-unification state. In most northern regions, on the contrary, the old paternalist order of the countryside was maintained, in some regions until the beginning of the twentieth century (Davis 1998, 217).

It is hence the modernity of the social conflicts of the early nineteenth century in the South that explains the emergence of the "iron circle of oligarchy," while northern (still mainly landed) elites, whose authority was as yet uncontested, could afford to maintain more distance from the state. When contested, the northern elites certainly did not disdain the state's help: Among the prominent factors contributing to the rise of fascism is the class war of northern latifundists against agrarian unionism. Northern Italy did not, however, experience this intimate symbiosis of political and economic power characteristic of the South.

The different insertion of regional elites within the state explains in a large measure the different development of civic culture in northern and southern Italy. This North–South divide has, moreover, also been actively reproduced. The post-war divide partly has its roots in the contingencies of the war, and particularly the contrasting experiences of the South, after 1943 under royal and Allied control, and the North, with its experience of resistance and the breakdown of authority in 1945, leading to a large-scale political mobilization unparalleled in the South. Political mobilizations in the South were confronted with a much more solid authority, or emerged a few years later, when the cold war context made their neutralization more feasible because the state's authority had been restored.

Policy decisions moreover played an important role in reproducing this difference in the post-war period. The post-war state, dominated by the Christian Democrats, was stronger and more interventionist than its predecessors, and its interventionism was much stronger in the South. Development in the North occurred with relatively little interference from the state. To develop the South, the state organized a large-scale public intervention, the *intervento straordinario* (extraordinary intervention), initiating an impressive process of state-led development from above. The *intervento straordinario* undoubtedly contributed to the modernization of the South and the drastic amelioration of its standards of living. At the same time, however, it took a form that was deleterious for the accumulation of social capital and degraded its already weak civic culture. Modernization policy uprooted much of its community culture and the grassroots forms of sociability and the social capital they provided, while the DC actively inhibited the creation of new forms of civic culture. It created a model of development based on the absence of universally accepted rules, where the state granted instead private favors through its clientelist channels. Much of the post-war development in the South concerned public works strongly conditioned by clientelism and patronage. As a consequence, their realization has frequently been characterized by high expenditure, low quality of execution and conspicuous waste (e.g., useless roads and buildings). The post-war South has thus experienced a sometimes drastic degradation of its public sphere—embodied in the massive abusive uses of its territory.

Rather than resulting from a culture inherited from its feudal past, southern lack of civicness should thus be understood as the outcome of its political history. This absence may have feudal roots but is mainly the consequence of the specific southern transition to modernity. It has its origins in the social crisis caused by the dissolution of its ancient structures in the early nineteenth century, which besides feudal structures also included many (especially but not only church-related) associations that could have offered a civic counterweight to the elites (Sabetti 1996). The continuity, and plausibly also the reinforcement in the post-war years of the North–South gap in civic culture, is thus above all the outcome of an initial important disadvantage, the dominance of southern society by the "iron circle of the oligarchy," absent or much less evident in the North, which has then been reproduced throughout the history of the unified state.

FOR A RE-INTERPRETATION OF NORTHERN CIVIC CULTURE

A critique of Putnam's approach also implies a reassessment of civic culture in the North. Putnam's argument on its historical continuity since the Middle Ages is at best hypothetical (Feltrin 1994), but he is undoubtedly right in highlighting the contribution of grassroots movements in the late nineteenth and early twentieth century (socialist, communist and Catholic) in its formation. It is clear that their role in this process is related to their relative independence of the oligarchic structure of the Italian state. He may, however, have underestimated the impact of the oligarchic Italian state structure on northern society. The higher quality of regional government, certainly related to regional civic tissues, probably also reflects their relative independence from central government. This is certainly the case for the most civic regions—Emilia-Romagna, Tuscany, Umbria—governed during Putnam's period of research by the Communist Party, in opposition at the national level. Northern regional governments did not, however, escape the degradation of central government and the rise of rampant corruption characteristic of the 1980s, a process underestimated by Putnam (Lupo 1993, 155–156). The weakening of ideological conflicts in the 1980s, observed by Putnam, rather than revealing a stronger civic culture of cooperation, should be interpreted in the context of a culture of sharing the spoils of corruption (Bettin Lattes 1993, 169).

The degradation of Italian institutions in the 1980s put into crisis the relation between grassroots civic culture and the public sphere in northern Italy. The political crisis of the early 1990s revealed the limits of civic culture in the North, especially in its small peripheral centers that have been particularly economically successful in recent decades. The economic development of these centers (often referred to as industrial districts) is strongly embedded in the local community and its social capital (Putnam 1993, 161). However, against Putnam's optimistic description of community life in those newly emerging centers as characterized by enlightened self-interest and liberal values, recent studies have revealed its frequently exclusionist and xenophobic culture, against outsiders but also against immigrants and deviants within the community. This culture found in the 1990s a political expression in the discourse of the northern Italian secessionist party Lega Nord, which campaigned for the right of a northern community to be protected from outsiders, the Italian state, southern Italians, cultural deviants and immigrants. The Lega Nord and its anti-liberal and xenophobic program have been particularly successful in many of these highly competitive northern communities (Cento Bull 1996).

This evolution questions the relation between social capital and civic culture in these communities. These industrial districts, where the market has become a strong mechanism of integration and solidarity, are only able to produce what Arnaldo Bagnasco has defined as "bounded civicness": a culture where solidarity functions only within the local community and whose scope is limited to the private sphere and the particularistic relations of the market in which its members operate (Bagnasco 1994). Its instrumentalization of family and social relations for economic goals moreover creates a tension with the overall reproduction of social relations, and the exclusive economic use of social capital may ultimately impoverish social relations (Bagnasco 1999, 117–118). Its is moreover difficult to perceive how such a culture can sustain public virtues, and their reproduction is indeed becoming problematic in those parts of northern Italy (Magatti 1998). What Putnam perceives as a problem for the South, the incompatibility of private and public interest, is thus also becoming characteristic for some parts of the North.

Re-evaluations of specific forms of northern civic culture should not lead to the formulation of new stereotypes on "northern culture": As in the South, regional culture in the North is characterized by a plurality of experiences. This crisis of civic culture has, for example, been strong in regions previously dominated by the Christian Democrat party, but much less outspoken in regions with a communist political tradition. Within regions formerly dominated by the Christian Democrats, the Catholic Church continues to play a role, both in offering an ideology of national integration and solidarity and in sustaining grassroots civic associations. Northern Italy (and Italy as a whole) has in fact recently experienced a noticeable growth of voluntary associations, and as a whole is probably not suffering from a decline in social capital. As for southern Italy, the weakness of its civic culture should moreover be related to the particular nature of the Italian state. As Loredana Sciolla argues, institutions and the way they function exert a powerful influence on the behavior of citizens and the formation of national "character." Northern bounded civicness and southern particularism should hence be understood in light of the Italian state's promotion of clientelistic and particularistic policies (Sciolla 1999, 608).

The emergence of such a bounded civicness in northern Italy does raise the issue of the norms and values sustaining civic culture. It suggests that political culture, by offering norms and values transcending private interests, may play a more important role than Putnam acknowledges. Putnam does highlight how the political mobilizations of socialist (later communist) and Catholic movements in civic regions have contributed to the initial formation and consolidation of civic culture. In Putnam's view, however, this political component is instrumental in creating an atmosphere of reciprocal trust and cooperation, but afterward becomes secondary (see also Trigilia 1988). The consequences of the crisis of the Christian Democrat party as a mediator between local and national interest and of its ideology of solidarity rather suggest the importance of this component. The political success of the Lega Nord and its anti-liberal and xenophobic political culture within northern communities, which are undoubtedly characterized by a strong presence of social capital, problematizes Putnam's optimistic vision whereby social capital enhances the development of an enlightened self-interest, sustained by liberal values. Those northern communities where such an illiberal political culture took hold do continue to be characterized by the presence of a community ethos and reciprocal trust, but these assets are combined with an illiberal culture of intolerance against outsiders and deviants and a weakening of public ethos.

The evolution of northern Italian industrial districts raises at a theoretical level the question of the compatibility of private and public interests, which is at the heart of Putnam's theory of social capital. Putnam's description of civic culture implies a vision of a society characterized by the presence of a rational and enlightened self-interest compatible with public interest. Like Banfield's theory of amoral familism, Putnam's definition of social capital assumes, on the one hand, that the defense of private interest is conductive to public virtues, and critiques, on the other hand, an ethos of private interest like amoral familism. Putnam's theory envisions social capital as a resource to relate and reconcile public and private, individual and collective interests. The case of northern Italian industrial districts reveals the limits of this approach: In the absence of an ethos of public interest and solidarity social capital will not be able to engender such reconciliation.

THE DEVELOPMENT OF SOCIAL CAPITAL FROM AN INSTITUTIONALIST PERSPECTIVE

Institutionalist critics of Putnam concur with him in relating the North–South differential in government capacities with differences in civic culture but disagree on his culturalist explanation of these differences. They highlight how Putnam's representation of southern Italy is partially inadequate: While this region does suffer from a lack of civic culture and inadequate government, Putnam's image of a Hobbesian society characterized by generalized distrust ignores the effective and strongly entrenched presence of forms of social trust and cooperation. They explain the South's problems as consequences of the negative impact it has undergone from the Italian state. As a consequence of its absolutist origins, the state has consistently played an active role in inhibiting the development of those forms of cooperation and civic culture that would have constituted a challenge of those vested interests with which the state collided. For reasons related to the particular political history of the unified Italian state, this pressure has been more pronounced in the South. Its impact on northern Italy is nevertheless also noticeable: it has caused government corruption and has favored the eruption of uncivic political movements that belie Putnam's overly embellished image of a civic region.

Without denying the importance of culture, the institutional perspective redimensions its role in shaping civic society. It highlights the interaction between institutions and culture, and draws attention to how culture is shaped by its institutional environment. It offers a more positive view on southern society, highlighting its capacities to generate social capital. It makes visible the resilience of networks of trust engendering social capital at a grassroots level and acknowledges traditions of civic culture and collective political mobilizations in the South. It highlights at the same time the problematic relation between social capital and civic culture. While for Putnam the presence of social capital easily leads to the development of civic culture, an institutional perspective reveals their more problematic compatibility. In southern Italy, the difficult transmission of social capital in the public sphere is primarily a result of institutional pressure. In northern Italy, the economic instrumentalization of social capital, in the absence of an ideology and institutions transcending private interest, has sometimes produced an uncivic political culture. Both cases reveal the difficult relation between grassroots reciprocity and trust and a civic culture of public trust, since the institutions of the Italian state discourage such a relation. Beyond the particularities of Italian history, this case draws attention to the role of government action. It certainly cautions against interpretations of Putnam's book as "a case study of society's *indifference* to government action: if social capital is 'path dependent', i.e., deeply ingrained in centuries of history and culture, then societies may have a broad tolerance for various types and degrees of state intervention" (Woolcock 1998, 153).

The partial failure of northern social capital to generate civic culture—paralleling in fact the presence of some forms of social capital in the South (organized crime and its social networks) that generate an uncivic culture—also suggests that norms and values play an important role in translating social capital into civic culture. Political mobilization and ideologies are thus not only important in creating reciprocal trust and in supporting associative life, as Putnam suggests, but also in providing norms and values that give social capital a public scope beyond private interests. The crisis of civic culture in the North is undoubtedly related to the erosion of the parties and their ideologies that mediated between private interests and public virtues, the Christian Democrats and the Communists.

An institutionalist perspective amends rather than rejects Putnam's conclusion that emphasizes the need, especially for the South, of building social capital. Like Putnam, it highlights the need to engender civic culture. Social capital is undoubtedly an important asset in this process, and the revival and renewal of associative life both in the South and the North will undoubtedly have an important role to play in it. The Italian case suggests, however, that social capital will only fulfill this role in the presence of norms and values transcending private interest. Only when mediated by ideologies expressing such norms and values can social capital engender a virtuous civic culture, and politics will hence play an important role in this process. Since the weakness of civic culture is related to the negative heritage of the Italian state, engendering and reinforcing it moreover requires a drastic reform of its institutions. Such reforms should be aimed at breaking its absolutist inheritance and its particularist culture defending abusive private interests. While Italy's uncivic heritage has its sources both in its institutions and in society, the production of a more civic society will analogously rely on the interaction of civic political mobilizations and institutional reform.

NOTES

1. Putnam's measures of civic culture may have underestimated southern civic culture: The upsurge of associative life in the South in the 1980s would probably modify one of Putnam's indicators of civic culture, the presence of associations, since Putnam's indicator dates from 1981 (Putnam 1993, 96). Overall, his critics have nevertheless accepted his assessment of differentials in civic culture. Putnam's opinion (not corroborated by data) that informal forms of social capital are also much more present in northern and central Italy is more controversial: It is one of the focuses of critiques of his unilateral representations of the South.

2. Whether an ethos of amoral familism really exists (or has existed) in southern Italy, has recently been a subject of much controversy. Some scholars argue that it plays a role in southern culture, as the common-sense explanation given by southern Italians themselves for their lack of a cooperative attitude (Davis 1970, 344). Others (Meloni 1977) interpret it as a discourse expressing the crisis of community values during the post-war transition toward modernity. Most students of the southern family are extremely cautious about the concept as defined by Banfield, either rejecting it altogether (Gribaudi 1993, 1996), or using it only for very specific cases and certainly refuting its use as a general concept to explain social behavior in southern Italy (Meloni 1997).

3. This attachment is also rather confusingly referred to as "amoral familism." As such, it is an example of the semantic shift the concept has undergone from Banfield's specific meaning to a generic description of real and/or imagined societal features of southern society deemed unmodern (Gribaudi 1996, 83–84).

4. Putnam's indicators of prefascist civic culture may have downplayed its presence in the South (Putnam 1993, 149). This is particularly the case for the indicator on the continuity of associative life between 1860 and 1920. It correlates with economic development in 1860 (lower in the South than in the North). It ignores how the traumatic effects of unification, the disintegration and dissolution of previously existing forms of associative life, especially when related with the Catholic Church, and several years of martial law against "banditry" certainly inhibited the development of associative life in the first years after unification.

REFERENCES

Alcaro, M. (1999). *Sull'Identità Meridionale. Forme di una Cultura Mediterranea.* Torino: Bollati Boringhieri.

Bagnasco, A. (1994). "Regioni, Tradizione Civica, Modernizzazione Italiana: Un Commento alla Ricerca di Putnam." *Stato e Mercato* 40, 93–103.

Bagnasco, A. (1999). *Tracce di Comunità.* Bologna: Il Mulino.

Banfield, E. C. (1967 [1958]). *The Moral Basis of a Backward Society.* New York: Free Press.

Bettin Lattes, G. (1993). "Le Radici della Cultura Civica nell'Italia Divisa." *Quaderni di Sociologia* 37(5), 161–171.

Cento Bull, A. (1996). "Ethnicity, Racism and the Northern League." pp. 171–187. In C. Levy (ed.), *Italian Regionalism. History, Identity and Politics.* Oxford: Berg.

Colombis, A. (1992). " 'L'invenzione' del Familismo Amorale." pp. 201–212. In F. P. Cerase (ed.), *Dopo il Familismo Cosa?* Milano: Franco Angeli.

Colombis, A. (1997). "Invece del Familismo: La Famiglianza." pp. 382–408. In B. Meloni (ed.), *Famiglia Meridionale Senza Familismo.* Catanzaro: Meridiana Libri.

Davis, J. (1970). "Morals and Backwardness." *Comparative Studies in Society and History* 12(3), 340–353.

Davis, J. (1998). "Casting of the 'Southern Problem': Or the Peculiarities in the South Reconsidered." pp. 205–224. In J. Schneider (ed.), *Italy's "Southern Question." Orientalism in One Country.* Oxford: Berg.

Donzelli, C. (1990). "Mezzogiorno tra 'Questione' e Purgatorio. Opinione Comune, Immagine Scientifica, Strategie di Ricerca." *Meridiana* 9, 13–53.

Feltrin, P. (1994). "Recensione di Robert D. Putnam, <La tradizione civica nelle regioni italiane>." *Rivista Italiana di Scienza Politica* 24(1), 169–172.

Ginsborg, P. (1990). *A History of Contemporary Italy.* Harmondsworth: Penguin.

Gribaudi, G. (1990). *A Eboli. Il Mondo Meridionale in Cent'anni di Trasformazione.* Venezia: Marsilio.

Gribaudi, G. (1993). "Familismo e Famiglia a Napoli en nel Mezzogiorno." *Meridiana* 17, 13–42.

Gribaudi, G. (1996). "Images of the South." pp. 72–87. In D. Forgacs and and R. Lumley, *Italian Cultural Studies. An Introduction*. Oxford: Oxford University Press.

Huysseune, M. (1999). "Putnam Interpreteren Vanuit een Italiaanse Context." *Tijdschrift voor Sociologie* 20(3–4), 283–301.

Lupo, S. (1993). "Usi e Abusi del Passato. Le Radici dell'Italia di Putnam." *Meridiana* 18, 151–168.

Magatti, M. (1998). *Tra Disordine e Scisma. Le Basi Sociali della Protesta del Nord*. Roma: Carocci.

Marselli, G. A. (1963). "American Sociologists and Italian Peasant Society: With Reference to the Book of Banfield." *Sociologia Ruralis* 3(4), 319–338.

Meloni, B. (1997). "Introduzione." pp. v–lxiii. In B. Meloni (ed.), *Famiglia Meridionale senza Familismo*. Catanzaro: Meridiana Libri.

Putnam, R. (1993). *Making Democracy Work. Civic Tradition in Modern Italy*. Princeton: Princeton University Press.

Ramella, F. (1995). "Mobilitazione Pubblica e Società Civile Meridionale." *Meridiana* 22–23, 121–154.

Romanelli, R. (1995). "Centralismo e Autonomie." pp. 125–186. In R. Romanelli (ed.), *Storia dello Stato Italiano dall'Unità a Oggi*. Roma: Donzelli.

Sabetti, F. (1996). "Path Dependency and Civic Culture: Some Lessons from Italy about Interpreting Social Experiments." *Politics and Society* 24(1), 19–44.

Sciolla, L. (1999). "Come si Puo Costruire un Cittadino." *Il Mulino* 48(4), 601–609.

Tarrow, S. (1977). *Between Center and Periphery. Grassroots Politicians in Italy and France*. New Haven: Yale University Press.

Tarrow, S. (1996). "Making Social Science Work Across Space and Time: A Critical Reflection on Robert Putnam's *Making Democracy Work*." *American Political Science Review* 90(2), 389–397.

Trigilia, C. (1988). "Le Condizioni 'Non Economiche' dello Sviluppo: Problemi di Ricerca sul Mezzogiorno d'Oggi." *Meridiana* 2, 167–187.

Woolcock, M. (1998). "Social Capital and Economic Development: Toward a Theoretical Synthesis and a Policy Framework." *Theory and Society* 27(2), 151–208.

CHAPTER 12

CONCLUSION: THE SOURCES OF SOCIAL CAPITAL RECONSIDERED

Dietlind Stolle and Marc Hooghe

There can be little doubt that societies can function even in the absence of those aspects of social capital that benefit the wider society. Distrust or mere particularized trust; the lack of weak, bridging ties and reciprocity; high levels of political apathy and cynicism; and corruption may not be the ingredients of an ideal society, but they can provide the basis for the emergence of a stable equilibrium. The classic example of this situation would be the "amorial familism" as it was described by Banfield (1958). In the village of Montegrano, there is little evidence of solidarity between nonrelated village dwellers: Solidarity and reciprocity remain limited to one's own kin. There is no confidence whatsoever in local office holders, and rightly so, as they indeed tend to use their function for the purpose of personal enrichment. The almost feudal social structure of the village is even sanctioned by the Roman Catholic Church, and as Huysseune shows in his chapter, the local rulers succeeded in using the resources of the Italian central state to strengthen their hold on power.

A touch of Montegrano—though in an entirely different context—can be found as well in one of the Northern regions in Sweden (Stolle, forthcoming). Citizens in one of the villages could not even agree to build a sidewalk along a busy street. This sidewalk could have prevented many accidents that occurred along the road over the last years. In this village, trust might go beyond the family circle, but it does not reach out to connect citizens for a common purpose. The people of the region experience a different web of social interactions and state–society relations than people elsewhere in Sweden. Suspicion of strangers, distrust of local politicians, bonding but no real bridging social interactions and recent corruption scandals characterize social life in this region. Finally, we have learned about the urban community of Dordrecht in the Netherlands, where generalized trust, political trust, informal societal networks as well as formal social participation just pale in comparison to other locations in the country (see de Hart and Dekker this volume).

As these very diverse examples from Italy, Sweden and the Netherlands show, the basic problem of distrusting societies is not instability but rather the failure to develop a comprehensive democratic system that enables citizens to fully exercise their rights of expression, conscience and participation. Research shows that these kinds of societies develop fewer chances for economic development, while in general their political system will be less responsive to citizens' needs and demands.

The existence and the relative stability of certain societies in southern Italy, northern Sweden and metropolitan areas in the Netherlands are not just interesting from an anecdotal point of view—they also teach us very important lessons. To begin with, we should not assume that patterns of sociability, generalized trust and reciprocity develop as a matter of course. There are obviously several examples, even in societies otherwise known as "high trust" countries, that demonstrate that citizens in certain regions and localities are unable to overcome collective action problems. On the other hand, the contrasting cases, such as parts of the Italian north, other communities in the Swedish south, as well as the village of Asten in the Netherlands, show that there are ways to reach a virtuous circle as well. In these places generalized trust is thriving, social interactions are relatively rich, community problems can be solved, relationships between citizens and politicians seem relatively healthy, and the economy is blossoming.

In examining these radically different descriptions of societies, the ultimate question is about the sources of this variance. How are virtuous and vicious circles of social capital, economic development and well-functioning public institutions generated? Although research shows quite convincingly that high-trust societies function better and are better equipped to attain their collective goals, we do not know whether trust can be created or should be seen as a result of historical traditions. In other words, how stable are these two equilibria? Where in the virtuous and vicious circles is there a point of departure from which societies can take off to rise (or to decline) to new levels and patterns of social capital?

The authors in this volume have attempted to provide an answer to these difficult questions. All of them were guided by the main question underlying this volume: How can we explain the emergence of generalized trust and other attitudinal components of social capital? We can distinguish their answers on the basis of where they see the foundation or springboard for the emergence of vicious and virtuous circles. As we suggested in the introduction to this volume, some authors see the spiral of these relationships evolving from a web of associations and, more broadly, from social interactions. Other authors step outside the realm of civil society to explore the institutional foundations of generalized trust and other civic attitudes.

THE NEWS OF SOCIETY-CENTERED APPROACHES

On the one hand, the development of civic attitudes and the ability to solve collective action problems is mostly seen as being located in various forms of social interactions, such as membership in voluntary associations. We introduced such approaches as society centered, because the attitudinal components of social capital are seen as clearly linked to and influenced by social interactions. Yet, if we are interested in aspects of social capital that benefit society at large, and not just a certain group of the population, so far we did not have sufficient knowledge about whether and how social interactions are most valuable for the development of such civic attitudes.

Society-centered approaches to social capital formation assume that civic attitudes and norms are the product of regular social and predominantly face-to-face interaction, as, for example, in voluntary associations. The major challenge for this claim is to demonstrate that social interactions really do have these beneficial effects. Moreover, we want to know about the characteristics of social interactions that influence participants' civic attitudes. In the first part of this volume, several chapters looked at these questions in depth and tested these propositions at the micro-, meso- and macrolevels. Whereas some authors approach this issue with an analysis of individual members of associations, and most importantly their civic attitudes and values (Mayer, Wollebæk and Selle this volume), others focus more explicitly on contextual effects that evolve from the associational experience (Hooghe, Molenaers, Stolle this volume), and still others emphasize the overall effects of associational density in regions or cities (de Hart and Dekker, van der Meer this volume).

The evidence presented in these chapters implies that the role of associations for the development of civic attitudes, norms and the ability to solve collective action problems outside the group has been exaggerated, at least by earlier versions of social capital theorizing. The relationship between membership and generalized trust is tenuous at best. Whereas Mayer in her chapter on France shows that the connection between these two phenomena does not exist, other authors' findings are more mixed. The Dutch data reveal that membership is related to trust only in the rural village of Asten but not in the city of Dordrecht. The Norwegian and the Belgian research both suggest that civic attitudes and membership are potentially related, but not without reservations. These weak findings that doubt the importance of voluntary associations are indeed confirmed by other research (Moyser and Parry 1997; Newton 1999; Van Deth 1997; Stolle 1998, 2001a; Hooghe 2003). Moreover, any correlational findings have to be subjected to further scrutiny, as we have to take into account the possibility that citizens, who developed civic responsibility and generalized trust, are far more likely to join voluntary associations and other types of social interactions. The actual question is whether these interactions have an *additional* socialization effect on the participants, beyond the effect of self-selection (see Hooghe, Stolle this volume).

Also this more specified test did not support any enthusiasm regarding the importance of associational life, as the additional membership effects are not as substantial as earlier accounts of social capital theory have suggested. In their attempt to distinguish between effects from face-to-face contacts and passive forms of associational belonging for individual members, Wollebæk and Selle found that face-to-face contacts are not superior in their influence on generalized trust. This strong finding questions the privileged role of direct and face-to-face interactions and their potential for developing trust and reciprocity beyond the associational setting. Moreover, more time spent in social associations leads to more trust for other fellow members, yet it does not contribute to more generalized trust, civic engagement and activities outside the group (Stolle 2001b). The problem is that there is no causal mechanism that successfully explains the transfer of trust for people one knows personally, such as the members of one's association, to people outside the associational experience. How are group experiences generalized?

Social capital theory suggests that the membership contact with citizens that represent a broad sampling of the population might be more conducive for generalizing trust to people outside of the association than contact with people like oneself. This reflects the important difference between bridging and bonding social capital. Yet associations might not be the best contexts in which bridging interactions are being produced. It is therefore not surprising that there is a lack of evidence for the importance of bridging types of associations (Stolle 2001b).

Another potential mechanism might work more successfully at the individual level: Citizens maintain several memberships in fairly homogeneous types of associations; however, it is the multiplicity of memberships that might ultimately create bridging contacts. Surely, multiple memberships in several sports or church groups might not necessarily present the ideal model of bridging social capital; however, citizens engaged in various different types of associations ought to be exposed to some level of diversity in their social interactions. Wollebæk and Selle certainly find multiple memberships important for generalized trust and other civic attitudes, yet also here these effects could be determined by self-selection. Real joiner natures might have different characteristics so that additional memberships do not have any effects on that person's civic attitudes. In addition, in this account as well, the causal mechanism remains unclear. What kind of diversity is needed for the development of generalized trust? Again, how are the various group experiences transferred to the outside world?

Hooghe's insights might solve some of these puzzles. He argues that membership in associations has incremental and reinforcing effects. In his theoretical account, socialization effects in associations can work when the members of an association converge in a process of value polarization. So, for example, when ethnocentrism is not very appreciated among the members of a book club, these members would probably strengthen their pre-existing anti-ethnocentric values through their social interactions. If we are interested in civic attitudes and behaviors, we will have to look for associations in which civic-minded people come together. In what might be called a cycle of "selection and adaptation," members self-select into these kinds of organizations, but subsequently they are being influenced by the values upheld by their fellow-members. This practically implies that socialization effects are more prevalent in homogeneous settings where value patterns converge more easily and that they are less pronounced than we sometimes think they are. So, no wonder some of the research does not find any significant effects, if membership can only under certain conditions lead to the strengthening of existing values. At the same time, the logic of the argument implies that under certain circumstances, for example, value congruence that converges on uncivic orientations, associations might reinforce these uncivic predispositions.

A similar finding, though based on a different causal mechanism, is presented by Molenaers in her chapter on Nicaragua, where she documents adverse effects of associations. Voluntary associations can be used to strengthen existing cleavages and exclusion patterns. Her research demonstrates that associations can be used for purely instrumental reasons, for example, by using outside donor money to develop clientelistic networks with potential voters. Even though the theoretical insight about the importance of value congruence represents an important addition in identifying the microcausal mechanism in the link between membership and generalized trust, we are left wondering about the extent to which associations can function as the *producers* of civic values.

The problem with this microlevel research might be that it only examines direct effects of membership or other social interactions on the individual member. Coleman argues that citizens' interaction can have effects far beyond those who actually participate, namely on those who don't (Coleman 1990). The above accounts take this, of course, into consideration, as attitudes such as generalized trust or anti-ethnocentrism benefit the society at large. However, there is a sense that social capital works best at the collective level and thus should be understood as a pure collective good. Putnam and Pharr have described these collective effects as rainmaker effects (2000). The claim is that in regions with stronger, dense and more cross-cutting networks of voluntary associations, there is a spillover effect from membership to the development of cooperative values and norms of citizens more generally, whether they are members or not. How exactly the spillover occurs—the causal mechanism behind this relationship—is still a puzzle, particularly because of the missing microlink. There is no apparent reason why a citizen who is not a member of any association whatsoever should become cooperative, simply because a lot of her/his neighbors are members of various kinds of voluntary associations. However, van der Meer (this volume) finds that particularly the regional density (but also the country level to an extent) of membership in new political movement organizations, interest groups and welfare organizations is related to higher generalized trust levels of nonmembers in these regions. His findings point us to the importance of collective effects of social capital that cannot successfully be captured in most surveys. However, his results are not entirely conclusive. If there is a positive correlation between membership and generalized trust at the macrolevel—which we might expect—we are still unclear about the final causes, since we do not have access to a reliable causal mechanism to explain why nonmembers could be more trusting in regions with higher associational density.

The research reported in this volume does not imply that associations are not relevant for the establishment of a democratic political culture; they only suggest that creating generalized trust and other civic attitudes (and the same can be said for political trust) is not the prime mechanism by which voluntary associations contribute to the strengthening of civic culture. However, there are other, namely *external* functions of voluntary associations that connect the citizens to the polity and allow citizens to get access to government and to political decision making (Warren 2001). Not only is the distance between a "big structure" like the state and the individual citizens too large to be bridged directly, without any intermediary organization (Streeck 1987), national or regional political entities mostly seem too abstract to allow for successful identification processes. If citizens are to develop affective ties with the political system, this process does not seem likely to happen in an anonymous and abstract fashion. Instead we expect associations and other intermediary organizations to play their role here.

Almond and Verba (1963, 265) already demonstrated that membership of voluntary association is strongly associated with feelings of political efficacy, which can be considered an assessment of the real political influence of the respondent. Members do not just feel more effective in politics; they also *are* more effective. Associations represent a crucial mechanism in establishing effective ties between citizens and the political system (Baumgartner and Leesh 1998). Membership, whether in political or in nonpolitical organizations, allows citizens access to the political sphere, and therefore associations can be considered as an instrument "to empower people." How is this expressed in the work presented in earlier chapters? The French study of Mayer shows that members of voluntary associations are more interested in politics, while they are also able to identify themselves more clearly with regard to the dominant political cleavages in the country. Interestingly, though, these political attitudes do not automatically translate into political trust. In fact association members in France are not more likely to trust politicians or political institutions compared to nonmembers. Research in other countries, however, usually reveals a positive relation between membership and political trust. Wollebæk and Selle, for example find that association members trust political institutions more than nonmembers, and they are also more civically engaged. However, in contrast to the expectations by social capital theory, they found far fewer differences between passive and active members, which indicates that associations do not necessarily socialize their members into different attitudes and values by the regular face-to-face interaction. Associations of various kinds, whether checkbook organizations or local groups, still give members information, a sense of connection, loose networks, as well as efficacy (Wollebæk and Selle this volume).

Again, the relation between political efficacy and associational membership can be the result of a process of self-selection. Those feeling more confident in the public and political sphere will be more strongly inclined to join all kinds of associations (Hooghe 2001). It also seems reasonable to assume that not every organizational type will have the same effect on political trust or political interest. In new social movements or trade unions, it seems likely that political issues will be discussed regularly among the members, and these discussions could further stimulate political interest. In other kinds of associations, however, talking about politics is actively discouraged because politics is considered as a potentially divisive issue (Eliasoph 1998). Associations also differ with regard to the intensity of their interaction with the political system, so there is no reason to expect that all associational memberships will be positively associated with political efficacy, of course.

In general, however, we have to take into account that contemporary mass-democracies create very few opportunities, outside the context of elections, for individual and unorganized citizens to participate effectively in the process of political decision making. As Gutmann reminds us: "Without access to an association that is willing and able to speak up for our views and values, we have a very limited ability to be heard by many other people or to influence the political process, unless we happen to be rich or famous" (Gutmann 1998, 3). Associations, interest groups and intermediary organizations are crucial mechanisms in the process of interest aggregation, thus enabling their members to play a role in the political system. The external effects of voluntary associations, however, are more difficult to study than the internal effects, as they often require us to go beyond survey research. If a neighborhood association in the depressed outskirts of the city of Dordrecht succeeds in obtaining collective benefits from the city council, all residents—whether they are members or not—will profit from these collective goods. If this association effectively channels neighborhood demands to the local political system, this could reduce the feeling of powerlessness in the area. Research, however would not necessarily reveal differences between members and nonmembers. External effects of associations have to be studied in a different type of research design: Above all, studies of multiple localities and regions should be pursued (see examples in de Hart and Dekker this volume; Onyx and Bullen 2001; Stolle forthcoming).

The literature on interest groups suggests that associations and groups are potential prime mechanisms to ensure responsiveness of the political system to citizens' demands (Berry 1984; Tarrow 1994; Baumgartner and Leech 1998). This instrumental or external function, more than the internal role of associations, might be the reason why we should include voluntary associations as key ingredients of a democratic political culture. It is quite striking that in their recent volume on the demise of political parties in Western societies Dalton and Wattenberg (2000) arrive at a parallel conclusion: External functions of parties are probably more important, or at least harder to replace, than their internal functions. One could think of ways how the internal mobilization, information and socialization functions of political parties, for example, could be taken over by other actors like the mass media or the education system. But Dalton and Wattenberg conclude that there are fewer alternatives available for the interest aggregation function that political parties traditionally fulfill. Although the political role of voluntary associations is not as well defined as the role of political parties, our conclusions with regard to voluntary associations are closely related to Dalton and Wattenberg's: We have no reason to assume that they are privileged institutions with regard to mobilization or socialization, but it is hard to think of functional equivalents for the instrumental or external functions of these associations.

However, this insight about the role of associations has important repercussions for social capital theory, as the socialization function was one of the foundations of an important link in the web between structural and cultural aspects of social interactions. Surely, we need associations and organizations to link citizens to their democratic system, though this insight results mostly from the research on political participation. The contribution of social capital research has been to redirect our attention to other resources that emphasize norms of reciprocity, generalized trust and various networks and ties between people that all have consequences for democracy. This redirection is still an important and welcome insight for research on political culture. Yet we need to search for more promising routes that lead to the generation of civic attitudes and values. If social interactions matter, the next step for this research is to move beyond associations to include the study of various other types of social interactions in a variety of social contexts. The most promising avenue here seems to be the analysis of bridging (as opposed to bonding) social interactions and their potential beneficial effects on trust. Such interactions might be more prominent outside associational life, for example in diverse neighborhoods (Marschall and Stolle 2001), at the workplace (Mutz and Mondak 1998), in informal networks and communities and in other settings. However, what we have learned in the first chapters of this book about membership in associations is that we certainly find these civic aspects represented in many voluntary associations, though associations are not the main *creators* of civic attitudes and behaviors.

THE NEWS OF INSTITUTION-CENTERED APPROACHES

The question, of course, is whether the study of institutions outside of voluntary associations and social interactions more generally might elucidate the institutional sources that are related to the creation of trust and other civic attitudes. In one way or another, the chapters in the second part of this volume attempted to test institutional explanations for the generation of the attitudinal components of social capital. Critical voices have long argued that the state and its institutions condition and structure the development of social capital (Berman 1997; Levi 1996; Tarrow 1996). Critics suggested that the state's monitoring capacity, its ability to grant and secure civil liberties and civil rights to its citizens, the level and length of experienced democracy and aspects of the welfare state are important for the development of generalized trust and other civic attitudes. Others have phrased this criticism differently: They pointed out how social capital is context dependent, and our task is to identify better the contexts in which social interactions are most beneficial (Edwards, Foley and Diani 2001). However, so far we do not have a good understanding about which institutional aspects of democracy and welfare states, for example, might be particularly conducive to social capital.

The chapters in the second part of this book try to fill some of these gaps. Indirectly or directly, the chapters end up refuting the claim that social capital is a resource that can be built and developed *only* in path-dependent fashions. The main message of the chapters is that *contemporary* aspects of institutions are also responsible for explaining the variation or patterns of social capital that we find in and among villages, cities, regions and nations. Huysseune tackles the argument against path dependency most directly. He argues that there is no indication that the political cultures of northern and southern Italy have been reproducing themselves continuously since the Middle Ages. Looking back, the history of southern Italy, and even Sicily, shows that these regions, too, have known periods of intense civic engagement, for example, in the second half of the nineteenth century and in the first part of the twentieth century. Given these temporal fluctuations, it seems very unlikely that medieval institutional arrangements can be held directly responsible for current differences in levels of social capital. To explain these differences, Huysseune argues, we rather have to take a look at what happened in the second part of the twentieth century, when the local strongholders, the Christian Democrats and the Catholic Church succeeded in using state funds and influence to strengthen their hold on power. The authoritarian rule of the central government in Rome, and the widespread practice of corruption, actually discouraged southerners from participating in civic engagement or from developing feelings of generalized or political trust.

The chapter on two Dutch localities by de Hart and Dekker takes an interesting turn in this debate. Instead of focusing solely on explaining the levels of social capital, the authors are more interested in identifying the relation between the various components of social capital, which are clearly context dependent. While in some Dutch municipalities membership in voluntary associations is indeed positively associated with trust, this is not the case in the community of Dordrecht. De Hart and Dekker demonstrate that the context of living in a depleted inner-city neighborhood and living in a cozy and well-off rural village has tremendous repercussions not only on the levels of social capital but also on its pattern as well. The authors use further research and focus group materials to speculate about the aspects of these different environments that could have mattered for the social capital differences: diversity, unemployment, infrastructure, and simply the local wealth of a community are likely to be behind these important variations. In other words, context matters, but we need to go a step further to ask *how*. What is the causal mechanism behind the relationship between social capital and local or institutional context?

Most of the authors in this second part of the book focus more precisely on the role of the state and government policy, and the chapters by Uslaner as well as Rothstein and Stolle are complementary in this respect. Even though Uslaner departs from a skeptical approach toward institutions, he shows that experience of long periods of democracy is strongly associated with trust (Inglehart 1997; Uslaner this volume). He also arrives at the finding that aspects of welfare states matter. Particularly, income inequality seems to prevent the development of trust, whereas trust blossoms in countries where governments have implemented more egalitarian programs. In fact Uslaner offers solid evidence for the existence of a macrolink between government policies and trust levels: Citizens who live in stable democracies with relatively egalitarian income structures are considerably more trusting than citizens in other countries. Uslaner does not reject cultural explanations: His analysis shows that, for example, religious traditions do have a bearing on present-day trust levels. But in addition to these cultural variables, the resources devoted to social policy and public education are positively and significantly related to generalized trust. These results too, however, can be questioned about the direction of causality at the macrolevel. As Uslaner acknowledges, we might as well argue that trusting societies have a tendency to develop a comprehensive welfare state, though he shows in his two-stage models that inequality is a persistent cause of trust, more than trust is a cause of inequality.

Rothstein and Stolle supplement this analysis by suggesting a micromechanism that could explain the nature of the macrolink. Their claim is that means-tested welfare states are more prone to corruption, abuse of power, arbitrary decisions from civil servants and bureaucrats, and, most importantly, systematic discrimination. The ideal of impartiality is seldom met in these means-tested institutions, which are beset by systematic inequalities. It seems evident that citizens, who experience this lack of impartiality, will not develop trust in those government institutions that discriminate against them. Furthermore, the observance and experience of political officials and other citizens who promote their own interests by means of corruption or fraud, as well as their own experience of discrimination, prevent the development of not only institutional trust but also trust in other citizens. If the causal mechanism that Rothstein and Stolle invoke and test by using Swedish survey data would be confirmed for other research settings, this would allow us to be more confident about the proposition that fair and equal state policies actually can strengthen basic trust levels among the population.

These chapters address two important aspects of welfare states that potentially matter for trust. On the one hand, they identified as crucial the policy *process* and the values that drive it, such as fairness or its absence; on the other hand, the findings point to policy outcomes, the results of which are more or less equality. These aspects are conceptually and empirically closely linked, even though the authors keep them distinct. Yet political systems accepting or even establishing strong income inequalities are more prone to use their powers in an arbitrary and potentially unfair fashion. Income inequality has many costs. Cross-culturally, there are very few examples of groups of poor people who succeed in getting their voices heard in the political system

(Piven and Cloward 1977). The problem for poor and economically excluded citizens is not just that they have fewer economic resources, but also that often governments will tend to neglect their demands. The issues that are raised by excluded groups (whether on the basis of economic, ethnic or religious discrimination) do not gain priority on the political agenda compared to the issues that are important to the well-off in society (Schlozman and Verba 1979; Verba, Schlozman and Brady 1995). Margalit (1996) argues that a decent society is one in which governments treat people in a "decent" and fair manner, avoiding any humiliation of specific groups within the population. Not only can poverty and income inequality by themselves be seen as unfair, but one of their consequences is that they enable government institutions and civil servants to treat poor people in an unfair manner, as well.

In the introduction to this volume we stated that the systematic socioeconomic differences we observe in countries with varying trust levels might offer us a clue with regard to the mechanisms responsible for the generation of basic trust. Newton (1999) observes that trust seems to be the privilege of "the winners" in society, those with ample financial, economical, cultural and educational resources. This would imply that societies that accumulate a lot of marginalized citizens will indeed have lower trust levels, since more people have no reason to develop trust, either in their fellow citizens, in political institutions, or in society at large. This implication is confirmed in the work by de Hart and Dekker (this volume). The feeling of discrimination, humiliation and powerlessness as it is described by Rothstein and Stolle (this volume), offers us a clue as to how we might understand this relation between inequality and distrust.

The evidence on the importance of institutional factors presented in these chapters might still be incomplete, since it is concentrated mainly on aspects of welfare states and economic inequality. Other aspects of state institutions, however, have a direct bearing on social capital as well. If governments do not succeed in effectively establishing the rule of law, ensuring enforcement of the law and monitoring that the law is being followed, then citizens might have reasons to distrust (Levi 1998). States, and especially courts or the police force, can function as third-party enforcers, thus creating a background setting in which generalized trust can develop. In this view, state institutions offer a degree of assurance that allows citizens to trust others who they do not know more easily (see Rothstein and Stolle 2002). Corrupt or ineffective regimes do not provide an ideal background for trust, as Uslaner (this volume) reminds us: "The most corrupt countries have the least trusting citizens. This is hardly surprising, since "kleptocracies" send clear messages to people that crime does pay."

Even though institution-centered accounts offer an interesting insight into the production of social capital, the problem with this approach, too, is that the evidence for causality remains tenuous. Institutional impartiality might build trust, but trust might also build impartial institutions. In fact the idea that the social policy process and social policy output might be responsible for the generation of trust flies in the face of Putnam's logic, which runs from social capital to institutional performance. Since longitudinal data about institutional characteristics and social capital are hard to obtain, the exact causal flow might remain a puzzle, or simply an unsolvable chicken and egg question. However, we suggest here that in order to get closer to an answer, we need to specify the causal mechanism in both causal claims. Given the Putnam logic from trust to institutional performance, we do not know how trusting people create better service performance and better politicians who are responsive. Do trusting citizens contact governmental officials more frequently to pressure them into good performance? Or is it that local politicians just reflect the culture of trust or distrust that prevails in their local societies? How exactly can the trust or distrust of citizens and their ability to cooperate influence governmental performance and as a result stimulate their confidence in politicians? The reverse logic is just as plausible, namely, the quality and inclusiveness of service delivery and the fairness of institutions can cause differences in institutional trust, which in turn influence generalized trust. However, the question here is how these experiences are generalized to the public at large. How are institutional experiences transmitted and socialized? What role do parents play in this socialization process of institutional values and trust for people?

In sum, there is obviously a strong relationship among government actions and institutional structures and social capital, and the theoretical and empirical evidence suggests that the flow of causality might run from local and national institutions to the generation of social capital. It is clear that the spread of generalized trust and norms of reciprocity are complex phenomena and cannot be explained by one factor alone. The fairness and equality of political institutions are embedded in and shaped by societal cleavages and the mobilization of these cleavages. However, whereas previous accounts of social capital formation have focused on the stability and path-dependency in the realm of civil society, these new insights about institutions enables us to see how contemporary factors influence the formation of civic attitudes. The future task of social capital research is to identify more clearly which aspects of familial, regional and national institutions create and possibly maintain low or high regional and national levels of social capital.

MAKING THE TRANSITION

The research assembled in this volume does offer new insights into how the generation of social capital might be actively promoted, and how societies could make the transition from vicious to virtuous circles. Society-centered accounts are not necessarily misguided, only the influence of social interactions seems more limited and more context dependent than was suggested in some of the previous research. This should not lead us to the conclusion that associations can be dismissed completely. In fact it is difficult to think of an effectively functioning democratic system without a vibrant associational life. We know, however, that associations do not work as a magic-bullet solution: More associations do not automatically translate into more social capital, as the chapters on France and, particularly, the Nicaraguan villages have demonstrated. This insight is important, because several development agencies now consider a thriving nongovernmental organization sector as a hallmark of a fully developed democracy. Moreover, the creation of associations by outsiders is highly problematic, as Molenaers shows, because they might just secure benefits for selected members while excluding others. Traditional and informal neighborhood networks, at least in the Nicaraguan villages she studied, tend to operate in a more open and fair manner, and thus can be seen as more effective instruments to create bridging forms of social capital. It seems clear from these and other examples that outside forces or state interventions cannot easily install community life (Ostrom 2000, 182).

The chapters on the institutional factors that influence social capital seem more optimistic: Government policies can stimulate or prevent people from participating in public life (Skocpol 1999), they can be used to strengthen the position of traditional powerholders (Huysseune this volume), but they can also be used to ensure income equality, and thus a more equal distribution of acting capabilities. Culture and path dependency do play a role in this process: As Uslaner demonstrates, government policies do not change trust levels overnight. Collective memories might have the effect that interaction patterns and group cultures are transmitted from generation to generation. It is not to be expected that eradicating corruption or ensuring a universal comprehensive social security system will rapidly or automatically lead to the development of higher trust levels. As Putnam (1973) rightfully observes, political culture tends to behave like a kind of heritage that populations take along from previous times, even when the conditions in which that culture was functional have long since disappeared. Political cultures are not immune to change, however, and government policies can be instrumental in furthering or preventing these changes. In this respect, the first responsibility of governments (and for that matter, of international agencies) seems to be to establish and enforce impartial and fair state structures, as well as to provide citizens with equal access to government services and equal chances to actively participate in social and political life.

REFERENCES

Almond, G. and Verba, S. (1963). *The Civic Culture*. Princeton: Princeton University Press.

Banfield, E. (1958). *The Moral Basis of a Backward Society*. New York: Free Press.

Baumgartner, F. and B. Leech (1998). *Basic Interests. The Importance of Groups in Politics and in Political Science*. Princeton: Princeton University Press.

Berman, S. (1997). "Civil Society and Political Institutionalization." *American Behavioral Scientist* 40, 562–574.

Berry, J. (1984). *The Interest Group Society*. Boston: Little and Brown.

Braithwaite, V. and Levi, M. (eds., 1998). *Trust and Governance*. New York: Russell Sage Foundation.

Coleman, J. S. (1990). *Foundation of Social Theory*. Cambridge: Belknap Press of Harvard University Press.

Dalton, R. and M. Wattenberg (eds., 2000). *Parties without Partizans*. Oxford: Oxford University Press.

Edwards, B., Foley, M. and Diani, M. (eds., 2001). *Beyond Tocqueville: Civil Society and the Social Capital Debate in Comparative Perspective*. Hanover: University Press of New England.

Eliasoph, N. (1998). *Avoiding Politics*. Cambridge: Cambridge University Press.

Gutmann, A. (1998). "Freedom of Association. An Introductory Essay." pp. 3–32. In A. Gutmann (ed.), *Freedom of Association*. Princeton: Princeton University Press.

Hooghe, M. (2001). "'Not for Our Kind of People'. The Sour Grapes Phenomenon as a Causal Mechanism for Political Passivity." pp. 162–175. In P. Dekker and E. Uslaner (eds.), *Social Capital and Participation in Everyday Life*. London: Routledge.

Hooghe, M. (2003). "Participation in Voluntary Associations and Value Indicators. The Effect of Current and Previous Participation Experiences." *Nonprofit and Voluntary Sector Quarterly* 32(1).

Inglehart, R. (1997). *Modernization and Postmodernization*. Princeton: Princeton University Press.

Levi, M. (1996). "Social and Unsocial Capital: A Review Essay of Robert Putnam's *Making Democracy Work*." *Politics and Society* 24, 45–55.

Levi, M. (1998). "A State of Trust." pp. 77–101. In V. Braithwaite and M. Levi (eds.), *Trust and Governance*. New York: Russell Sage Foundation.

Margalit, A. (1996). *The Decent Society*. Cambridge: Harvard University Press.

Marschall, M. and Stolle, D. (2001). "Race in the City: The Effects of Neighborhood Composition on Generalized Trust." Paper presented at the 97th Annual Meeting of the American Political Science Association, San Francisco, August 30–September 2.

Moyser, G. and Parry, G. (1997). "Voluntary Associations and Democratic Participation in Britain." pp. 24–46. In J. van Deth (ed.), *Private Groups and Public Life*. London: Routledge.

Mutz, D. (2002). "Cross-Cutting Social Networks. Testing Democratic Theory in Practice." *American Political Science Review* 96(1), 111–126.

Mutz, D. and Mondak, J. (1998). "Democracy at Work: Contributions of the Workplace Toward a Public Sphere." Paper presented at the Annual Meeting of the Midwest Political Science Association Meeting, Chicago, April 23–25.

Newton, K. (1999). "Social and Political Trust in Establish Democracies." pp. 169–187. In P. Norris (ed.), *Critical Citizens*. Oxford: Oxford University Press.

Onyx, J. and Bullen, P. (2001). "The Different Faces of Social Capital in NSW Australia." pp. 45–58. In P. Dekker and E. Uslaner (eds.), *Social Capital and Participation in Everyday Life*. London: Routledge.

Ostrom, E. (2000). "Social Capital: A Fad or a Fundamental Concept?" pp. 172–214. In P. Dasgupta and I. Serageldin (eds.), *Social Capital*. Washington D.C.: World Bank.

Piven, F. and R. Coward (1977). *Poor People's Movements*. New York: Pantheon.

Putnam, R. (1973). *The Beliefs of Politicians*. New Haven: Yale University Press.

Putnam, R. and S. Pharr (eds., 2000). *Disaffected Democracies. What's Troubling the Trilateral Countries?* Princeton: Princeton University Press.

Rothstein, B. and Stolle, D. (2002). "How Political Institutions Create and Destroy Social Capital: An Institutional Theory of Generalized Trust." Paper presented at the 98th Annual Meeting of the American Political Science Association, Boston, August 31–September 3.

Schlozman, K. L. and Verba, S. (1979). *Injury to Insult*. Cambridge: Harvard University Press.

Skocpol, T. (1999). "Associations without Members." *American Prospect* 10(45), 1–8.

Stolle, D. (1998). "Bowling Together, Bowling Alone: The Development of Generalized Trust in Voluntary Associations." *Political Psychology* 19(3), 497–525.

Stolle, D. (2001a). "Clubs and Congregations: The Benefits of Joining an Association." pp. 202–244. In K. Cook (ed.), *Trust in Society*. New York: Russell Sage Foundation.

Stolle, D. (2001b). "Getting to Trust: An Analysis of the Importance of Institutions, Families, Personal Experiences and Group Membership." pp. 118–133. In P. Dekker and E. Uslaner (eds.), *Social Capital and Participation in Everyday Life*. London: Routledge.

Stolle, D. (forthcoming). "Communities, Social Capital and Local Government: Generalized Trust in Regional Settings." In P. Selle and A. Prakash (eds.), *Investigating Social Capital*. New Delhi: Sage India.

Streeck, W. (1987). "Vielfalt und Interdependenz." *Kölner Zeitschrift für Soziologie und Sozialpsychologie* 39, 471–495.

Tarrow, S. (1994). *Power in Movement*. Cambridge: Cambridge University Press.

Tarrow, S. (1996). "Making Social Science Work Across Space and Time: A Critical Reflection on Robert Putnam's *Making Democracy Work*." *American Political Science Review* 90, 389–397.

Van Deth, J. (ed., 1997). *Private Groups and Public Life*. London: Routledge.

Verba, S., Schlozman, K. L. and Brady, H. (1995). *Voice and Equality*. Cambridge: Harvard University Press.

Warren, M. (2001). *Democracy and Association*. Princeton: Princeton University Press.

About the Authors

Joep de Hart is a researcher at the Dutch Social and Cultural Planning Office. He received his Ph.D. in sociology from Nijmegen University. His publications include books on youth subcultures, religion, social cohesion and civil society.

Paul Dekker is a researcher at the Dutch Social and Cultural Planning Office and a professor at Tilburg University. He is involved in (comparative) research on the non-profit sector, civil society, political behavior and social and political attitudes.

Marc Hooghe teaches at the Universities of Brussels and Antwerp (Belgium), and he is a research fellow for the Belgian Fund for Scientific Research. He holds Ph.D.s in political science (Brussels) and sociology (Rotterdam). He has published mainly on social capital, voluntary associations and political participation.

Michel Huysseune is a researcher at the Department of Political Science at Vrije Universiteit Brussel (VUB). His Ph.D. thesis (2001) focused on the relation between the political discourse of the northern Italian party Lega Nord and scholarly discourses on Italy's North–South divide.

Nonna Mayer is research director at CEVIPOF (Center for Studies of French political Life, Sciences Po Paris)—CNRS (National Center for Scientific Research) and teaches at Sciences Po where she is in charge of a Ph.D. program in political sociology. She has just published a book on the electorate of the extreme-right party Front National (Paris 2002).

Job van der Meer studied political science and history at Leiden University, the Netherlands. Since 1998 he has been a Ph.D. candidate at the Department of Public Administration at Erasmus University, the Netherlands. He is currently completing his dissertation on "Communitarianism and Political Support in Modern Democracies."

Nadia Molenaers teaches political theory, governance and development at the University of Antwerp and social and cultural anthropology at the Free University of Brussels. She received her Ph.D. in political science from the Free University of Brussels.

Bo Rothstein is the August Röhss professor in political science at Göteborg University. He has been a visiting scholar at the Russell Sage Foundation, New York, and at the Center for European Studies at Harvard University. He has published mainly on the welfare state, corporatism and social capital.

Per Selle (Ph.D. University of Bergen 1987) is Professor of comparative politics at the University of Bergen and Senior Researcher at the Stein Rokkan Center for Social Studies. His research interests include voluntary organizations, political parties, political culture and environmental policy.

Dietlind Stolle obtained her Ph.D. in political science from Princeton University (2000). She is an assistant professor at the Department of Political Science at McGill University, Montréal, Canada. She has published mainly on social capital, associational life, generalized trust and political consumerism.

Eric M. Uslaner is a professor of government and politics at the University of Maryland-College Park (USA). He received his Ph.D. in political science from Indiana University in 1973 and has published primarily on legislatures, elections and public opinion.

Dag Wollebæk is a doctoral candidate at the Department of Comparative Politics, University of Bergen. His research interests are voluntary organizations and democratic theory.

INDEX